ENGAGED IN WAR

Captain (acting Major) E. Stanley Goodland MC 1/5th Bn Somerset Light Infantry. Photograph taken in Cairo in July 1919. A Territorial Soldier, he started the war as a 2nd Lieutenant. (Letter 19/18)

ENGAGED IN WAR

THE LETTERS OF STANLEY GOODLAND

Somerset Light Infantry
1914-1919

TWIGA BOOKS
GOMSHALL

First published in 1999

Twiga Books
Twiga Lodge
Wonham Way
Gomshall
Guildford
GU5 9NZ

ISBN 0 9528625 2 2

Typeset by Typestyle, Newmarket
Printed and bound by
Intype London Limited

FOREWORD

The index to this book has more references to Frank Urwick and Harry Milsom than to any other of Stanley Goodland's fellow officers; and their surviving sons write this foreword in tribute to a friendship between the three which lasted from the time of these letters until they died. As well as a sacrosanct annual reunion there were everyday contacts. The Goodlands and the Milsoms lived within a mile, and were in and out of each others' houses throughout the period between the wars. The Urwicks' house in Somerset was a staging-post for what was then a long drive the Milsoms regularly made between London and Cornwall, where the Urwicks would come to spend holidays in the overcrowded Milsom cottage (and Mary Urwick's brothers, the two Moores who also feature in these letters, would come with their families to stay nearby). Goodland was godfather to Milsom's elder son, Mary Urwick godmother to the younger, and Milsom was godfather to Goodland's son.

There had been a fourth friend. Gerald Banes Walker was best man when Milsom married in India in 1915, was godfather to a child who lived only long enough to be christened, left a legacy for any future child, and was killed in 1917 in the action in which Milsom was wounded. References to him in these letters (especially 17/37) suggest that the strength of these friendships, between men who had not even met before the war, came largely from Goodland himself. Nor was it only between the officers that personal loyalties lasted. Milsom was not well enough to go to the battalion reunion in the year of his golden wedding; but he received a round robin signed by more than two dozen of those who remembered having been present so far away and so long before.

Goodland was always 'Uncle' rather than Stanley, probably not only because he was older than his fellow subalterns but also because of an unfailingly calm and avuncular manner. One of us remembers him in a quiet world caressing a piece of 18th-century furniture and gently explaining what was specially pleasing about it. The letters show him holding to his own quietness in a world which needed the constant reliability of which these friendships were one manifestation even more than it needed the bravery and stamina which gained his Military Cross and Croix de Guerre. He saw things through, and that must be why no commanding officer throughout the war felt able to send him on home leave.

S.F.C. Milsom
A.C.M. Urwick

July 1998

PREFACE

The preparation of these letters for publication has been an enriching experience. My brother and I had always been aware of their existence, had been allowed to look in the box and see the bundles of old envelopes and understood they had been written by Father in the First World War, when he was serving overseas and never once had been allowed home leave.

With our retirement, a growing interest in family history and the recognition of the value of primary sources, we began to realise that we should do something about these letters. The initial task of transcription was undertaken by my husband, Tom: we shared the checking and correcting and sent the drafts off to brother David. The majority of the letters are in pencil, often written on pages torn from a field note book, perhaps from a dug-out in the front line and under difficulties; 'I am very short of candles and the wind keeps blowing this little bit out.' There is a constant note of anxiety about letters not arriving or not being received at home; they were a true life-line between the extraordinary conditions of war and the normality of home. There are obvious gaps where letters must have gone missing and two miraculous survivals, with the envelopes marked 'salved from submerged mail' and still (mostly) legible.

Having transcribed the letters, we could then read them as a continuous narrative, which raised all sorts of questions; who were these people he was referring to? why was a territorial regiment sent to India? why did serving soldiers have to rely on parcels from home for soap and camp cutlery? why was the campaign in Mesopotamia (Iraq) such a muddle and so expensive in lives? why were troops sent on a winter campaign in Palestine in summer uniform? We have discovered a lot of answers; to some questions there are none.

David, with his career in teaching and a large library of books of reference, was able to provide information from official and contemporary sources and has written the introduction to each year of letters. To supplement this, Tom and I paid visits to the British Library (official publications, newspaper library, India Office Library) and David to the offices of the local press in West Somerset. At a meeting with Tony Urwick (whose father is also a part of this story), he suggested that the regimental War Diaries might be useful. David joined Tom and me for visits to the Public Record Office where we found these diaries for 1917 to 1919 and that the majority of them had been written by Father as Adjutant (and a very conscientious and efficient one too). As we moved further along the road to publication we were able to call on the typing and computer skills of David's wife, Gill and son, Andrew.

We are happy to put these letters before a wider public because we feel that they present a vivid and personal picture of one of the major events of the twentieth century. The campaigns in Mesopotamia and Palestine have, rather unkindly, been designated as 'side shows' and do not command the interest or volume of words which have been devoted to the Western Front.

The human picture that emerges from the letters shows a man who was getting established in his profession as a 'dealer in fine art' and had just become engaged to be married, who was prepared to leave it all and respond to the call to arms. The letters reflect the change from initial enthusiasm and excitement to a dogged acceptance of a job to be done. The stark contrast in a soldier's life is made between the 'thrilling' (his word) moments of attack and advance and the dreary days in cold and wet (or hot and sandy) conditions, attended by unwelcome insect life. The reader begins to understand the sadness and depression following the loss of friends, the pride at being awarded a decoration, the gratitude for Elsie's constant letters (none of which survive), the agony of knowing his mother was terminally ill and that he would not see her again, the pleasure and comfort of a few days leave offering a hot bath and a bed with sheets.

The year 1919 must have been difficult for both of them, the hope of reunion being endlessly deferred. The war was over but there was still work to be done, and Father had promised his colonel that he would stay until the end. There is an uncharacteristically immoderate outburst against the Egyptians, but it was hard for him to be sent off campaigning again, with a collection of unwilling soldiers from a variety of regiments whose hopes of demobilisation were suddenly dashed.

Some phrases have a particular poignancy; from a letter of January 1919; 'I really think I've forgotten how to talk to a girl - the last time I spoke to one was in India going on two years ago.' And from November 1915: 'If anything happens to me I should like you to have it [a watch] if it is recovered from my belongings as it should be.' Some of these letters must have been very hard to receive.

The strengths of both Stanley and Elsie come through in the letters; they didn't talk about their wartime experiences to us (we should have asked), but shortly before his death, at the age of 90, Father told David about the attack on El Jib, divulging the name of the man he and his colleagues blame for the death of their friends, an episode still clear in the mind after nearly 60 years.

This publication of the letters is dedicated to them both.

Ann Noyes (née Goodland) and Tom Noyes,
David and Gill Goodland,
Andrew Goodland
1998

A NOTE ON SOURCES

This book is based on the letters of Stanley Goodland, now owned by his family but soon to be offered to the Imperial War Museum. The holograph text is followed and quirks of spelling and punctuation are preserved.

The prime printed source is *The Book of Remembrance of the 5th Battalion (Prince Albert's) Somerset Light Infantry* (hereafter *'BoR'*). This was published at the Chiswick Press in 1930, with a print run of 500 copies. In it, the story of the 1/5 Battalion's record in India, Egypt and Palestine was written by Stanley Goodland and Harry Milsom. The 2/5 Battalion's service on garrison duties in Burma is described by a group of officers including Stanley Goodland's brother, Harold.

Internal evidence bears out the claim made when the *BoR* was published that its authors had been able to consult 'battalion records.'[1] It is safe to assume that these included the War Diary of the 1/5 Battalion from May 1917 to December 1919, when it was part of the Egyptian Expeditionary Force. This is now in the PRO, file WO 95/4690. From October 1917 most of the daily entries were written and initialled by Stanley Goodland.

Two more sources need notice here. The first, unprinted, is Harry Milsom's account of his experience in the Palestine campaign in October and November 1917. The second, privately printed, is Frank Urwick's record of the same period written from the perspective of the 1/5 Battalion's commanding officer. Extracts from these two sources will be found in the Appendix.

References will be found in the footnotes. The bibliography lists the works consulted.

---

[1] See *Somerset County Gazette*, July 12th, 1930.

ACKNOWLEDGEMENTS

The preparation of these letters for publication has been a family enterprise, as described in the Preface. Members of the extended family have also been consulted and have offered information which has added to our understanding; we would like to thank Christine Armstrong née Hyde, whose expected arrival and birth were much in the mind of her uncle; Mary Burns née Goodland, who remained in England when her mother went to join her father in Burma (and came back with another baby); Joyce Jones, both of whose parents are part of the story and Peter Rumjahn, son of Amy née Hyde. Two others, not part of the family but closely related to this history, are Tony Urwick and Toby Milsom, sons of Frank Urwick and Harry Milsom, who have kindly contributed the Foreword.

We thank them all.

We would also like to thank the staff of the various departments of the British Library, the Public Record Office and the offices of the Somerset newspapers.

EDITORS' NOTE

Stanley Goodland's letters are printed in full. In normal circumstances his hand was easily legible but some of the letters have been difficult to decipher. However, editorial intervention has seldom been necessary. His departures from standard spelling and punctuation have generally been preserved.

PLATES and MAPS

PLATES

Frontispiece

Section I - between pages 44 & 45
Section II - between pages 96 & 97

All illustrations are from photographs in the family archive except for,
in Section I, *The Tatler* illustrations, from its issues of July 14th, August 4th and
September 22nd 1915, in the British Newspaper Library, Colindale.
In Section II, the *War Diary* of 1/5 Bn Somerset Light Infantry is at the Public
Record Office, WO 95/4690

SKETCH MAPS

ORDNANCE SURVEY MAPS
(reproduced by permission - OS MC/103/98)

CONTENTS

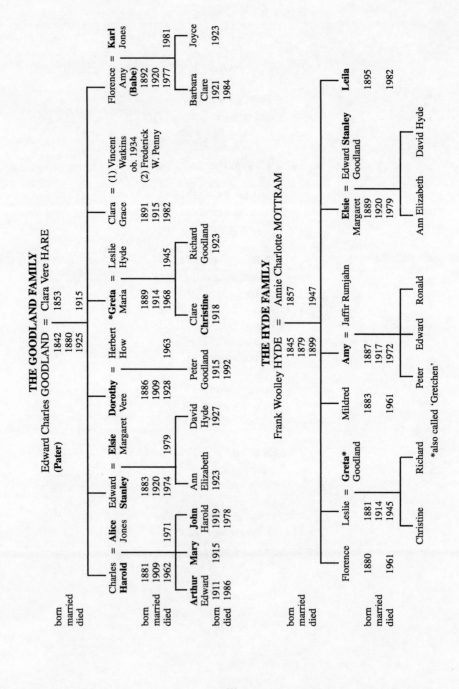

THE GOODLAND FAMILY

THE HYDE FAMILY

CHAPTER ONE

1914

Family Background.

On her death in 1979 Elsie Goodland's children inherited a Marshall & Snelgrove dress box containing bundles of the treasured letters she had received from her fiancé and future husband Stanley Goodland, on war service in the East, 1914-1919. These letters, each tucked into its original envelope, form the starting point of this book.

Elsie Margaret Hyde was 25 years old in 1914; Stanley Goodland was 30. Each came from late Victorian families of six. Elsie was the fifth child. Her father, a bank cashier in Manchester, died in 1899, when she was ten. Her mother, Annie Charlotte Hyde, née Mottram, brought up her only son, Leslie and five daughters at Hale near Altrincham, Cheshire.

Edward Stanley Goodland was born in Taunton in 1883. He was the second child of Edward and Clara (née Hare) Goodland. Harold, two years older, was his only brother; they had four younger sisters. Their father was the owner of Charles Goodland and Son, coal and builders' merchants, a Taunton firm established in 1830 with depots in four - later, in more - towns in West Somerset and Devon.

The young Goodland brothers went as day boys to Taunton School, known then as the Independent College, established to educate the sons of Nonconformists. Some of Stanley's prizes survive, including a copy of Prince Ranjitsinghi's *The Jubilee Book of Cricket,* awarded for the IV Form English Essay in 1897. Photographs show him as captain of cricket and football teams.

It seems that as a younger son Stanley had no prospect of a career in the coal trade, in which his brother later distinguished himself, but one of his mother's brothers was a partner in Franklin & Hare, goldsmiths and silversmiths in Taunton, and it was presumably with a view to eventually joining this firm that Stanley went to London as an apprentice to the Goldsmiths & Silversmiths Company, of Regent Street. This, at any rate, is what developed when he returned to Taunton in 1908; the business now became Franklin, Hare & Goodland, with premises on The Parade, Taunton and a branch in Minehead.

Nothing is now known of Stanley's time in London, though a faint memory suggests he played cricket for the Finchley club. Back in 'God's own county' he was chosen to play three times for Somerset in 1908. One of these matches was the occasion of the taking of the team photograph; Stanley stands at the right of the back row with such eminences as Sammy Woods and LCH Palairet seated at the front. An all-rounder at club level, Stanley was not asked to bowl for the county; his highest score was 42 not out. He played for Somerset only once more, in 1909, against Sussex at Hove, years later telling how, after he failed to catch CB Fry, a newspaper correspondent next day reported that the batsman had offered a difficult chance in the deep, 'which was not accepted.'

Acting and singing were further interests. Stanley belonged to the Taunton Amateur Operatic Society, being cast in comic character roles. The *Somerset County Gazette's* anonymous reviewer regularly praised his performances in the Society's annual show. With this experience of the amateur stage Stanley was the officer singled out by his colonel to organise and perform in regimental entertainments when, as will be shown, war service took him to garrison duty in India.

* * * *

It was Unitarianism that brought the Cheshire Hydes and the Somerset Goodlands together. The Hydes worshipped in the then remote chapel, founded in the late 17th century, at Hale Barns (now near the M56 and the runway of Manchester airport). Taunton had a strong nonconformist tradition and the Goodlands were pillars of Mary Street chapel, with its fine 18th century interior and imposing late Victorian schoolrooms. Mrs Edward Goodland was president of the Taunton branch of the League of Unitarian Women. Stanley, her younger son, was the leader of a Bible class at Mary Street and her elder son, Harold, was in May 1914, the president of the Annual Assembly of the Western Union of Unitarian churches, held in Ilminster.

The two families met because Elsie Hyde and Greta Goodland were schoolfellows at Channing House, Highgate, a Unitarian foundation. The exchange of holiday visits led to the engagement of Greta to Leslie Hyde and they were married on May 16th 1914, in Taunton. Family legend has it that for some time before this Elsie and Greta's brother Stanley had secretly committed themselves to each other but had kept quiet about it for fear of stealing the thunder of the bride and groom. In the evening of the wedding day some of the party went for a drive to Cothelstone Hill on the Quantocks, travelling in scrubbed out horse-drawn coal carts fitted with benches, and there Stanley and Elsie declared themselves. Much was to happen before their own wedding day in September 1920.

At the time of her engagement Elsie had been working for more than a year as nanny to Ronald, the first child of Dr & Mrs Brown of Minchinhampton, Gloucestershire, where Dr Brown was in general practice. She had obtained this appointment after completing a nine month's course in Nursery Nursing at the Princess Christian College at Fallowfield, Manchester. There were eventually three children for Elsie to look after. Ronald was six weeks old when she joined the household in 1913, Barbara was born in September 1914 and Alison in 1919, too late to retain any memory of Elsie's care; but the two older ones remembered her with great affection, while Mrs Brown's annual reports to the Princess Christian College speak glowingly of her character and abilities.

2

Military Background.

In keeping with the provisions of Haldane's Territorial and Reserve Forces Act of 1907, the old Volunteer battalions in Somerset were disbanded in 1908 and re-formed as the 4th and 5th Battalions, Prince Albert's Somersetshire Light Infantry, the 5th being based in Taunton, with drill halls in many smaller towns in South and West Somerset.

Before August 1914 the role of the Territorials had been limited to Home Defence, but the alarming scale and rapidity of the German invasion of Belgium and Northern France, and the lengthening casualty lists, provoked drastic changes in the raising and deployment of manpower. On August 21st Lord Kitchener ordered the creation of a New Army of six divisions, soon to be followed by many more. Territorial soldiers were now encouraged to volunteer for service overseas, the presumption being that this would mean garrison duties in Gibraltar, Malta, or India. On September 23rd Major-General CG Donald, General Officer Commanding 43rd (Wessex) Division, of which the 1/5 Somersets were a part, was interviewed by Kitchener at the War Office and as he later related 'got a little bit of a shock when he said: "I want you to take your Division to India, will they go?" I said, "Well, sir, I do not think anybody has thought much about it, but I am perfectly certain that if you want them to go to India they will go there right enough." He replied, "Very well . . . tell them from me . . . that by going to India they will be performing a great Imperial duty. I have to bring white troops back from India to Europe and I must replace them there by white troops from Home."' [1]

So the 43rd (Wessex) Division sailed for India and by way of the Straits of Gibraltar and the Suez Canal[2] reached Bombay on November 9th and 10th. The long voyage was completed in safety. The U-boat menace had not yet developed, the German surface raiders *Goeben* and *Breslau* remained in friendly Turkish waters and the Emden, of the German Asiatic Squadron, which had operated in the Laccadive and Maldive Islands area in late September and early October had turned eastward and was sunk while landing a party on the Cocos Islands on November 9th.

When the 43rd (Wessex) Division arrived in India the British garrison was being severely depleted by the departure of regular battalions of European and Indian troops to Europe and East Africa. As a former Commander-in-Chief, India, Kitchener believed that a minimum of eight regular European infantry battalions,[3] one cavalry regiment and some artillery units was needed to preserve order in that vast country and to ward off attacks of the tribesmen on the North West Frontier. It therefore fell to the 43rd (Wessex) and other Territorial Divisions to adapt themselves to soldiering in a hot climate and to learn to play their part in the preservation of the British Raj.

---

[1] Major General Donald, quoted in Everard Wyrall, *The Somerset Light Infantry* 1914-1919, Methuen 1927, p.34

[2] The 1/5 Somersets claimed to have been the first Territorial Battalion to pass through the Canal. Light Bob Gazette, vol xxiii, no 1, April-June 1920, p.24.

[3] Among them the 2nd Somersets, who to their 'bitter disappointment' served in India throughout 1914-1918. See Wyrall op. cit. p.371.

Stanley Goodland: from Salisbury Plain to the Punjab, August to December 1914.

The 1/5 Somersets began their annual camp at Bulford, Salisbury Plain, on July 26th 1914. The Goodland brothers attended; Harold was already commissioned in the rank of Captain and Stanley was appointed Second Lieutenant on July 30th, being gazetted on August 29th. He was ten years older than many of the other subalterns, now his fellow officers, who delighted in calling him 'Uncle', then and for the rest of their lives. On August 30th the commanding Officer, Lt-Col EF Cooke-Hurle, paraded the battalion and conveyed the War Office request for voluntary overseas service. All the officers stepped forward and 650 of the 950 other ranks, but now arose the urgent need for new recruits to replace those whose age, fitness or commitments had caused them not to volunteer. On September 1st Lt-Col Cooke-Hurle sent out his officers to those parts of Somerset where they were well known, with instructions to return to Salisbury Plain on Saturday September 5th with the necessary number of recruits. Stanley Goodland was sent to the Minehead area and the issues of the *West Somerset Free Press* of September 5th and 12th vividly record details of his activities. After a tour of local villages on September 2nd Stanley followed Lord St. Audries' introductory address by speaking to the 'large attendance' at the Auction Field, Williton. Twenty nine men enlisted that day. On Thursday the 3rd Stanley spoke at a meeting on the Esplanade, Watchet where 14 men were attested, three of them employed by the Great Western Railway. Later that evening there was a meeting in the Church House, Crowcombe, at which seven men gave in their names. On the Friday Stanley and his team concentrated on Minehead and its immediate area, to such effect that on the 5th Stanley returned to Salisbury Plain with more than double the number of recruits he had been commissioned to find.

Over the subsequent five weeks Stanley's letters tell of the intensive training a Territorial battalion required, the rumours about postings at home and overseas and the 48-hour embarkation leave granted to all ranks when the destination of the 1/5 Somersets was known. On October 9th Stanley and the 1/5 Somersets sailed from Southampton to their adventures in the East.

The Letters Written in 1914

No. 14/1

Plume of Feathers Hotel, Minehead
Sept. 4th. 1914

My dear old Elsie:

I was sent down here last Wednesday for 3 days to try to raise 40 recruits or more for the Battalion - willing to serve in active service.

I am glad to say that up to the time of writing I have signed on 86. I am returning with them to Salisbury Plain 8 o'c train tomorrow.

Many thanks dear old girl for the box of cigs. you sent me. I will write soon, am very busy. Best love dear

from Stan.

*****

No. 14/2

Durrington Camp, Salisbury Plain
Sunday Sept. 6th. 1914

My dear old Elsie,

Many thanks for your last letter which was sent on to me at Minehead. I got back safely last night and am dead tired - one had to work day and night to get our recruits in and had a splendid response. I got 94 in my district and we all gathered together at Taunton yesterday morning and marched 350 strong (all raw recruits got in 3 days) down the Town and they gave us a tremendous send off.

I am learning to ride a motor bike belonging to another officer and when I can manage it I shall sometimes be able to borrow it. I wonder if I could then meet you for one afternoon somewhere, I must study a map for I am quite at sea and dont know in the least the best point to meet. Perhaps I could just get right into Minchinhampton but I dont know how far that is. I had no time to see my people yesterday and it was all such a rush so apart from spending a few hours at home on Tuesday night it was by no means a holiday. We have so many applications for recruits that a reserve battalion is being formed and posted at Taunton. There are already 400 men there and Harold[1] has been sent back to command them - he will have a very responsible job and very hard work. The Babe[2] arrived home yesterday evening but I did not see her - I believe they got a wire saying she was in London and so there was great excitement. I dont know any particulars but I

---

[1] Charles Harold Goodland (1881-1962), elder brother to Stanley, served throughout the war in 2/5 Battalion, Somerset Light Infantry, in Burma and India. Brought to the notice of the Government of India for valuable services rendered (*BoR*, p.112).

[2] Florence Amy Goodland (1892-1977), known as 'the Babe', 4th and youngest sister to Stanley, married Karl Jones of Mumbles, South Wales, in 1920. On July 30th 1914 she left England to attend a course at the Dalcroze College of Dancing near Dresden. Caught in Germany by the outbreak of war she succeeded, on the second attempt, in crossing the Dutch frontier. A long account of her experiences was printed in the *Somerset County Gazette*, September 19th, shortly after her return.

hope she is well and I am anxious to hear all about her experiences. There is no news yet of any move but I hope they will put us into barracks soon - it is so very cold at night and lonely during the day. It was real good to get between some sheets for three nights and get some warm baths.

I am enjoying the cigarettes so much dear - thank you so much. Best love dear old girl

from Stan

Now there is a chance of our going abroad everyone has to be inoculated with typhoid germs. I am going to be done on Wednesday & suppose I shall be laid up for 48 hours.

*****

No.14/3

5th. Somersets, West Down Camp, Salisbury Plain
Sept. 19 1914

My dear old Elsie

Ever so many thanks for your most welcome letter, and I am sorry I have not written lately. I have been away shooting at Bulford all this week and have returned late everyday. I am glad to say I have passed all the shooting tests and have got my marksmans certificate so thats all right. I got over my first innoculation all right and this evening I am due to take my second dose. It seems necessary to be done a second time ten days after the first. The doctor says I shant feel this one as the first gave me such a bad time. I do hope he will be right. We changed camp yesterday and marched over here (6 miles from Durrington) it is a good thing because we had been on the old camping ground a long time and the [word missing] were getting very dirty. We are now a hundred miles from any-where and right in the most exposed part of the Plain. Unfortunately the man who had the motor bike has left us to join another battalion for the time being so I am done out of my lessons, isnt it a shame. Since I last wrote we have been having a very rotten time and the weather has been gastly. I sometimes wonder if I shall ever be warm and comfortable again but the bed stockings your mother so kindly gave me are the greatest comfort to me. Most of the days I was shooting it was wet and windy and I had to lie prone on the damp ground for hours but I suppose one gets hardened to almost anything and really I am keeping awfully well. Thank goodness some of our troubles will soon be over for in a few weeks we are going to Bournemouth and are to be billeted in the town. It will be lovely to have a real roof over ones head again. Nothing is fixed yet of course about our ultimate destination but it seems fairly certain that we are booked now for some service out of the country and after all we may see some fighting.

I dont think anything will be done to us until Xmas or the New Year but Lord Kitchener said in the House of Lords that he was relying upon the territorials in a few months - Perhaps this terrible war will be over before we are wanted, I do hope so for everybody's sake.

6

You have been having bad weather too and I am sorry you got so wet blackberrying, you must look after your throat this winter. I am sure you must be very busy now and I hope Mrs. Brown is keeping well. I am afraid I shant be able to go up to see Gretchen[3] for a long time to come. Bournemouth is so far from the North but I hope when we do get settled into our Winter quarters I shall be able to get home for a few hours. It will do mother so much good to visit Gretchen and I hope she will put in some time with Dorothy[4] too on her way back.

Mother[5] has had a very anxious time lately, but she has borne everything splendidly. I must not stay for more now so good bye dear. I will try to write again next week. With many thanks for the letters which I much enjoy, and best love

from Stan

*****

No.14/4

5th. Somersets, West Down Camp, Salisbury Plain
Sept. 23 1914

My dear old Elsie

Thank you ever so much for your two letters and birthday present. It was awfully sweet of you to remember me and I shall enjoy the pipe so much and have started it going already. The baccy is fine too, I cant afford it myself and it is a great treat.

It was kind of you to send me two letters too thanks so much for the good wishes. I spent a strange birthday but the postman brought me several letters and parcels which were a great consolation. I have many letters to write so this must only be a short one. I have a lot of duty today. I am quite well again now only some bothering rheumatism in my shoulders. But I am warmer at night now with the bed stockings from your mother and some more blankets from home.

Amy[6] very kindly remembered my birthday and sent me a lovely box of cigarettes, I must send her a line. No more news of our movements I wish they would send us into billets I will let you know at once if we are moving.

Well old girl ever so many thanks for all your kindness to me and much love from Stan

*****

---

[3] 'Gretchen' was the family name for Greta Goodland (1889-1968).
[4] Dorothy Goodland (1886-1928), eldest of the Goodland sisters, married Herbert (Bert) How in 1909. Also known as 'Do.'
[5] Clara Vere Hare had married Edward Charles Goodland in 1880.
[6] Amy Frances Hyde (1887-1972) sister to Elsie, 4th child in the family, married Dr Jaffir Rumjahn MB, ChB, of Liverpool, on September 8th 1917.

No.14/5

Dear old Elsie,

Just a hurried line to tell you we are ordered off to India immediately. The General[7] was summoned to the War Office yesterday & Lord Kitchener told him that we had been selected for Indian Service. We should probably go next week. It is a frightful rush but I hope to go home for a day. I have wired to stop mother going tomorrow. I was sorry to do this but I must see her before I go. It means entirely new kit and there are a thousand things to do. I dread the sea voyage but I hope I shall be well enough to enjoy the latter end. Next to going to France Indian service is supposed to be the greatest honour the War Office can bestow upon a regiment.

Lord K. said that after a while he would probably relieve us with other troops and send us to the Front, so we are likely to see some service after all. At any rate India will be a great experience for me. Goodnight old girl I will try to write again. Best love

from Stan.

*****

No.14/6

Elm Grove[8], Taunton
Sept 28th. 1914

My dear old Elsie

I am home on 48 hours leave, I left yesterday morning (Saturday) and have to motor back this morning. We sail on Thursday but they wont tell us our port neither would they say what part of India we are going to.

I am sorry I shall not be able to see you but you see how impossible it is so this must be Goodbye as I expect I shall not be able to write again. If I am well enough I will write on the voyage and try to post it somewhere where we call. I dont know if we go via Suez Canal or round South Africa I wonder what you think of it all. I havent got a letter from you but I expect I shall find one at camp. It is a dreadful rush and I have so much to buy and pack and see to, Goodbye old girl, keep well and happy. I will send you my address for letters as soon as possible and hope you will be able to write me each mail and I will answer them whenever possible. With love and all good wishes from your old pal,

Stan.

*****

---

[7] Major General Colin George Donald (1864-1939). Served in the Afghan War 1879, South African War 1899-1902, GOC Wessex Territorial Division 1911-1914, Inspector of Territorial Forces in India 1914-1915. Western Reserve Centre in England 1915-1917 (BoR pp.11-12, & *Who was Who* vol III).
[8] No. 1 Elm Grove was the Goodland family home.

No. 14/7

5th. Somerset L.I., West Down Camp, Salisbury.
Oct 5th. 1914

My dear old Elsie

You will be surprised to hear from me again from the Plain but our departure has been delayed for a few hours for some private reason

We have had rather a dreadful time for everything was packed up for us to go on Saturday and now we are pigging it terribly - we should go on Wednesday or Thursday for certain and I should be so glad. This uncertainty and countermand is very tiring. We sail from Southampton and a line addressed to me c/o the Embarkation Officer Southampton would find me probably. Our station in India is Jhansi, right in Central India very hot and full of snakes but a fine sporting centre so we should have a good time.

Please write me a letter to Jhansi so that I get it when I reach there. I think it will be a long railway journey from Bombay. The War Office are very scared and we have to be ready to move at a moments notice. They say there are 3 German submarines submarines in the English Channel which cant be located and this is the reason for our delay - but I suppose the troop ships are not quite ready yet. I got your letters quite safely so many thanks and I have already enjoyed the helmet it is so beautifully warm I shall take it to India in case we bivouack some day. I may be able to write again before we go but it is very uncertain, anyhow heres wishing you Goodbye again I wish I could have seen you, but never mind, I shall be home again soon I hope

Goodbye old dear, best love

from Stan

*****

No.14/8

Telegram 7.45 am. 9th.Oct. 1914
Southampton

To Hyde, The Uplands, Minchinhampton
Goodbye and love sailing Kenilworth Castle[9] Stan.

*****

---

[9] Union Castle Mail Steamship Co Ltd, mixed cargo/passenger liner, reg. tonnage 7185, built Belfast 1904, usually on Southampton-Cape Town-Durban run.

No.14/9

Union Castle Line R.M.S. Kenilworth Castle
Wednesday 14th. Oct. 14
At sea, a few hours from Gibraltar.

My dear old Elsie,

We have just been told that there may be a chance of getting letters off at Gib. but they will be censored so I can only send you a few lines. You will be glad to know that I am an excellent sailor up to now and of course am enjoying every minute of the voyage - We were lucky right from the start - when we reached Southampton we found the 5th. Somersets were to sail in the Alnwick Castle[10] a small tub of a thing with very good quarters for the men but only cabins for 12 officers - and so all the junior officers were transferred to this splendid ship Kenilworth Castle in charge of our senior major.[11] We are living in luxury and ease with no men to look after and only watch duty once in five days. This is just like a swagger hotel and we are fed like princes and after camp life it is simply splendid! I will try to get a letter posted at Port Said which is our first stopping place. We are going very slowly and I'm told we should be on the sea for six weeks. Many thanks for letter which I found at the docks.

Best love

from Stan.

*****

No.14/10

Union Castle Line, R.M.S. Kenilworth Castle
at sea Oct.21st. 1914

My dear old Elsie

It is just sun rise - 5.15 am. a curious time to be writing letters you will say but I am Officer of the Watch tonight and have been keeping vigil. The sunset [sunrise] is priceless - I have been on the top deck watching it - it is right in front of our bows so we are going due east.

I think I told you in the letter I sent from Gibraltar that we are so lucky to be in this ship and have no duty except every five days we take our turn as officer on duty - it is my turn now - I am tired of reading so I am scribbling a few letters. Every two hours I have to do a round of the ship and it takes nearly an hour so you can imagine what a big place we are living in.

We are somewhere between Malta and Port Said and our ships log tells us we are 2,700 miles on our journey. I'm told that we shall be at Port Said in two days and I hope to get this posted then. I wrote you from Malta on Sunday last but the sea was so rough that the little steamer that came out to collect our mail couldn't get near enough to us to get the mail bag - so it now lies in the ship post office and you will probably get two letters together - that is if the censor will allow it.

---

[10] As *Kenilworth Castle,* reg. tonnage: 3796.

[11] Major RH Brutton TD, died in India of pernicious malaria January 15th 1916 (*BoR* p19).

Since Gibraltar the journey has been full of interest - for some days we steamed along quite close to the African coast and we waited some hours outside Malta and all longed to land for a while to have a look at the place. Here our silent English warships left us for the Adriatic they say and now the Frenchmen have taken charge of us until we reach Aden - then we shall have an extra strong escort for the Indian Ocean in case the Emden[12] is waiting for us.

It has been a glorious trip so far - we had some rough days about Malta and several wonderful thunderstorms at night but through everything I have felt as fit as a fiddle and haven't missed a meal - which is the best sign of all. We are not quite cut off from the world for wonder of wonders we are still in touch with the wireless station in Cornwall and get a Marconigram each day - the news is very short but it is better than nothing.

The days go by very quickly - we just get up at 6.30 and do an hours physical drill before breakfast and during the morning we have military lectures and are all learning semaphore signalling. There are heaps of jolly deck games - cricket etc. but the sun is so strong now that one spends most of the afternoon in a deck chair in the shade. After dinner we play bridge or have a sing song. There is a fine library in this writing room so there is plenty to do.

With us on this boat are the 4th. Wilts. with Lord Radnor in command - the 7th. Hants, the Hants R.F.A. and the Divisional Staff, about 3,000 all told - in the 7th. Hants are 4 old boys of Taunton School, two of them are men of my time, so through them I have made a lot of new friends. I am looking forward very much to seeing the Suez Canal and I hope we shall be allowed to land at Port Said altho' this is very doubtful. We are quite a big fleet and have to keep together for obvious reasons so we go along rather slowly and shall take some time going through the canal. I wonder when we shall get to our journeys end - Im told we have 3 days train journey when we reach Bombay. I will try to post you another letter as soon as we touch Indian soil. The sun is up above the sea now and the Mediterranean is a glorious blue - looking out of the writing room windows I can see the lines of transports and beyond the evil looking cruisers and destroyers. I must do another round of the ship now and see the sentries are not sleeping at their posts. It is so difficult even yet to realize that we are steadily steaming towards the mysterious East but it is a great experience! Goodbye dear old girl I so look forward to your letters at Jhansi.

Best love

from Stan

*****

---

[12] On November 9th 1914 the German cruiser *Emden* was destroyed by HMAS *Sydney* on Keeling, one of the Cocos Islands. She had sunk two Allied warships off Penang and fifteen merchant ships in the Bay of Bengal and around the Maldives. HMAS *Sydney* was escorting Anzac troopships heading for Suez.

No.14/11

My dear old Elsie.

New and very strict regulations have been issued today and I am only allowed
to send you a few lines to tell you I am very well indeed and having a good and
very interesting time. I hope you got my other letters (4 altogether) posted prior
to this. It may be three weeks or so before I am able to write you again but I'll do
so when ever possible, Best love dear

from Stan

*****

No.14/12

5th. Somerset L.I., Jubbulpore, India
Nov. 18th. 1914

My dear old Elsie,

At last I am able to sit down to write you a decent letter but you will be
surprised to see that it is addressed from Jubbulpore. When we arrived at Bombay
we were told that our plans were altered and that after all we were not going to
Jhansi.

We thought ourselves awfully lucky as this is a fine station and one of the most
coveted in India but to day we hear that we are shortly to be moved up into the
Punjab and that Umballa will probably be our station - at first we were told that it
would be in six weeks time but now I hear that it may be as soon as 10 days time.
The Government seem to think that if there is any trouble in India it will come
from the North West Frontier and so most of the available troops are to be
concentrated in the Punjab. But perhaps in case these orders are changed again
you had better address letters here - marked "please forward" with the regiment
marked very distinctly. I hardly know where to begin this letter but first of all I
must thank you ever so much for your two letters and the four papers which
reached me from Jhansi two days ago - they were my first letters from England
and youve no idea what a joy it was to get a mail again. It was awfully sweet of
you to think of sending the papers - thank you so much dear. It is sad so many
fine men are being killed in the war and your friend Lieut. Rushton looks such a
nice chap - I can quite realize how busy your days are now with such a large
family and the nurse[13] gone away but I hope you will keep fit for this winter and
not get any throat trouble.

I am so well and up to now the climate suits me down to the ground - I was
always a hot weather man! The officers are good chaps and we have great times
together - there is a certain exclusive comradeship among soldiers which is
delightful - they have knick-named me "Uncle" - I am so much older and fatter

[13] Barbara Brown was born in September 1914 and the 'monthly nurse' would have gone leaving
Elsie to care for the baby as well as Ronald aged 18 months.

than the other subalterns and I sometimes have to fight their little battles for them. I fancy the last letter I sent you of any length was from Port Said after that we were quite cut off from the world and the strict orders were that we were not to write to our friends or relations any particulars whatever of our whereabouts. We were lucky in being allowed to land at Port Said - it was fascinating and wonderfully picturesque but so smelly that we were thankful to get aboard ship again - there is a peculiar smell in the East but I suppose we shall get used to it - In the native quarters here it is just as bad. I shall always remember my trip down the Suez Canal - we passed partly at night & partly by day. At night each ship had a huge search light at her bow lighting up the sandy barren dessert for miles around - it was very weird.

Half way through we had to pull into a siding to let a lot of transports pass us with Indian troops on board bound for the front (and some days later in the Red Sea we passed close to 40 more transports with their battleship protectors - all with Indian troops for France - it was a great sight and British hearts felt very proud - there was a cheering and counter cheering and some one would shout "are we down hearted" and the stentorian reply would come back "No oh oh" - and then to the singing of "Tipperary" and "God Save the King" we passed on!) At last we reached Suez and here it was we were stopped for five days. At this time the Allies were clearing all the Austrian German shipping out of the canal & its ports and it was most exciting - also the trouble with Turkey[14] was getting acute and already they had threatened to destroy the entrance to the Canal. We were kept under arms and were spoiling for a fight but more Indian troops came up and were landed and put on guard and so we were sent on into the Red Sea. It was frightfully hot here - it was impossible to stay in ones cabin and sleep was out of the question except in a camp chair on deck. At last we came to Aden and we were able to land here and see the sights while some of the transports coaled. I was laid up for two days here - the effects of vaccination - I had such a bad arm. Here I got some ostrich feathers for you - I am wondering how to get them to you or whether I shall keep them and bring them back?[15] I wonder if you can ever make use of them - if they are not fashionable now perhaps some day they may be! We steamed into the Indian Ocean at last and did not see land again for a week but then to our great joy we sighted Bombay and I am sure everyone was delighted and thankful for we had been just five weeks at sea.

Bombay gave us a great reception - in fact I cannot speak too highly of the reception we have been given everywhere - it is really splendid and makes our job much more pleasant. We were three days in the troop train and this was the worst part of the whole journey - we reached Jubbulpore thoroughly dirty and tired.[16] I must tell you next more of my work and daily doings but you can think of me

---

[14] Germany had for some years been putting pressure on Turkey to align herself against Britain. Great Britain declared war on Turkey on November 5th 1914.

[15] The ostrich feathers were stolen from his kit in India but later replaced (Letter 17/17). The replacements were received by Elsie and worn on her hat on her wedding day.

[16] Stanley remembered that when the Battalion reached Jubbulpore it did not make a good initial impression. Accustomed to the Light Infantry's 140 paces to the minute the Battalion was confused when led from the station to the barracks by the band of another unit which played at 120 paces to the minute.

comfortably settled in a bungalow with four other fellows and we share all the expenses - I will send you along some snap shots as soon as I can. We have some lovely shady trees and a large compound all our own. Lovely little grey squirrels run up and down the trees (the Hindus worship these) and there are monkeys who throw things at you coming up the drive, at night the jackals come round and make a horrid noise. The only thing I fear is the mosquitos & they are very deadly here & carry malaria with them - already some of our Tommies are laid up. I sleep under a mosquito net at night and they buzz buzz round it all the time.

Today my Indian uniforms have come thank goodness and I discard my thick English khaki. The new things are made of khaki drill and we even wear short trousers like hockey shorts - it is so cool with bare knees but we all felt quite shy for a day or two (I dont think), Every day I have an hours lesson in Hindustani & I hope to pick up the language very soon - it may be useful some day. We get the war telegrams each day - I wish the news was better - the progress seems so slow doesnt it!

Thank you again ever so much for your letters & papers & I am longing to hear from you again soon. With best love & all good wishes for Xmas dear old thing.

from Stan

*****

No.14/13

Nebudda Club, Jubbulpore
Dec. 3 1914

My dear old Elsie

Ever so many thanks for your last mail letter & the Tatler which I enjoy ever so much and read every word. We have been living in a packed up state for 10 days and it has been most uncomfortable. I wonder when our wanderings will cease. We leave for Umballa[17] tonight (Thurs) and do not reach our destination until next Monday! When we are settled again in Umballa I will write you another long letter - you will probably get this about Xmas time - it seems impossible to send you the old old wishes but let us hope for better times and that we may meet again soon as in the good old peaceful days. We have been turned out of our mess for days for all our things had to be packed and are living at this Club. The best bed I can find is a hard wood floor and a blanket. But after all this soldiering it takes a lot to upset me and I'm glad to say I am keeping wonderfully fit. I expect Amy is staying with you now, how very nice for you and I hope she is much better.

Excuse more now old dear. I hope my next will be more interesting and I'll try to send you some snap shots too.

Best love and many thanks again for your letter and papers.

from Stan

*****

---

[17] Umbala or Ambala: city north of Delhi with garrison cantonment.

14

No.14/14

5th. Somerset L.I. Umballa, Punjab.
Dec. 8th. 1914

My dear old Elsie

Just a few lines to tell you I am safe and sound at Umbala or Ambala or Umballa - which ever you like. I only hope we are permanently settled now for these long train journeys are very trying and it is so expensive to fit up fresh bungalows.

You will be glad to hear that I am still very fit indeed and am getting on so well with my soldiering that I have ever so much more confidence and am happier than ever in my work. We are in quite different country now to Jubbulpore - it is far colder, for away Simla way we can see the snow capped heights of the Himalayas - the country is much rougher and the people speak no English and look so fierce that I always carry my revolver with me after sunset. The men have very fine barracks - roomy and high and the drilling grounds are excellent but our own bungalows are very inferior to our Jub. ones and are over run with huge rats and insects which I've never seen before - still all these things come in the life of a soldier I suppose and all one can do is set ones teeth and go on. We passed through Jhansi on our way up and picked up the letters - many thanks dear for the one you sent me posted on Nov. 12th. I am sorry the little boy[18] has been so ill and that Mrs. Brown has had other trouble too but I hope every thing is better now. I will try to send you a longer letter next mail - we have to work very hard now and I shall get less time for writing - we hear that we are to go back to France in March and we have a lot to do by that time. Goodnight old girl I hope you are quite well and free from throat trouble

Best love and all good wishes

from Stan.

*****

No.14/15

5th. Somerset L.I. Ambala
Dec. 31st. 1914

My dear old Elsie

I can only send you a few lines this week as the mail goes tonight and I have had no time - the week before Xmas I was away in the hills with my company on a bivouacing expedition returning on Xmas Eve. I spent the Xmas holiday as a guest of H.H. the Maharajah of Patiala[19] and tomorrow I am off again for several days bivouacing - next mail I hope to send you a long letter. So many thanks dear for the letters and papers - its awfully good of you and I am sure the pipes will be fine when they arrive - You can somehow always pick out a good pipe.

---

[18] The little boy was Ronald Brown, aged about 21 months.

[19] The Maharajah of Patiala died in March 1938 aged 46. He had been President of the Cricket Club of India and had been a 'free scoring batsman' before poor health compelled him to give up active participation in the game. (*The Wisden Book of Cricketers' Lives*. Compiled by Benny Green, Queen Anne Press, 1988, p.689.)

It has been a strange Xmas but I have had a wonderful time and I'll tell you all about it in my next - I am keeping very fit & I do hope you are altho I'm sorry you are so thin - I can still trouble the scales to the tune of 13 stone.

Its New Years Eve old dear - goodness knows what's going to happen in 1915 - it will be a great year & lets hope we shall meet again before it has run its course.

Best love and all good wishes,

From Stan.

*****

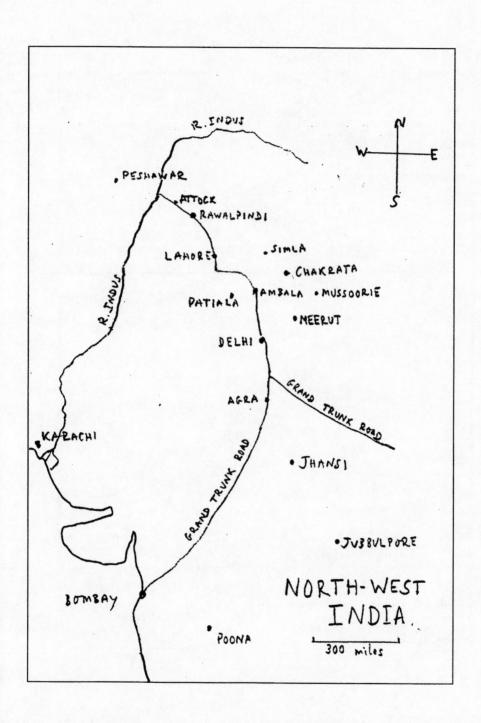

NORTH-WEST
INDIA.

300 miles

LOWER
MESOPOTAMIA

Scale

MILES 50 40 30 20 10 0   50   100 MILES

CHAPTER TWO

1915

The Background.

As the transports taking the 43rd (Wessex) Division to India steamed through the Eastern Mediterranean diplomatic relations between the Allies and Turkey steadily worsened, which was not surprising given Germany's sedulous cultivation of friendship with the Muslim world. Hostilities began in the first days of November 1914 and war was declared formally on November 5th. In anticipation of such a development the British Admiralty had long been voicing concern for the security of the oil-fields of the Anglo-Persian Oil Company. Persia was a neutral but weakly governed country in which British, Russian, Turkish and German diplomats and agents competed for influence. The 140 mile-long pipeline to the refinery at Abadan, near the head of the Persian Gulf, ran dangerously close to the border with the Basra province of Turkish Mesopotamia. Even before the end of September the India Office in London had telegraphed the Viceroy of India, Lord Hardinge, warning him to prepare an expeditionary force for operations in the Gulf and on October 18th the 16th Brigade of the 6th Indian Division set sail from Bombay, with orders to occupy Abadan and, should war with Turkey break out, Basra as well.

Basra was then a town of 60,000 inhabitants and the centre of the Turkish administration of the southern half of Lower Mesopotamia. The 16th Brigade landed at the mouth of the Shatt-el-Arab on the day after the declaration of war and was soon joined by the other Brigades of the 6th Indian Division. After some sharp fighting the British occupied Basra on November 21st and Qurna, forty miles further on, where the Euphrates joins the Tigris, early in December. For the next four months there was little military activity but while the Turks were preparing a counter-attack in the hope of recovering Basra, the British began to experience the problems of campaigning in a country which was extremely cold at night and exceptionally hot by day,[1] which away from the river banks was flat dusty desert or, after a rainstorm, a glutinous morass, a country which in spring was swamped by the flood waters of the two great rivers, whose twists and turns and mudbanks made navigation difficult at other times of year. Some of the Arab sheikhs had loathed the Turks and welcomed the British, but in a lawless society the local people exploited every chance of looting; camps and river traffic were continually sniped and the dead and wounded of both sides were stripped of their possessions if stretcher or burial parties failed to reach them quickly.

The Indian Government in Delhi and Commander-in-Chief in Simla were accustomed to suppressing internal disorder and fighting frontier wars, but had no experience of sending expeditions overseas. One of their worst mistakes was the

---

[1] The difference between day & night temperatures could be 50° Fahrenheit; see H Birch Reynardson, *Mesopotamia, 1914-15*, Melrose, 1919, p.215.

lamentable under-estimate of the necessary provision of medical services to cope with the thousands of men who fell victim to heat and sun stroke, dysentery and fevers as well as those wounded in battle with a stubborn enemy. Administrative under-funding and incompetence was compounded by disagreements between Delhi and London as to the consequences of the capture of Basra. Would the pipeline and the refinery be safe only if the Turks were driven out of the entire province they had ruled from Basra and, perhaps, from Baghdad, 500 miles away? How important was the Mesopotamia campaign to the defeat of Turkey, which would greatly benefit the Serbs and the Russians? The attack on the Dardanelles, launched in April 1915 in the hope of a quick breakthrough and the capture of Constantinople was, from London's perspective, the best means of achieving a victory that would make a Mesopotamian campaign irrelevant. The Government of India's appreciation of Mesopotamia's importance was radically different. Success there would enhance British prestige and the establishment of a protectorate would strengthen the security of India's western frontier by increasing British influence in the Gulf. In May 1915, at an anxious time of major military operations in France and the Aegean and the political crisis from which emerged a coalition Government in London, Delhi's views prevailed - with the dire consequences which unfolded in the next twelve months.

The Turkish counter-stroke against Basra had been delivered in April but was repulsed at the hard fought battle of Shaiba, giving the newly arrived Commander-in-Chief, General Sir John Nixon, the opportunity to put Delhi's forward policy into effect. On May 31st the 6th Division under Major-General Townshend's command brushed aside the Turkish defences on the Tigris north of Qurna and after a four day pursuit occupied Amara. It was a brilliant achievement but it extended by about 85 miles the precarious line of communication up which came military stores, food and mail and down which at the height of the hot weather came the increasing numbers of the sick, either to the makeshift hospitals in Basra or, in severe cases, to ships sailing for India.

By the end of August the worst of the hot weather had passed. Once more Sir John Nixon could not stand still; the Turks were re-grouping at Kut, the next town up-river from Amara, and the dream of a victory parade in Baghdad was enticing. Having prised the Turks out of a well-entrenched position Townshend entered Kut on September 28th; he was now 380 miles from the Gulf and 120 miles short of Baghdad. General Nixon's persistent demands for reinforcement had been met by the promised arrival, at an unspecified date, of two Indian divisions withdrawn from France for future garrison duty in Baghdad, so despite Townshend's misgivings about his weakness in numbers - he had no more than 12,000 men - and the unreliability of river transport with the flow of the Tigris at its annual lowest, Nixon ordered him to march on Baghdad whose capture would compensate for the stalemate on the Gallipoli peninsula. The Turks were waiting for Townshend at the ancient Arch of Ctesiphon, 23 miles short of his prize. After a three day battle in which some of the Turkish position was taken, at heavy cost, Townshend had too few fit survivors to press home any advantage, and on November 23rd his depleted and exhausted division was compelled to turn back and head for Kut, fighting rearguard actions, enduring forced marches and losing some valuable river craft. Nixon told Townshend to remain in Kut as his presence there would deter a Turkish advance on Amara or Basra. Townshend had enough food and ammunition to hold out for some weeks and a relief force would soon arrive to break up the siege. A determined assault on Christmas Eve was repulsed and the Kut garrison remained confident that the British forces gathering at Ali Gharbi, halfway to Amara, would reach them early in the New Year of 1916.

Stanley Goodland in 1915: India & Mesopotamia.

Stanley's experience of life as a subaltern officer in India on and off duty, in barracks, on exercises and his musketry course, was interrupted by his plunge into active service.

The 2nd Battalion, the Dorsetshire Regiment, was a regular unit previously stationed at Poona (now, Pune) and was the British component of the 16th Brigade, thus claiming to be the original and longest-serving battalion in Mesopotamia. Its record of service, written by CT Atkinson, can be found in the composite *History of the Dorsetshire Regiment, 1914-1919*.[2] The 2nd Dorsets were heavily involved in all the early fighting of the campaign. In November 1914 three officers and 21 other ranks had been killed in action and 149 men wounded. A steady trickle of sick men was sent back to India. At the battle of Shaiba, outside Basra, in April 1915 the colonel and three more officers were killed, 15 more being wounded, while 37 other ranks were killed and 115 wounded. By mid-May a further 133 men were in hospital with heat-stroke or fever.

It was this sorely depleted battalion which on May 25th welcomed a draft of eight officers and 232 men, composed of detachments from the Wessex Division, each of one officer, one sergeant, one corporal, two lance-corporals and 25 private soldiers. *The Book of Remembrance* lists the names of Stanley Goodland's detachment from the 1/5 Somersets which, with a similar detachment from the 1/4 Somersets led by Lt GWR Bishop, was posted to A Company. The newly-arrived Territorials were thrown into action almost at once, though the 2nd Dorsets and all the 16th Brigade did not lead the advance up the Tigris, reaching Amara on June 5th, 48 hours behind the vanguard. Here 'there was much sickness, both fever and dysentery being prevalent. Lieut Goodland and over 150 men were invalided to India.'[3]

Stanley's letters record his slow recovery from the severe attack of enteric fever which had forced him to give up after 'about a fortnight' in Amara. After four months of hospital treatment and convalescence he was back in uniform again, at Poona. It was by strange twists of fate that a Somerset Territorial commissioned only in July 1914 now found himself 15 months later the officer in command of the Indian depôt of the Dorsets, a pukka regular regiment. The army postal service kept him in touch with the men he had left behind in Mesopotamia, now commanded by Sergeant Eno, who were reinforced by a further draft of two NCOs and 13 privates in September. The detachment was fully involved in Townshend's

---

2 published by Henry Ling Ltd., Dorchester, 1932.
3 Atkinson, op. cit. p.185.

arduous campaign; the *Book of Remembrance*[4] traces its part in the distinguished record of the 2nd Dorsets. Some were killed, many more were wounded, and others probably fell sick; when the siege of Kut began only three out of the six NCOs and 15 of the 38 private soldiers remained on duty. Sergeant Eno was killed on December 10th; he was posthumously awarded the DCM for bravery in the field. When Kut surrendered the surviving two NCOs and seven privates became prisoners and of these only Lance-Corporal AV Nichols and Private EM Taylor emerged from Turkish captivity in 1918. Of the Dorsets all 12 of the captured officers, including Lt Bishop of the 1/4 Somersets, survived imprisonment in Turkey, but only 70 of the 350 other ranks who were marched out of Kut were alive to be repatriated at the end of the war.

Stanley's prediction in his letter of November 6th that he would be re-united with his men on about December 15th was unrealisable. He left Poona on the day Townshend turned back from Ctesiphon and the siege of Kut was formed soon after his arrival at Basra. He was under no illusion as to his chances of survival; enteric fever had failed to kill him but an ounce of 'Turkish Delight' might do the trick. His sombre mood was intensified by his anxiety for his mother dying of rectal cancer. The issues of the *Somerset County Gazette* of December 25th and January 1st 1916 record her death on December 22nd and funeral on Christmas Eve, but it was many weeks before her younger son heard the dreaded but expected news.

---

[4] pp. 25-32.

The Letters Written in 1915

No.15/1

5th.Somerset L.I., Ambala
Jan 7th. 1914 [sic]

My dear old Elsie

I have been living on the shooting range with my company since the Xmas holiday and I am writing this sitting in a trench with rifles banging away all round me so it isn't easy to collect my thoughts - but the mail goes tonight and if I don't write in this way you wont get a letter this mail. Many thanks dear old thing for your letters addressed to Jubbulpore and Madras which came quite safely. None of us ever went to Madras - it is another of the wild rumours that fly about. You will be glad to know I am still wonderfully well touch wood! Most of our officers have been laid up with something or other but I keep on splendidly but I musn't boast. I am glad you got my first letter from India safely & hope the others Ive written reach you in due course. Unfortunately the captain of my company Timms[5] has broken his arm and Ruck[6] has gone to Meerut for a months signalling course so I have the company on my own for some time to come and I find there is plenty to do and I dont get any time now for sport and haven't been out with a gun once since we came to this God forsaken place. We had a real good time at Xmas and now are hard at work for there is much to do before March comes - When you get this letter I shall probably be away in the country on a three weeks company training so think of me then. The week prior to Xmas I was away training with my company and we had a very rough time. We are having a spell of cold weather that lasts some 3 or 4 weeks. Otherwise it is very hot here during the day but at night it is bitterly cold and the winds sweep off the mountains just like Switzerland.[7] When bivouacing we got very little sleep and I found your woolly helmet such a comfort. I didn't realize India could ever be cold! Well I got back to barracks on Xmas Eve in time to sing[8] at a hospital concert and we all had to spend Xmas day with our companies Church parade of course and then a big dinner with the men and the usual speech making and singing - In the evening we had a special do at our own mess - It was very strange Xmas Day and for the first time since I was a soldier I got a bit of a hump. I hope I shall never have to spend another Xmas Day out of old England. We had plenty of paper chains and decorations and even mistletoe and holly but there is no place like home especially at Xmas. We had compensations awaiting us for the Maharajah of Patiala has sent us an invitation to go over (26 miles away) to his place to stay with him for two days cricket!

---

5 Capt AS Timms, awarded MC. Officer of the 1/5 Battalion, SLI (*BoR*, p.74).

6 Lt CFL Ruck, also Officer as above. (*BoR* p.13 'officers proceeding overseas.')

7 In January 1914 Stanley had enjoyed a skiing holiday in Switzerland.

8 Stanley had been a member of Taunton Operatic Society. The *Somerset County Gazette*, April 18th 1914 acclaimed his performance as Ravennes, one of the thieves in the comic opera 'Erminie.' See plate, section I, p.2.

And so at sunrise eleven of us set out and we spent a wonderful two days and were treated every bit like royalty. We were met at the station by elephants and rode on these huge things up to the Palace which is of course a most gorgeous place and it would take me ages to tell you all the wonderful things we saw. We had two full days cricket and of course I enjoyed every minute of this altho we were beaten we made 391 in our two innings which was quite good considering we were all out of practice and the Maharajah had his two pros Tarrant[9] and J.W. Hearne[10] against us The Maharajah is only 23 but is a huge man - he is going to get up some pig sticking for us in February and I hope we shall be able to get two more days leave as they say it is the finest sport in the world. I took some photos at Patiala and I hope some day to send you some but there isn't a man to develop films in Ambala and I get no time to do it. I hear Harold is coming out to Burmah with his battalion[11] - he will be hundreds of miles from me and I dont expect we shall meet. Fancy last year this time I was in Switzerland - all this seems like a dream to me. I wonder where I shall be next Xmas Well old dear I must see to my men now so will say Goodbye best wishes for the New Year and much love

from Stan

*****

No.15/2

5th. Somerset L.I., Ambala
Feb. 2nd 1915

My dear old Elsie

Ever so many thanks old thing for your last letter dated Jan. 7th. and the Punch and Bystander which are so much enjoyed and for the two lovely pipes which came quite safely last mail - really you are too good to me altogether. I havent used them yet for they look so nice in their little case but I have always found you an expert in pipes and Im sure I shall enjoy many many smokes from them.

I am so very sorry to hear that your mother[12] is laid aside with appendicitis and do hope she is stronger now and that if an operation is necessary she will come through all right - It must be an anxious time for you old thing but try to keep cheerful through it all. I believe 1915 is going to be a devil of a year for most people and the 'cheery' souls of the world simply must keep their peckers up. I must try to find time to write to your mother. Talking of cheery souls I will send you with this a photograph which is very interesting and awfully good I think -

---

[9] Frank A Tarrant, Australian born all-rounder, made a great name with Middlesex, 1905-1914. Back in Australia he played for Victoria in the 1920s, retiring at the end of the 1926/27 season. In 1935/36 he took an Australian team to India under the auspices of the Maharajah of Patiala. He died in 1951 aged 69.

[10] John William ('Young Jack') Hearne died in 1965 aged 74. He was a Middlessex professional from 1909 to 1936 and played for England in 24 Tests. He was 'one of England's greatest all-rounders' (*The Wisden Book of Cricketers' Lives*, op. cit. Tarrant, p.375. Hearne, pp.411 & 875).

[11] The 2/5 SLI embarked at Southampton on December 12th 1914 on the chartered ship *Ionian* for Bombay, thence by rail to Calcutta, across the Bay of Bengal on the transport *SS Thongwa* and up the River Irrawaddy to Meiktila, about 80 miles south of Mandalay (*BoR* pp.83-84).

[12] Mrs Annie Hyde survived her attack of appendicitis and lived until 1946.

I'm sure you will think I look as happy as ever - it was taken in our bungalow compound on Xmas morning our servants had come for their Xmas boxes and insisted on presenting us with sugar cakes and placing chains of flowers round our necks - it is a quaint Indian custom indicating loyalty. The men are our personal servants - water carriers, sweepers, gardeners, etc. The man in white on my left is my headman and the little boy sitting by my left leg is "Tiger" my dressing boy, errand boy, boot boy, and odd job boy. His English is delightful and he always calls me "My Lord"! The other officers are of course Capt Timms in centre and Ruck. Youll want a magnifying glass to see all my moustache for I cut it regularly every week. Well old dear I have had a very busy time lately I forget if I have told you that Timms is laid up with a broken arm and Ruck is away for a course in signalling at Meerut so for the last month I have had to run the company on my own. It has been a very important month for we have finished our musketry and done most of our company training - For my pains the Colonel[13] has recommended me for my second star and the papers have already gone to the War Office so all being well I shall be a full lieutenant in due course - I suppose it will take a month or so before I am gazetted - it is very nice and besides makes quite a difference in pay! We are hard at the final stages of training now and on Feb. 12th. we go out to camp for two weeks - The first week we are under canvas and the second one we have to live in trenches - can you imagine me old thing? I expect I shall miss my antique furniture dont you? It may be impossible to write while in camp for we are eighteen miles away in the jungle and cut off from everything but I will if I can. In addition to all my military work I am as busy as can be with a musical & dramatic concert which the General's wife has asked me to run for her in aid of the War Fund - It is to be on the 9th. and I will send you a programme as soon as they are printed. I told the Colonel I hadn't the time to do it but he said that anything coming from the General or his missus was practically a command so that settled it! The first part of the show is a pierrot party about 6 ladies and 6 men I think - all in red white and blue costumes - I am singing Hey Ho! cant you hear the screams and 'Up from Somerset' The second part is a one act play called 'Make Believe' which I am producing at very short notice - it is for four people two ladies and two men I am an unsuccessful author. I hope it will go all right - of course I enjoy it but it means a good deal of night work which is a nuisance just now and I wish one had more time! We get very little war news through now - the telegrams to the Indian papers get shorter and shorter - I hope we are doing well but one longs for a really big thing! I fancy Lord K is preparing for some coup in the Spring and I only hope his new army comes up to expectations. When we do advance in earnest the loss of life must be simply awful - I wonder what the people who said this war would be over in 6 months are thinking now - Why we have left old England 4 months now and the time has simply flown!

I have had some letters from Harold the last was written on a river steamer as they were going up to Mandalay - he tells me the good news of the safe arrival of

---

[13] Lt-Col EF Cooke-Hurle DSO commanded the 1/5 Battalion SLI throughout the war until ordered to report back to the War Office in February 1919.

Arthur's[14] sister and I am longing to hear more particulars and only hope everything is going along well. I can guess you have had a busy time keeping house & looking after your family - but I hope you are keeping well through everything - Goodbye old thing many thanks again dear for all your letters and papers & the lovely pipes - with best love

from Stan

*****

No.15/3

5th.Somerset L.I., In Camp, Ambala
Feb. 23 1915

My dear old Elsie

Here I am in camp sitting in the shade of a friendly palm tree writing my mail. Thank you so much old thing for your last letter and most welcome papers - We are 18 miles from Umbala here and right away from civilisation but there are 400 men and 14 officers so we are a large and very happy family. The letters and papers were sent out to us and we eagerly awaited the messenger.

The papers you sent have simply been fought for by the other officers and I have read every word several times over. We are having a slack day today for we have been out all night the last two nights practising digging trenches in the darkness.

I can tell you it has been a job. On Thursday we send our tents back to our base and then for a week we live in our trenches - the nights are still very cold but the days are stoking up and are a good deal warmer than the hottest of our English summer days. I hope you enjoyed your weekend at home - but Im sure you did - I am rather anxious to know why you are on sick leave and suppose it is your poor old throat again perhaps I shall hear all about it in your next letter. Goodness knows what will happen to us old thing - last week we were told to be ready to sail from Karachi on March 19th. and yesterday we heard that the Viceroy[15] of India refuses to release any more troops from this country and that we are to stay here over the hot weather - Orders seem to change every week. The fact is lots of things have been happening out here which never get into the papers at home and Im not allowed to say much about it - there has been serious trouble among some disloyal Sikhs[16] at Lahore which is not far from here and we have been warned that we must be ready for any emergency - You cant trust the natives one bit.

---

[14] Arthur, first child of Harold & Alice Goodland born on November 11th 1911. His sister, Mary (later Burns) was born on January 15th 1915.

[15] Charles Hardinge, Baron Hardinge of Penshurst, PC, KCMG, KCVO, 1858-1944, Viceroy of India 1910-1916, censured by Commission of Enquiry into Mesopotamia Expedition (*DNB*) succeeded by Frederick John Napier Thesiger, 1868-1938, 3rd Baron & 1st Viscount Chelmsford, Viceroy of India 1916-1921 (*DNB*).

[16] Many Sikhs living and working abroad were lured back to India by the revolutionary Har Dayal with promises of German arms and the understanding that disaffected units in the British Army would defect and kill their British officers. There was a secret meeting in Lahore on February 12th and a plan for a country-wide rising on February 21st, which failed to occur. (*On Secret Service East of Constantinople*, Peter Hopkirk, John Murray, 1994, pp.68-71, 81 & 82.)

I am always wishing this terrible war would cease - it is simply sickening - today news has come of a great Russian[17] defeat and another air raid in Colchester and several English merchantmen sunk - it looks very serious but thank goodness we are holding em in the west! My birthday wishes will come very late and Im so very sorry - fancy you 26 now - how old we are all growing! I hope you had a happy birthday dear & lots of presents and good wishes. I must write to the mater now. I do hope Mrs. Hyde is getting on and how was Gretchen - please let me know

Best love and all good wishes

from Stan

*****

No.15/4

5th. Somerset L.I.,Ambala
March 24th. 1915

My dear old Elsie

Time goes so quickly and I have had so much to do lately that I havent written to you very regularly but even so I am afraid some of my letters have gone astray - Yours too unfortunately dont always reach me - you wrote one mail that you were ill and going home all in a hurry with a mysterious pain which you would write and tell me all about - but I never got that letter so Im quite in the dark. But last mail your letter came saying you were better but that the pain was still rather a mystery to the doctors - Im glad to hear you mother is getting on too - I wrote her a few mails ago but I dare say my letter never reached her. I wonder if you ever heard of the safe arrival of the lovely pipes - Im sure I wrote to thank you for them - Ive had one in use for some time now and its a beauty. Thank you also - old thing - for all the papers you send me out - it is awfully sweet of you and Im sure I read every word. You'll be glad to hear Im still very fit indeed and feel as hard as nails and to my great delight my weight is going down for I'm now quite a fairy at 12st 7lb. and my word weve got Indian weather now - the last fortnight each day has got hotter and in the middle of the day it is dangerous to be out of doors - the mosquitos are biting savagely at night and the heat has brought out thousands of mysterious insects that Ive never seen before.

Im afraid, old thing, the Regiment is not going to France this Spring after all - we have been waiting patiently for our sailing orders which came and were cancelled indefinitely - the fact is there is a good deal of trouble here but Im not allowed to say anything about it but the Government of India is having a very anxious time and I dont think at present any more troops will be allowed to leave this country - We have our own part to play out here and I suppose we must be content but you can quite understand how we all long to do more. As a rule the British Regiments who are stationed in the plains are sent to the hill stations but I think if we have to remain in India that we shall have to remain here and Ambala is one of the hottest stations out here so we have trying times ahead - But Im

---

[17] Russian forces were defeated by a German Army under Ludendorff near the Mazurian Lakes (Russo-German border, East Prussia) in early February 1915.

certain it wont be safe to allow troops to leave Ambala which is full of unrest at present. I shall get some change however for Im going to Rawal Pindi (400 miles north east) on April 2nd. for I have to report myself there on the 5th. Easter Monday for a months course in musketry and Frontier Fighting - its the same course that is given at home in the depots at Hythe Woolwich etc. Of course I am looking forward not only to the change but especially to the course which will be very valuable to me and Im delighted the Colonel is sending me with a man called Lieut. Rawlings[18] from Wellington. I shall be staying at Flashman's Hotel but please address letters here - in any case I suppose by the time you get this my visit may well be nearly over. It will be very much like school again for there are 3 exams! and I was never very good at these as you know.

Thank goodness our time of hard training is over now and we have come through Kitcheners Test[19] with excellent results. In spite of many hardships the men are splendid and the only thing Im suffering from is sore feet which are much better now thanks to Condy's fluid and boracic powder![20] But 120 miles in 3 days takes a bit of doing for a man of my age and infirmities!

Unfortunately towards the end of the Test we were caught by tremendous thunderstorms - all one night we were lying out in the drenching rain and the next night we were marching all through the darkness with the rain simply streaming down and our cotton uniform is not very water tight and we weren't allowed to take overcoats. Ive been sleeping in strange places and my night experiences would fill a book - I perhaps have something to look back upon and ponder over if I live to be 100. Im sending home some large photos which you will enjoy seeing - I cant get more than one copy of each so Ive asked mother to let you see them - they are of my company and a large group of all the officers and football team etc. We have 'Sports' on April 10th. and Im Secretary so Ive got that to bother me now - the original date was April 3rd. so I should be in Pindi on the 10th. so thought how to get an assistant but I shall have to do all the dirty work. I dont know what time I should have at Pindi but Ill write as often as possible. I do hope you are all right now - I shall think of you at Easter and hope that Gretchen[21] and Leslie will be down with you

Best love old girl & many thanks again for your letters & papers

from Stan

*****

---

[18] One of the officers listed as proceeding overseas in 1914 (*BoR* p15). Mentioned in Despatches (*BoR* p.73).

[19] Three days of arduous manoeuvres under simulated battle conditions.

[20] Potassium permanganate solution, one time popular disinfectant. Boracic acid powder, soothing & drying agent.

[21] Greta, née Goodland, and her husband Leslie Hyde.

5th. Somerset L.I., Rawalpindi
April 7th. 1915

My dear old Elsie

Many thanks old girl for your last letter, (March 10th) which has been sent on to me from Ambala - You dont say how you are so I hope your pain has quite gone and that you are ever so fit again. I came along here last Sunday and we are settled down to a really hard course but I am glad to be able to see this part of the country which is by far the most interesting and picturesque of any I have yet come across. Last week I went over to Multan[22] with Frank Calway[23] and the weekend before I spent in the hill country around Simla so by the time I reached Pindi last Sunday I had done about 2000 miles in the train and was jolly tired of it.

We went to Multan to see the grave of poor Buster Deane[24] an old Taunton School boy who died there last December and we made arrangements for the erection of a tomb stone, etc. He joined the ranks of the Devons last August and came out the same time as we did - he was a great strong chap but he got hold of fever somehow or other. I went up to the hills with a jolly party and we had a very good time. I am anxious to see as much as I can of the country now Im out here but it is very expensive worse luck - and I'm sure I shall be poor for the rest of my days for I cant do all these things on subalterns pay. But Simla is glorious and to go up from the plains as I did is just like getting into another country and its very much like Switzerland - only vaster and grander. Up here it is very wild and I hope to go up to Peshawar and the Khyber Pass before I go back to the Regiment. I hope I shall get through the course all right - I find it very difficult and the army instructors have no mercy - I have to do a lot of home work - It's just like being at school again and it's very irksome at times. I shall be here until the first week in May and then go back to Ambala. I am glad Gretchen and Leslie will be with you for Whitsun and hope you will manage a few days holiday at Taunton afterwards for Im sure you deserve [it]. I heard by cable yesterday of poor Mr. Franklin's[25] death and its a great blow to me but of course not altogether unexpected - I dont know what will happen to the poor old business for Im sure I shall never be happy there without him and so if you hear of anyone who wants a bright young fellow after the war is over dont forget me!

There ought to be some good commercial jobs going in London when things settle down again and I expect I shall have to make a fresh start for there are many

---

[22] City in Punjab (now Pakistan) with garrison cantonment.
[23] Capt FHF Calway, Adjutant when the Battalion left for overseas. Stanley succeeded him as Adjutant in October 1917: see letter 17/26. On leaving the 1/5 Somersets Frank Calway became Brigade Major of the 233rd Infantry Brigade, an appointment which enabled him to keep in close touch with his old Battalion. War service interrupted his lifelong connection with the silk industry in Taunton. He was chairman of Somerset County Council at the time of his death, aged 70, in 1956.
[24] 'Buster' Deane, Charles Gerrard, only son of Edwin Deane LRCP of Bronshill House, Torquay, died of fever in Multan. (*Somerset County Gazette*, December 19th 1914.)
[25] Mr TH Franklin of Franklin, Hare & Goodland, Antique Dealers & Silversmiths of Taunton, where Stanley had worked, died April 5th 1915 aged 63. He had been active in many Taunton organisations.

lean years in store for the antique trade I'm afraid but there is heaps of time isn't there to think these things out! I must write to Mother now last mail I heard she was in bed and not at all well. I expect Alice[26] and her family were rather too much for her. I have spent a strange Easter and I must say it hasnt been nice and at times I get very homesick but I really think the war is moving in our favour everywhere now and I quite hope to see you again before 1915 is out.

Best love old girl and many thanks for all your letters and papers.

from Stan

*****

No. 15/6

5th. Somerset L.I., Rawalpindi
April 14th. 1915

My dear old Elsie

I'm afraid I've no time to write you a long letter this mail but I'll send you a few snap shots instead which I hope you'll like and I will write on the back what they are.

We are having such a busy time up here and I haven't felt so done up since I started soldiering. I didn't realize there was so much theory in the thing and I must say my brain is very muddled at present with all this stuffing - We had our first exam today and I hope I've done all right - we get another tomorrow and two next week. It's just like sweating up for the matric! But I'm still awfully well and think all the 'learning' will be very useful when I get back to the regiment!

Best love old thing and many thanks for your letter (March 18) and the papers - it is sweet of you to send them.

from Stan

*****

No. 15/7

Rawal Pindi Club, Rawalpindi
April 21 1915

My dear old Elsie

Just a line this mail to thank you very much old thing for your last letter and the papers. I have read with great interest the thrilling description of the fighting round Ypres.[27] How wonderfully our men did against frightful odds.

We are kept awfully busy here and I shall be so glad when this course is over for we have simply been living on musketry the last three weeks and I'm fed up with it. But I'm learning such a lot that will be very useful to me but it is a bit strenuous in this terrific heat. We are out field firing most mornings now so have to attend afternoon lectures and in the evening write out our notes properly so there isn't much peace but we make the most of our weekends. Last Sunday

---

[26] Wife of Stanley's brother Harold.

[27] The First Battle of Ypres, October and November 1914. The Second began on April 22nd 1915.

eleven of us went to Murree[28] 7,000 feet up in the mountains and got into 3 ft. of snow there scenery was magnificent - from Murree we took ponies and went 20 miles along the Jhelum[29] pass into Kashmir - it was just like Switzerland only wilder and grander and after the heat of the plains the air was like champagne. Today I've had a long letter from Harold who seems to be having a good time in Burma - it must be delightful country where he is and he says he is putting on flesh I think I shall melt quite away before the hot weather is over!

I hope you are very fit now dear girl - I am inspite of everything - how I wish this horrible war would end and tho' at present we seem as far away as ever from a final result - Best love dear

from Stan

*****

No. 15/8

5th. Somerset L.I., Rawalpindi, India
April 26 1915

My dear old Elsie

Many thanks old girl for your letter and papers by this mail just arrived and I've news for you this week for in a few days I'm off on active service. It appears that in recent fighting in the Persian Gulf the Norfolks and 2nd. Dorsets suffered heavy casualties and the Territorial Battalions serving out here have been asked to supply drafts immediately. Yesterday the Colonel wired me asking[30] if I would go in command of our detachment and of course I replied "yes gladly" and I expect to sail from Karachi in 10 days time. I return tomorrow to Ambala after sitting for my final exam here and there will be a hundred and one things to do and to get ready and the proper equipment of the men is so very important. This may be my last opportunity for some time old girl of writing to you but I'll send a line whenever I'm allowed if its only one of those terrible official postcards. But of course letters from old England will be more acceptable than ever now and should be addressed

Lieut. S. Goodland
5th.Somerset L.I.
Attached 2nd. Dorset Regiment
Indian Expeditionary Force
Persian Gulf

The letters already in the post for me will be sent on from Ambala and I hope to get them all in due course. Persia isn't an ideal spot to do service in and the climate is pretty bad the next 4 months but I'm awfully fit and strong and this is probably one reason why I've been chosen for the command. My great regret is that I shall be severed from the old Regiment and the many friends I've made but in these times soldiers musn't be choosers and of course I'm awfully pleased with

---

[28] Hill station north of Rawalpindi.
[29] Town now in Pakistan on present Kashmir border, also River and pass into Kashmir.
[30] Stanley recounted that the Colonel had first offered the posting to the Senior Subaltern who had 'declined the honour.'

being selected. I'm sorry I haven't time to write a long letter - my mind is so full of many things (I dread the rotten old exam tomorrow) and my heart beats faster today in anticipation of fresh experiences ahead - I must write to mother too and its rather difficult - I only hope she won't worry or be too anxious about me as I'm afraid even now she is far from well.[31] I will send a little photo with this - the Colonel wanted to have one of all his officers but I'm afraid the native photographer wasn't very expert! I shall always be thinking of you, old pal, and if thoughts have wings (as the song says) your ears will often tingle - What to do with all my things is a great problem for I'm only allowed to take 35lb. of baggage including my valise and blankets! But it's no use worrying over these trifles is it. Now don't be anxious about me old girl or think things because you don't get news of me - I feel I shall come through all right and we shall meet again before many months are over and I shall be telling you all my experiences safe and sound in dear old England once again - So long dear with best love

from Stan

*****

No. 15/9

Sind Club, Karachi
May 17 1915

My dear old Elsie

Here I am dear at Karachi and we embark in a couple of hours time. I have seized the opportunity of coming to the Club for a bath and a good meal. We have been a week in the troop train and it has been 'hell.' It's only a 2000 mile journey but the heat has been awful across the Sind Desert and we have only been able to travel at night. Last night we stayed at the Rest Camp here but the frogs (great big slimy ones) and mosquitos were so numerous that we got no sleep. Will you make me a present - old girl - you said you'd like to didn't you! I want a looking glass and knife fork and spoon. The looking glass is made of highly polished metal and the knife fork and spoon are all in one and fold up. I saw the advertisement in an old Bystander[32] and they are sold by John Pound & Son Oxford St., London. The glass is 2/6 and the kf&sp is 3/6 - I hope you wont be cross with me for asking but these things will be so useful and I think they will come all right by parcel post. I will send you another line as soon as I can - Ive had no English letters for two weeks but I expect they'll turn up one day - I hope so.

Cheero! old girl best love

from Stan

*****

---

[31] Stanley's mother was very ill and died December 22nd 1915. There are frequent references to her illness in subsequent letters and his concern at being so very far away from home. He did not receive the news of her death until February 5th 1916.

[32] There are several references to periodicals: *Bystander, Tatler, Sketch,* and *Punch*.

30

No.15/10

To Goodland. Elm Grove. Taunton.
Copy of Telegram received from Military Secretary - War Office - begins -
Lieutenant E.S.Goodland 5th Somerset L.I. attached 2nd. Dorsets reported sick -
sailed on Hospital Ship *"Madras"*[33] 8th. July - Officer - Special G.F. Records
Exeter

*****

No.15/11

Coluba Hospital, Bombay
July 30 1915

[Envelope readdressed to Borth,[34] N.Wales, with note on the back in Mrs.
Brown's writing: "I say, this is a bit of Xmas!"]

My dear old Elsie

First I must thank you ever so much for all your letters and papers - I did not
get any mail for nearly 2 months and when I eventually found it at Basra on my
backward journey there was quite an accumulation. I shall never be able to thank
you enough for writing so regularly and for all the papers you have so kindly sent
me out - they have helped me to spend many happy hours but I'm afraid I have
cost you a lot of money and you have to deny yourself all sorts of things on my
account - But there - old thing - I'll try to make it up to you some day when the
dear old peaceful times come again.

I wonder how much news you have had of me and my doings? I'm so sorry I've
had no chance of writing to you - I have only been able to send a few lines to
Mother occasionally and I doubt if these letters all reached their destination! No
doubt you have heard I've been ill and am now in the Military Hospital in Bombay
- and so much has happened to me since I last wrote you from Karachi that I
hardly know where to begin. First of all I had better tell you I am practically well
again now and only lack the proper use of my legs. Since leaving Amarah Ive
made a wonderful recovery[35] and am being fed on all sorts of fattening things
now and am getting huge again and want some real hard exercise again badly -
But Im not allowed to walk yet for there is a danger of getting enteric legs[36] so
I'm carried out on to the balcony of this ward every day. We are right on the sea
and look out over the Arabian Sea - the monsoon gales spring up almost every day
and the huge waves break against the foundations of the hospital. - it is a grand
sight & besides we get sunsets which are indescribably beautiful.

So old dear you must cease to be anxious about me any more for I'm doing
famously. I am now wondering what will happen to me. In a very few days I
expect they will have a Medical Board on me to decide my future. Sometimes

---

[33] British India Steam Navigation Co. Ltd. Reg. tonnage 4237.

[34] Welsh Coastal village north of Aberystwyth where the Hyde family went on holiday.

[35] Enteric Fever was a lay term used for infections by both typhosis (typhoid) and paratyphoid
bacilli, of which there were three strains: Paratyphoid A was most prevalent in the Middle East and
India.

[36] Muscle degeneration may occur in cases of enteric fever - there was also a risk of thrombosis of
the veins in the lower extremities. From *Synopsis of Medicine*, H Letheby Tidy, 5th edn, 1920.

they send enteric cases home and I shall press for this for several reasons but I'm afraid I shan't be successful - probably they will make me take a couple of months sick leave in a hill station and if so I shall try to go back to the Regiment which is at present at Dagshai near Simla[37] and in the lower Himalayas - I shall enjoy being back among my old pals again - they wont allow me I am sure to go to Burma to see Harold for its such a long journey - it takes eight days from Bombay! I feel it is my duty to get back to my men in Mesopotamia as soon as I possibly can get quite fit and this is what I shall try to do if I can't get back to England. All that passed up in the Gulf seems a horrid nightmare now altho the time was so short. First of all the sea trip from Karachi was gastly and I arrived at Basra quite a wreck! and then almost immediately we had to go into action and were fighting practically every day for a fortnight without undressing and only getting bully beef and biscuits, water taken from the filthy Tigris river which was in full flood - we were covered in fleas & things & I wonder everyone didn't get fever! But the battle was glorious and I shall never forget it all and was amply repaid for all the hardships - we kept the Turks on the run for 150 miles & ultimately captured Amarah & nearly 1000 prisoners!

After being in Amarah about a fortnight I had to give up - I struggled against the fever for several days but absolutely couldn't get up one morning & so was taken off to hospital on a stretcher. I was really ill for 4 days and nearly left my old bones in the Garden of Eden but they kept me alive on brandy and spoons full of milk. I had malaria too & was very delirious but made a grand recovery & here I am all alive but not kicking much yet. The news of poor mother was a great shock to me & I'm always thinking of her now and wondering. Fortunately I am in communication with Harold now & rely upon him for the latest news. All my mail will still go up to Basra & goodness knows when I shall get it. Of course I did not hear of mother's illness until I reached Basra & it seems just too dreadful & unfortunate that Harold & I are so far away, thats why I want to get home so much. Mothers life has been so wonderful - active & unselfish she deserved a happy & peaceful autumn of her life & now this has come! I only hope she will not suffer much pain when the end does come! But it seems terrible that when we return it will be to a motherless home & Im sure I dont know what the poor old Pater [38] will do when he realizes it all - these are dreadful times and a year ago we were all so happy.

I hope you will be able to go down to Elm Grove mother will enjoy seeing you & it will cheer her up & I wonder when you are having any holiday & wherever you go I hope you will have a good time and a long rest and mind you look out for enemy aircraft.

We are very comfortable here there are 4 of us all enterics and weve been together about 6 weeks now - one is an Artillery Major and the others are R.A.M.C. Captains - jolly nice men all of them and we share a nice big ward - the

---

[37] Himalayan Hill Station, summer capital of India. The Viceroy and members of the Viceregal Council with their staffs retreated there from the heat of Delhi in the summer months. The name is also used as shorthand for Indian Army GHQ.

[38] Edward Charles Goodland (1842-1925). Married 1880. He was blind from an accident in childhood but took an active part in the family firm of Charles Goodland & Son, Coal Merchants.

Sisters are such good sorts & take so much trouble for us - at Amarah the hospital was dreadful - just a hut built of reeds and no beds!![39]

I get into trouble if I write too much so I must dry up. I hope you will be able to read this scribble.

Hoping you keep well & again let me thank you for all your letters & papers.

Best love

from Stan

*****

No. 15/12

The Station Hospital, Poona
Aug 6 '15

My dear old Elsie

Just a few lines to tell you I was moved up to this hospital yesterday but please address letters c/o Messrs Cox & Co. for the present. I am still getting on wonderfully well and am thankful to say that I can walk about 20 yards with the help of a couple of thick sticks - I shall soon be running about again but my poor old knees are still very weak & sometimes refuse to work. Ive got a huge appetite & always seem hungry which is the best possible sign and with all this inactivity Im getting so fat! The Colonel doctor told me this morning that I must go to a convalescent home at Wellington[40] - it is a very healthy hill station in the Madras district & quite near Cootamunda [Ootacamund] which is the Simla of Southern India - I shall probably go before a Medical Board next week - they tell me that England is out of the question as I could not travel by P & O alone & there are no hospital ships running now - they wont even let me go to Burma to stay with Harold but I hear he is to be moved shortly to Rangoon which is a very unhealthy place and wouldn't do for me at all. I am glad to say that I hear from Harold regularly now and he sends me on his home letters which I am so glad to have - I hope to get my own mail soon but suppose I must be patient a bit longer. The last news from home is very distressing - Harold sent me a letter he had just received from Dorothy a very gloomy letter indeed and I cannot help feeling that the end is not far distant now. Dorothy says that mother complains now of a pain at the bottom of her back - this sounds very ominous - it is terrible really & makes me so anxious and unhappy. I wish to goodness I could get home soon while the dear old mother is still alive. Im so very glad you have been down to see her and it was good of you to make the long journey for such a short visit. I shall be anxious to hear what you really think about it all - I suppose Grace and Vincent[41] are married by this time. I dont approve of war weddings least of all this one but I musnt be selfish, I suppose I can keep a discreet silence. I only hope they will be very happy but there must be a certain sadness hovering over the start of their new life

---

[39] 'A large number of mud and reed huts in long rows stood on the plain covering an area of about a quarter of a square mile. These were the wards.' Martin Swayne, *In Mesopotamia*, Hodder & Stoughton, 1917, p.103.

[40] Large military establishment; the Camberley of the Indian Army, south east of Ootacamund, Madras Province.

[41] Grace Goodland (1891-1982). 3rd sister to Stanley, married Vincent Watkins, January 31st 1915.

which they wont easily forget. Lets hope it will all turn out for the best. I hope you are keeping fit old thing and that your babies havent been too troublesome during the hot weather - you ought to have a long holiday and I do hope you get it & that youll have a good time dear and a long rest wherever you go and that the sun may shine for you! Please dont be anxious about me - I am making a good recovery & I am ever so well cared for and am given everything I want. I should probably be at Wellington a month or so and then go back to the old Regiment for a month and then I hope to be quite fit for service again. With best love old girl

from Stan

*****

No.15/13

The Station Hospital, Wellington, Southern India
Aug 20th.1915

My dear old Elsie,

Here I am old thing still in hospital and very tired of it all and fed up with things in general - but I think they will let me out soon as I am quite convalescent now and they are only holding me to see if Im a carrier of infection which Im sure Im not. I was at Bombay until Aug. 4th and then was sent to Poona and a week ago came on here. The journey was very interesting and I came through some really gorgeous country but 3 nights and days in the train was rather a trial and I arrived here a bit of a wreck. But here I am up 8000 ft in the South Western Ghauts and in a perfect climate - I feel the cold so much after the Gulf that I have a fire every evening after tea in my little ward - it doesn't seem a bit like India and I feel better and stronger every day and hope soon to go long walks over the downs. Today to my great joy I got a bundle of letters from the Gulf and yours up to July 1st. many thanks dear old thing for all your letters and the papers too. I so enjoy the Tatler and always read those Letters of Eve - do you ever read them - I think they are so smart & amusing! It was so kind of you to send me the looking glass and knife spoon and fork and the baccy and I have no doubt the parcel will turn up if I am patient. I thought afterwards that I ought not to have asked you to spend your hard earned money on me and I do hope the railway shares are keeping up! I am thinking of you now at Borth with your people and hope you are having a good restful holiday and fine weather I am sure you must enjoy being with your own kith and kin again. I dont quite know what the future has in store for me - I hope in about two weeks I shall go before my Board and I expect they will make me take 6 weeks or two months sick leave and very likely I shall go into a hotel or Club here for a while for Im sure there cant be a healthier place in India. After my leave is up I suppose I shall go back to Mesopotamia but I hear strong rumours that the Somersets are going on service to Europe this autumn and if such is the case of course I want to go with them - but everything is very undecided at present and at any rate you can think of me at Wellington for some little time yet. As far as I can gather from Harolds letters poor little mother seems gradually to get worse and Im so afraid it will be a long and painful ending for her - it is a great trouble to me and I am always thinking of her. Im sure your short visit brought her a lot of pleasure and it was so kind of you to go down. One can do nothing and its all so very sad - and what a year this past one has been - it seems like an

34

eternity and so much has happened that my memory sometimes cant keep pace with it. The weeks go by and still the war brings 'no change' its terrible really. Its true the Russians have had a big defeat and the Germans seem invincible in the East but it does not alter the ultimate result but unfortunately prolongs the awful struggle - Im quite convinced now old thing that it will be a long war and there are many weary anxious months ahead. I will write you again soon & will let you know what my plans are - there is just the chance of Harold and I meeting somewhere say at Madras before I return to service. Well cheerio and heres my best love to you

from Stan

*****

No. 15/14

The Station Hospital, Wellington
Sept 2 1915

My dear old Elsie

I was so delighted to get your two letters this week via Ambala - thanks so much. I am so sorry you have had a poor time in Bognor and hope you have had a very good time at Borth to make up for it all. Thanks so much old girl for the Sketch also safely received. I hope you soon got quite better & you mustnt bathe any more - what a pity Mrs. Brown got ill and I hope if you had to take the two kiddies[42] home you reached Minchinhampton quite safely but it must have been a job!

Well old thing I am getting on splendidly and can walk quite a long way now - I had a long buck[43] with the Major doctor this morning and he says I am quite fit and free from any infection but he says he must keep me here a month from the date of entrance and so that will take me to about Sept. 15th. He says I ought then to have a months sick leave and strongly advises me to spend it up here in this delightful country and I shall probably decide to do this - he says that after that I shall be well enough for anything and quite ready to go back to the Gulf if I am ordered there.

The news of poor Mother gets more & more distressing and now the pain has come I imagine the end will come soon - it is very very sad & I am always thinking of her and wondering when the terrible day will come - the poor old Pater seems to be bearing up wonderfully well through it all. In Harolds last letter he suggests we should arrange to meet before I leave Southern India and I hope we shall be able to manage this in October - he would probably come over and meet me at Madras. This will be something to look forward to. I hope you have got my letters all right and I will often write to you now I am in India again. I wish we could get the Dardanelles[44] and then the Balkan States would make up

---

[42] Ronald & Barbara Brown.

[43] Hindi for 'talk', 'chatter' (examples in *Kim*, Rudyard Kipling, first published 1901).

[44] In February & March 1915 British and French Allied fleets tried to break through the Dardanelles with Constantinople (Istanbul) as the objective. The Straits were heavily guarded by mines & shore batteries. The attempt failed. On April 25th landings were made on the Gallipoli peninsula. After a bitterly fought campaign with heavy casualties, this attempt also was abandoned and the Anzac and British forces were evacuated in December 1915-January 1916.

their minds to join us -a big success there I am sure would influence the whole war. Well old thing heres my love to you and all best wishes

from Stan

*****

No.15/15

The Station Hospital, Wellington, Madras
16 Sept 1915

My dear old Elsie

The weeks go by and here I am still in hospital. I was hoping very much to get out this week but now they have put off the Medical Board until Monday 20th. If the Board passes me as fit and recommends me for a months sick leave the report will go to Headquarters in Simla and take a day or two to get officially passed so Im afraid it looks as if I shall spend my birthday[45] in hospital after all. I am very tired of hospital regulations and the isolation especially as I feel quite well now. Fortunately another enteric officer has arrived and we are able to pass our evenings playing poker patience and picquet.

My great consolation is that while I am ill I get £3 per week from my Insurance people at home and hope to get £50 out of them which will be very useful for my sadly depleted exchequer - Ive paid in to the Society for years and never got much out of them but of course I shall be amply repaid now. Many thanks old thing for your last letters written from Borth Im so glad you had such a good time there and hope you feel all the better for your holiday. Yesterday a very delapidated parcel arrived with the baccy cigarettes metal glass and spoon etc. Everything quite safe and undamaged - my best thanks dear for all the things which are greatly appreciated - I am just able to enjoy a pipe now and the 3 Nuns[46] is a great treat - the parcel took just 3 months getting to me. I hear from my men in the Gulf they have had another fight and have advanced 40 more miles up the Tigris to a place called Al-Gharbi - they are now only 270 miles from Baghdad. I think they will have a big battle soon at Kut-al-Amarah where the Turks are at present digging themselves in. The Somersets are still at Dagshai and are always expecting to get their orders to pack up and be off - I fancy tho that at present they wont be spared out of India - only this week there has been a big show on the N.W.Frontier above Peshawar[47] in which nearly all the 8 Regiments of Regulars who are left out here were engaged and at any time it is thought that the whole Frontier may be ablaze with war. I suppose little is given in the English papers of these doings - the principal enemy is a tribe of Mohmands about 10,000 strong - the tribe is chiefly composed of Pathans who are devils to fight and who are well armed - all the world seems mad and thirsting for blood - in far Tibet there is fighting between

---

[45] September 22nd.

[46] Brand of pipe tobacco, see copy of advertisement in 'The Tatler.' See plate section 1 p.4.

[47] Peshawar: A grand Jirga or open air meeting of 3.000 tribal leaders and elders was called at Peshawar. They were informed by Col George Roos-Keppel that Delhi had decided to reward their loyalty by increasing their subsidies. After that, while a further 25,000 tribesmen looked on, they were treated to a bombing display by aircraft of the Royal Flying Corps. (Peter Hopkirk, op. cit. p.188.)

the Chinese and Tibetans and there is talk of rebellion in China[48] against the Manchurian Dynasty - Ive been reading a little volume of Robert Browning and came across the well known quotation "Gods in his Heaven - alls well with the world". I sometimes wonder how the really religious people explain away the happenings of the past year - and surely the little faith one has is sorely shaken. The war goes on and we make no progress - it is very hard to be patient - my chief interest is in the Dardanelles - for a long time Ive thought that our chief advance would come from the Mediterranean - I think we shall probably first hold the enemy in the West and when we get Constantinople there will be an advance of millions of men from the south of Austria - I mean that Italy Servia and probably Roumania will join hands and we shall put a million or so men and surely nothing can stop us getting right up to Budapest and Vienna and if necessary into Germany - It's a little consoling to work out these schemes and I hope it wont bore you.[49]

The news of poor Mother gets more and more distressing and Im always expecting to hear the end has come - it is really terrible and so sad that she is suffering so much. Im very glad Gretchen is down there now but every day I am expecting the fateful cable. It is really beautiful up here and Ive never in all my wanderings seen such lovely scenery - I was very lucky in being sent here. Well, goodbye old thing, ever so many thanks for all your kindness - letters papers and the parcel With best love

from Stan

*****

No. 15/16

Atherstone, Coonoor, Madras
Oct. 6 1915

My dear old Elsie

I cannot thank you enough for your delightful birthday present which came this mail - you could not have sent me anything more useful than the handkerchiefs & tie and I shall in future be an awful knut[50] - I shall enjoy the smokes too - it is naughty of you to spend so much money on me and I ought to be very cross really! The two little pipes (in case) that you gave me are my constant companions and have been through everything with me and are smoking 'just proper' now. Many thanks, old thing, for your letters and papers and good wishes which I can assure you are very much appreciated. You will be glad to know, dear, that I am feeling ever so well now - never better in my life - and I am thoroughly enjoying my leave which I regret to say is too quickly slipping away.

I came away from hospital on my birthday - it was a present from the Major doctor - and I am very comfortable in this boarding house which is near

---

[48] China: the revolt against the Manchu Dynasty had taken place in 1912 with the deposition of the last Emperor, the boy PuYi, by Sun Yat Sen.

[49] This summarises the strategy of the 'Easterners' (including Churchill) who thought the 'Westerners' would never break the German hold on the Western Front in France and Belgium.

[50] Slang meaning 'toff', elegant gentleman "Tatler". See plate section 1 p.7.

Wellington - I get two rounds of golf every day nearly - and sometimes tennis or a long walk and sometimes a picnic in rickshaws which is great fun.

I am as red as a berry and if you saw me now you would never believe I had been ill and would think me a dreadful fraud. I come before another Board in a weeks time for my leave ends on Oct 23rd. The doctors are sure to pass me fit for duty and will wire to Simla for my orders and I shall be very anxious to know. I think it very probable that I shall be sent to Poona which is the Dorset depot and if this is so I shall almost certainly find myself in the Gulf again before long - You will have seen in the papers that they have just had another big fight out there and thank goodness we've gained a great victory[51] - The Dorsets led the attack and up to now I see 12 officers have been hit and I am wondering how many of my men came through safely - all the officers in my Company are wounded so I suppose I should be very thankful that I am safely lodged in India instead of lying out there with an ounce of Turkish lead inside me! But it has always been a great trouble to me to have had to leave my men in the Gulf and shall feel it only my duty if I am sent back to them - I can only hope for better luck next time but I think in such times as these one's life is not one's own but one's country's. But I am anticipating! At any rate I have promised to send Mother a cable if I go back to the Dorsets so you will perhaps hear by the time this reaches you.

I have had no home mail this week and am therefore very worried and anxious about Mother - the last letters have been very sad and depressing - I am hoping to see Harold before I leave Southern India but do not know yet if he will be able to get over to me in Madras. I do hope so - I'm so glad Gretchen and Leslie have been at Elm Grove and hope perhaps you may be able to go down again soon - it makes her so happy to have people she is fond of about her! You have had a very busy time lately and I hope you will not knock yourself up - I imagine it is getting cold & cheerless in England now and the leaves are falling - I am always wondering when I shall see the old country and the dear old friends again! I cant foresee the end of this terrible war and I think we have many many anxious months ahead! but lately the news is better and in Flanders weve go[t] superiority of artillery fire at last and are able to get a move on! I will write you very soon giving you my latest news and telling you my orders - Again ever so many thanks dear for all your goodness & heres my best love and all good wishes from your old pal

Stan

*****

No, 15/17

Club of Western India, Poona
Oct 29 1915

My dear old Elsie

Here I am old girl back in uniform and on duty once again - I am staying at this palatial club which has the reputation of being the finest in the world - it is quite

---

[51] The Turkish force holding Kut el Amara was attacked on September 26th and after several days of fighting with heavy casualties the town was occupied.

a splendid place and we are fed in best English fashion and it is so nice to be able to get bacon and eggs for breakfast.

I left Coonoor with many regrets and after a very long and hot journey reported myself at the Dorset depot on the 23rd.

After the lovely air of the hills the plains are simply stifling and I must say I feel a little shakey at present - but in a few days no doubt I shall get used to it all again - I was immediately pitch-forked into commanding the Depot for Capt Miles had to be sent away to recover from malaria - there are 350 men at the depot and only another officer with me so it is no small job - my days start at 5 am and I'm busy all the time - the men are mostly convalescent from the Gulf or recruits and odds and ends of other Regiments which are on service out of the country. I thought I should be settled in this job for some time and was looking forward to the experience and to making new friends in Poona but my hopes were dashed to the ground for very soon a wire came ordering me to return to service in Mesopotamia with the next draft! This draft will be ready in about two weeks time and then it will only be a question of waiting for a suitable transport and so after all - old thing - I shall be spending my Xmas on service - perhaps in Baghdad - who can say? I cant say I am looking forward to it but you know my views and I'm so thankful to feel fit again and able to do my bit - besides I have always felt that my place was back amongst the men I originally took out to the Gulf - I shall send a cable home when I know when I am actually leaving Bombay - so you will hear - and then please send letters again through the India Office marked Indian Expeditionary Force 'D.'

Further particulars of the last fight at Kut el Amarah are coming through and I believe our people had a perfectly awful time and suffered from lack of water so much - I believe our total casualties were about 1750 and of these the Dorsets lost 61 killed and 300 wounded so must have been in the thick of the fight - the list of men is not completed yet but up to now I have been officially told of 9 casualties amongst my own draft - 6 wounded and 3 missing - I'm afraid the latter are almost certain to have been killed - I am so sorry about it but I hear they fought splendidly and of course it was a great victory for our force. Thanks ever so much dear for your last letter and all the papers you sent me. I have been very interested of course in reading what the English papers say about the P Gulf show and at last the public are allowed to know a little of what is going on out there. The Poona season is just over and the last Race Meeting was last week - but there are a great many English people here and of course a good deal of military activity. I shall be very anxious to hear in your next letter what change you found in Mother and all about your visit to Elm Grove. I'm afraid she suffers terribly now but she is wonderfully brave through it all - I wonder when the end will come and only wish it were possible to get home to see her again before returning to service. Well good night & cheerio

With best love

from Stan.

*****

No. 15/18

My dear old Elsie

Since last mail I have had a wire from Simla ordering me to be ready to sail from Bombay with my draft on Nov. 24th. This may yet be altered but at any rate I thought I'd write as often as possible now for goodness knows what chance there will be on service. So - old thing - by the time this reaches you you can think of me once again on the briny and this time as there is no monsoon - it should be a very nice trip. I dare say it will take quite three weeks for me to reach the Regiment from Bombay for as you know they are several hundred miles up the Tigris - and the river trip from Basra is a very slow one. I reckon I shall reach my men - all being well by about Dec. 15th. just in time to settle down for Xmas. I must not tell you much about the campaign in case I get into trouble with the Censor - but things are expected to happen out there and it looks as if there will be some hard fighting - thousands and thousands of fresh troops are being sent there this month. I'm told by men who were out there last winter that the nights are bitterly cold but the days of course are always hot- unfortunately we are allowed very little kit indeed and always have to wear thin khaki drill but I'm going to smuggle out the woolen helmet you kindly gave me and also those bed stockings your mother sent me and which were such a comfort to me on Salisbury Plain. You know how I hate the cold - but I think it must be nothing compared to the awful heat of last June.

I am not quite strong even yet but I have a good fortnight to pick up - this week the men at the Depot persuaded me to play in a hockey match but I had to give up at half time - but I'm going to take my draft at dawn tomorrow for a 20 mile route march and I think I shall manage this all right - I am anxious to get my feet hard again but it is a nuisance to have to train all over again.

I have been so very interested in all the papers you have so kindly sent me out- at last some recognition is being given to the Persian Gulf campaign - all the latest accounts show that the fight at Kut el Amarah was a very big show and the Turks quite reckoned to hold up our Force there for six months - but it took just 3 days to get through. I was so glad you were able to get down to Taunton to see poor mother - surely the end must come soon for this suspense is really awful. Dorothy wrote this mail to say Mother had to stay in bed now as she was in so much pain and I'm afraid she will never get up again whatever can be done?

I must go to bed now for I have to be about at 4 am in the morning.

Heres my best love to you & cheerio

from Stan

*****

No. 15/19

Club of Western India, Poona
Nov. 12 1915

My dear old Elsie

Thank you so much for your last long letter and the most interesting papers. I have no further news about my sailing so I have to live in a state of packed-up-ness which is very uncomfortable but it is necessary to be prepared to move at a few hours notice - I am very busy these days - the Depot has increased to nearly 400 so there is always plenty to be done - but I'm glad I've got something to occupy my mind otherwise these last few days of waiting would be very trying. I am troubled about poor Mother now as I fear she must suffer a great deal - I am expecting any day now to get a wire from Harold telling me the news that the cable from home has come - all the last letters - yours and the Paters - indicate that the end can't be far off now. It will be a very sad Xmas at home and very different to the dear old piping times of peace.

It is awfully good of you - old thing - to always want to be sending me things but you simply musn't spend any more money on me - the papers must be ruinous. I think I've got all my kit now and we are really allowed to take only very very little in service. But an occasional cake of coal tar soap and a tube of Kolynos tooth paste would be the greatest luxuries but don't send more than a couple of cakes and 1 tube as everything melts in that god-forsaken country. I'll write again next mail. Heres my best love to you and cheerio

from Stan

*****

No. 15/20

Club of Western India, Poona
Nov 20 1915

My dear old Elsie

I hate saying goodbye to anyone - much less to the few people that matter - so this is a letter to wish you au revoir and to send you greetings and my love.

I leave Poona on Tuesday 23rd and sail from Bombay on the 25th. but you will probably have heard this because I sent a cable home this evening.

I am very busy now and the last days will be crowded but I know better what things to take out this time and I am very well off for equipment and I have had my trusty revolver overhauled. I wrote home some time ago to a friend in the wholesale watch trade for a screw cased wrist-watch with a luminous dial and it came last mail and is a little beauty. If anything happens to me I should like you to have it if it is recovered with my belongings as it should be - You could arrange this with Harold as I should like to feel you have this remembrance of me - but I musn't anticipate trouble must I - but I can't help feeling there is a possibility for this time I know what I'm going out to. But I'm awfully fit and well now - old thing - and feel able to stand any amount of hard service and if only I can dodge the 'Turkish Delight' I'll come back to you with a whole skin yet. You must not expect to hear from me very often but I'll write a line when I can and I shall be thinking of you all the time. No news of poor Mother again this week. I have been expecting a cable daily and it is a great trouble to me. Well - heres cheerio & my best love

from Stan

*****

No. 15/21

Hotel Majestic, Wodehouse Road, Bombay
Nov. 24 1915

My dear old Elsie

These are just a few final lines - I have just arrived at Bombay once again and we embark at dawn tomorrow and are due to sail at 9.30am. I am going away feeling ever so fit and am looking forward to the second chapter of my great adventure. I shall always think of you and thank God for you and your friendship which means more to me than I can say. I will write when I can

Au revoir - a cheerio and much love

from Stan

*****

No. 15/22

S.S.Bankura,[52] at sea
Nov. 30th 1915

My dear old Elsie

Just a few lines to send you Xmas and New Year greetings. This has been a really delightful voyage and but for the thought of the things at the end of it, it has been quite a pleasant trip. Strange to say it is the same ship I came out in last May but the conditions are so different that I sometimes wonder - Is this the same ship? Is this the same Arabian Sea?

We should probably reach Basra tomorrow and are eagerly awaiting news of our movements - the morning we left Bombay the papers issued a telegram announcing a big battle[53] 20 miles from Baghdad and that we had met with a severe resistance and that the battle was proceeding - we have of course had no news since and are therefore very anxious and wondering if we shall be in time to take part in the triumphant entry into the city!

This ship is full of men returning to the British and native Regiments and we also have a lot of horses on board for the cavalry. I'm glad for their sakes that it has been good weather but poor things they are in narrow stalls and not allowed to sit down.

Harold wired the last thing to say there was no news of poor Mother - however does she keep alive? I should be much happier in my own mind if I could go into service knowing that she was peacefully laid to rest - perhaps there will be a cable

---

[52] British India Steam Navigation Co. Ltd, reg. tonnage 1905, built 1912 at Whiteinch.
[53] Ctesiphon.

42

at Basra? I got a cable from home just before leaving Poona wishing me Good Luck - it was very kind of them. We are steaming up the Shatt al Arab now and it seems very familiar - but the country round is not under water now as the floods have gone - the Arabs are busy picking their dates and along the river banks thousands of turtles are playing about! Well heres cheerio old thing & my best love

from Stan

Postscript: I heard today that they wont send papers regularly right up to the front but keep them at Basra so please therefore dont send the Tatler as they may only be wasted

CHAPTER THREE

1916

The Background.

At the New Year of 1916 the urgency of the need to relieve Townshend's besieged force in Kut dominated British strategy in Mesopotamia, but the practical difficulties of launching the campaign were daunting. Lieutenant-General Aylmer was now in charge of relief operations, but the Tigris Corps he commanded was in poor shape. Battalions which had already served for months in Mesopotamia needed to absorb and train the drafts which replaced the many sick and wounded. Newly-arrived battalions were required to adjust at once to the hazards of local conditions. Brigades were composed of units unused to working together. Behind the front line the number of river craft above Basra fell sadly below requirements and the port facilities on the Shatt-al-Arab were inadequate for the efficient landing of reinforcements and supplies.

Ali Gharbi, on the Tigris half way between Amara and Kut, was the base from which the relief force set out on January 4th, marching up the left bank (that is, the northern bank, the trend of this stretch of the river being from West to East). A tough battle led to the capture on January 9th of the village of Shaikh Saad, more than twenty miles on, but at the cost of 4000 casualties including 400 dead. On January 13th and 14th Aylmer's army crossed the Wadi, a small tributary of the Tigris, only to come up against the Hanna defile, a strip of nominally dry land 12 miles long and less than a mile wide lying between the Tigris left bank and extensive marshes. The Turkish position at Hanna was vulnerable to enfilading fire from the right bank but the frustration of all attempts to span the broad river with a pontoon bridge ruled out such at attack for the moment. Four miserable days of high wind and heavy rain were followed by a drier spell and the launch on January 21st of the frontal attack on Hanna, where the Turks were now well dug in behind barbed wire. Heavy rain returned in the late morning and lasted all day and the following night. The Turks held their ground against successive waves of British assault; once more casualty figures rose and the inadequate medical services were overwhelmed, hundreds of wounded being left in the mud to suffer or die of exposure to the rain and the cold. One eye-witness observed: - 'for collective misery the night of the 21st is probably unparalleled since the Crimea in the history of sufferings endured by the British Army.'[1] Aylmer's effective force was terribly depleted; for example of the six battalions of the 35th Brigade, already under strength on the morning of the 21st, four suffered more than 50 per cent casualties, the worst 92 per cent.

Blocked on the left bank, aware of Townshend's dwindling supplies and anxious about the predicted flooding season, Aylmer next built up his force on the Tigris' right bank. A long night march took the bulk of his army by dawn on March 8th to what seemed to be striking distance of the prominent mound known

---

[1] Edmund Candler, *The Long Road to Baghdad*, Cassell, 1919, vol. I, p.96.

Telegraphic Address:
"Feathers," Minehead.

P.O. Telephone
No. 8.

Proprietor:
G. THRISTLE.

Plume of Feathers Hotel,
Minehead, Som.

Sept 4th 1914

My dear old Elsie.

I was sent down here last Wednesday for 3 days to try to raise 40 recruits or more for our Battalion - willing to serve on active service.

I am glad to say that up to time of writing I have signed on 86. I am returning with them to Salisbury Plain by the train tomorrow.

Many thanks dear old girl for the box of cigs. sent on to me. I will write soon. Am very busy.

Best love dear

From Stan.

The first letter in the collection. The style does not alter, Stanley's fiancée was 'My dear old Elsie' from first to last. (Letter 14/1)

Stanley's interests before the war.

i. Skiing in Switzerland, January 1914. Switzerland provided a standard of comparison for mountains and wild scenery encountered on his travels. (Letter 15/1)

ii. Acting as Ravennes in *Erminie*, performed by Taunton Operatic Society in 1914.   (Letter 15/1 note)

iii. Stanley was working for Franklin & Hare (later '& Goodland') from 1908.

The Officers of the 1/5th Bn. Somerset Light Infantry at Ambala (India) January 1915. Lt-Col Cooke-Hurle is in the centre of the middle row, with Major Brutton and Captain Calway on his right. On his left are Major Kite, and Captains Urwick, Major, Timms and Watson. In the back row Lieut Goodland is third from the right and Lieut Banes Walker stands behind the colonel. 2/Lieut Milsom sits on the right of the front row.

These two advertisements are from *The Tatler*, sent regularly by Elsie. Three Nuns tobacco is gratefully acknowledged in Letter 15/15. Coal Tar Soap was requested by Stanley in Letter 15/19 and Letter 17/21 describes how he was looking forward to 'a bathe in the jolly old Jordan with a cake of Coal Tar'.

The Regiment at Chakrata; the location of this splendid photograph was identified for us by the British India Office Library. Stanley rejoined the Regiment there in July 1916 after convalescence following his second tour of duty in Mesopotamia.

(Letter 16/11)

The Knut: I want to see the neatest thing you have in stockings

Shop-Walker (absent-mindedly): I'm afraid she's out just at present, sir

A cartoon by George Belcher from *The Tatler* of September 22nd 1915 using the word 'knut' to denote a man-about-town. Stanley uses the word to describe himself and his fellow officers.   (Letter 15/16)

India, 1915 Written on the back of this photograph in Stanley's writing is 'more Knuts'. Stanley is in the middle, with Harry Milsom on his right. One of the others is likely to be Gerald Banes Walker who was killed in action in November 1917.

(Letter 15/16)

PROGRAMME.

1. QUARTETTE ..."Sweet and Low."......*Mrs. Whitty Miss McGregor, Capt. Goodland, Mr. Sanders.*

2. SONG. ..."Indian Love Lyrics."......*Mr. Evenmett.*

3. DUET ..."Somewhere a Voice is Calling"......*Mrs. Whitty and Mr. Sanders.*

4. SONG ..."Up from Somerset."......*Capt. Goodland.*

5. CELLO SOLO ......*Mr. Walton O'Donnell.*

6. ..."I'll make a man of you"......*Miss George, Mr. Cole and Troupe.*

7. SONG ..."Chanson de Florian."......*Mrs. Carr.*

8. SONG ..."Ruben Ronzo."......*Mr. Sanders.*

9. SONG ..."O, Wandering Breeze."......*Mrs. Whitty.*

10. SONG ..."Pierrot Land" [in character]......*Miss McGregor.*

11. SONG ..."Damon."......*Miss George.*

12. ..."The only way."......*Mr. Rogers and Troupe.*

Accompanist—*Mrs Maynard.*

INTERVAL.

"COLLABORATORS"

Duologue

BY

Daisy McGeoch.

Characters.

Mary ... ... Mrs. Jesse

Reginald ... ... Captain Goodland

God Save the King.

This entertainment was put on in August 1916 at Mussoorie and 'raised £50 for Mespot'. Stanley sang and acted and 'Mrs Jesse painted all the programmes and we got 2/6 each for them'. A copy survives, including the colourful little picture called 'Sunset in the Rains'.

(Letter 16/11)

as the Dujaila Redoubt, three miles south of the river and about nine miles east of Kut. Confusions in crossing a waterless and featureless desert in the dark meant that the attack was delayed and the crucial advantage of surprise was lost. Though parts of the Turkish defences were reached the Dujaila Redoubt was not captured and Aylmer, having suffered 3500 casualties was compelled to withdraw, to be swiftly replaced in command of the Tigris Corps by Lieutenant-General Gorringe. Reinforced by the 13th Division, commanded by Major-General Maude, composed of Kitchener's New Army soldiers who had already fought at Gallipoli, Gorringe concentrated once more on the left bank of the Tigris and when he attacked Hanna on April 5th he found that the Turks had abandoned their lines, only to fall back on two equally well prepared positions from which the fighting on the next day did not dislodge them. The Tigris was now running high to overflowing and the British right flank was threatened with inundation from the rising waters of the marshes.

Townshend had at first overestimated the speed at which his rations would run out and by doing so had prompted the Tigris Corps to expend its strength before it was sufficiently strong and organised. By mid-April he and his men, though surviving on very short rations, were near the end of their tether. Gorringe made two more attempts to reach Kut, one on the right, the other on the left banks of the Tigris but without success and the attempt of the gunboat *Julnar* to break through the Turks' river defences failed on the night of April 24th/25th. Two days later Townshend met the Turkish commander to discuss surrender terms; on the 29th the Turks entered Kut and 10,000 British soldiers passed into captivity. Their tragic adventures and sufferings cannot be recounted here.

The inability to rescue Kut and the dawning realisation in the United Kingdom of deficiencies in the organisation of the campaign - especially in the provision of medical services - had wide repercussions. The British were unable to resume the offensive in Mesopotamia until December 1916. By then the War Office in London had taken away the directing of the campaign from the Government of India. In August the Home Government appointed a Royal Commission to examine and report on the reasons for British failure. General Nixon's term as Commander-in-Chief in Mesopotamia had ended in January; his successor, Lieutenant-General Lake, lasted till August when he was replaced by Major-General Maude who built on and expanded the logistical improvements Lake had originated. At last the port and ship repair installations near Basra were properly developed, the number of river craft greatly increased, medical services were adequately supplied and staffed and narrow gauge railways were built, including a line from Qurna to Amara. Lines of communication were better protected by barbed wire and patrols. Modern equipment was issued; each battalion was supplied with eight Lewis guns and each brigade was supported by a Machine Gun Company with sixteen Vickers guns. The Royal Flying Corps, so essential for reconnaissance operations, was given modern machines and soon established mastery of the air. Showing that he meant business, Maude escaped from the pressure of administrative problems by moving his headquarters from Basra to a point about twenty miles below Kut.[2]

---

[2] Brig-Gen FJ Moberly, *The Campaign in Mesopotamia*, 1914-1918. HMSO, 1925 vol. III, pp.30-36, p.68.

The campaign to recover Kut began in December 1916 and was concluded victoriously in February 1917, after Maude's army contrived to cross the Tigris from the right to the left bank a few miles upstream of the town. This time there was no denying the British in their advance on Baghdad, which was entered on March 11th. Thereafter the campaign continued for the remaining eighteen months of the war, ending with the British at the gates of Mosul. The operation which began in November 1914 with the arrival of one brigade of the Indian Army ended four years later, after the loss of nearly 100,000 casualties, with British and Imperial forces at a ration strength of half a million. The value of their contribution to the eventual outcome of the First World War can be left to military and political pundits to debate.

Stanley Goodland in 1916: Mesopotamia & India.

In the second or third weeks of December 1915 Stanley Goodland reached Ali Gharbi, the headquarters of the newly formed Tigris Corps. After a period of staff work he was attached on January 3rd 1916 to the 1/5 Buffs (East Kent Regiment). This was a Territorial battalion, part of the Kentish Brigade of the Home Counties Division, which after a year in India had sailed for the Gulf early in December.[3] It had to acclimatise itself rapidly to Mesopotamian conditions, for it was fully involved in every attempt of the Tigris Corps to relieve Kut, from the march on Shaikh Saad on January 4th to the last desperate attacks at the end of April. Particularly in the first 18 days the Buffs were in the thick of the fighting, as the casualty figures show. Appointed Adjutant of a battalion he had only just joined, whose organisation was shaken by its appalling losses Stanley Goodland, recovering from his flesh wound, must have had an uphill task but it was at this time that he struck up a life-long friendship with Captain (later Lt-Col) John Body[4] who led the 1/5 Buffs after its colonel had been wounded and the second-in-command killed.

For the second time fever, now accompanied by jaundice, forced Stanley to report sick and in late May he left his friends in the Buffs and briefly returned to the same Bombay hospital to which he had been sent in 1915. A partial recovery soon enabled him to join the 'jolly old Somersets' at Chakrata, where his colleagues must have been interested to greet the only member of the battalion to have experienced active service. Lt-Col Cooke-Hurle turned to Stanley for help in preparing the departure of the draft of two officers and 150 NCOs and private soldiers which on October 20th left for service with the 1/4 Somersets in Mesopotamia. Stanley's temporary spell as Adjutant foreshadowed the permanent appointment made in October 1917. He had shared his secret - about being recommended for a Military Cross in recognition of his bravery in rescuing the wounded colonel of the 37th Dogras on January 21st 1916 - only with Elsie; neither his family nor his 1/5 Somerset friends had been told. The decoration was gazetted on December 22nd and the news reached Meerut at Christmas.

---

[3] Colonel RSH Moody, *Historical Records of the Buffs*, 1914-1919. Medici Society, 1922, pp.66, 123.
[4] 1875-1945, JP, DL, DSO & bar, OBE *Tonbridge School Register* ed. HD Furley, Rivington 1951, p.185.

The 1/5 Buffs remained in Mesopotamia to the end of the war, still commanded by John Body. The Battalion was the first to enter Baghdad and one of its officers hauled down the Turkish flag at the Citadel and hoisted the Union flag.[5] Though it suffered casualties before and after the fall of Baghdad it was never again subjected to the grievous losses and extreme weather experienced from January to April 1916, the months of Stanley Goodland's attachment.

---

[5] Moody op. cit., p.197.

The Letters Written in 1916

No. 16/1

I.E.F. "D"1.
Jan 7 1917 [sic]

My dear old Elsie

Just a line to tell you I am very well indeed and quite safe up to now - It has been impossible to write to you before and some day soon I hope to write you a long letter telling you all that has been happening in this country. I was simply delighted to get some English letters for the first time today and 3 from you - many thanks old thing - this brings you the best of New Years greetings. I wonder what it holds for us all. Poor Mother - it is wonderful how she lives on - I have had no news of her death yet - it is a great trouble to me. Best love old girl

from Stan

*****

No. 16/2

Field Hospital I.E.F. 'D'
Feb 1 1916

[The envelope is marked 'E.S.Goodland Lieut 2nd.Dorsets]

My dear old Elsie

I am very sorry I have so few chances of writing since leaving India - I wrote you last from Ali Gharbi[6] about Xmas time & hope you got it and now I am in hospital once again but this time thank goodness with no serious trouble. We have had a terrible time and very hard fighting and I was lucky enough to come through everything safely until the 21st. when I was hit through the left thigh I am glad to say it is only a flesh wound and it was a nice clean pointed bullet so it is healing very quickly and I hope to be about again in a few days but I expect I should be lame for a little time.[7] In spite of everything I am really very well but so tired and absolutely worn out. I think I told you that I arrived just too late to join up with the Dorsets - poor devils - they have been shut up in Kut since early Decbr with very little stores. I got as far as Ali Gharbi where the relief force was being concentrated and for some weeks I had a very busy time and lived with the General[8] at Headquarters and was a great knut On Jan 4th. the great advance began and on the day before I became attached to the 5th. Buffs who had just arrived from India. Some day I hope to tell you of the wonderful time we have passed through - from the 4th. to the 21st we have had no rest for we were fighting night & day. I did not take my boots off or clothes - didn't wash shave or clean

---

[6] This letter does not survive.

[7] 'Lieut Stanley Goodland wounded. His numerous friends in West Somerset will earnestly hope the wounds are not serious. It is surmised that Lt Goodland is with the British column advancing to the relief of our forces in Kut.' (*Somerset County Gazette*, February 5th 1916.)

[8] Either Major-General GJ Younghusband, GOC 7th Division or Brig-General GBH Rice GOC, 35th Infantry Brigade.

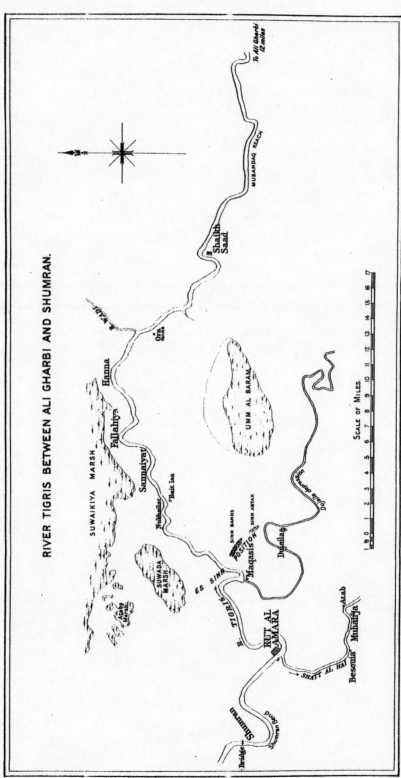

RIVER TIGRIS BETWEEN ALI GHARBI AND SHUMRAN.

SCALE OF MILES.

THE HISTORICAL SECTION OF THE COMMITTEE OF IMPERIAL DEFENCE.

Ordnance Survey 1924

my teeth - I had quite a beard and you wouldn't have known me - Can you imagine the state we were in? Operations ended on the 21st (the day I was hit) for the weather was awful and the country practically under water - How we suffered -it has been bitterly cold and often we had to be out in the desert at night or in the trenches in our thin Indian clothes with no blankets & often no food or water and nearly always wet through. Those few of us who remain now wonder how ever anyone is left alive - I can't tell you any particulars but I'll tell you this much the Buffs started out on the 4th with 650 men and 29 officers and at the end of the fighting on the 21st. there were 88 men and 2 officers left counting myself - other regiments have suffered equally and it is a great disappointment to us that at present at any rate we have not been able to relieve Kut and we have tried so hard. I have only had one mail and in it was a letter from you dated Dec. 9th. I suppose all my letters and parcels are in the Kut bags and until we get there I must be patient (we are only 22 miles from Kut now - isn't it aggravating)

Poor Tom Clatworthy[9] was killed quite close to me on the 6th - I was very cut up about it for I had been with him a good deal those last few days he was alive and we used to talk over all the old home news - I had some narrow escapes for once I was shot though my water bottle and again through my shoulder straps - Some day I will tell you of a particularly exciting adventure - I am always wondering of course if poor Mother is still alive it is hard times to be cut off from news in this way isn't it. I will try to write again soon - don't worry about me - old girl.

Cheerio and my best love

from Stan

*****

No. 16/3

I.E.F. 'D'
Feb 5 1916

My dear old Elsie

Only today I have heard about dear Mothers death[10] - Harold cabled me on Dec 23rd but the message has never reached me and his letter that he wrote at the same time only came to hand this morning. You have no idea of the conditions prevailing in this country and the almost unsurmountable difficulties and the post & telegraph people seem unable to cope with things - At any rate for a long time private wires have not been delivered above Amarah but I do think they might have sent on my cable or put it in an envelope & posted it to me as I tried to arrange.

The news altho expected has come as a great shock and I feel very sad and helpless and thoroughly miserable - We have lost the very best of Mothers and no one will know not even we her children all she suffered for us and her constant thought for our welfare. I find it difficult to write but you know how I loved her

---

[9] While in India with the Somerset Light Infantry Tom Clatworthy was given a commission as 2nd Lieut in the Indian Army and attached to the 37th Dogras. He was killed on January 6th in the action of Shaikh Saad. He was aged 30, the eldest son of Mr Eland Clatworthy of Trull, Somerset.
[10] Mother's death: December 22nd 1915.

and what I must feel about it all. I am thinking so much now of the poor old Pater - it must be heart breaking to see him without his lifelong mate - he is an old man and I am very much afraid his strength will fail him. I feel so unhappy about it all and that is why I naturally turn to you best of friends. Please write and tell me everything - I was so glad to get a letter from you (Dec 9th) but it is only one up to now and no Xmas present that you mention - ever so many thanks - but there must be many more somewhere which I am looking forward to getting very soon. I should like a long pow wow with you now for there is so much to tell you - I have wondered very much lately if we shall ever meet again. I dont want to appear despondent but I dont think it is possible for any one to go through a second time all weve been through since Jan 4 with a whole skin - I have had the most extraordinary good luck and I think a little goddess of good fortune has been looking after me and I hope she won't be frightened away. Candidly I have seen enough and I wish this old war would end - Altho I really dont want it to now until we can say we are top dog. I wonder if we can smash the enemy in every theatre of war this coming Spring - what do you think - its men we want - thousands and thousands of them! And now old girl I am just dying to tell you a great secret about myself - you musn't tell a soul and I haven't even mentioned it to my own people in case of disappointment - I have been mentioned in despatches and recommended for a 'Military Cross' or "helping his company with great gallantry and coolness during the actions Jan 4th to 21st and on the 21st altho wounded himself going out about 150 yards in front of our advanced trenches and bringing in a wounded officer of the Dogras under heavy fire."[11] What do you think of that - old thing. It really looks better on paper than it was but it was a very exciting adventure - Towards the close of the days fighting on the 21st we had orders to retire about 300 yards to take up a position for the night and I saw this poor chap out there in front of us and managed to crawl out to him on my right side (for my left thigh was bleeding and painful) and drag him back a few inches at a time - in doing so I was hit through the water bottle and through the shoulder of my coat - it all sounds like a book or a play now and cant you imagine poor Lewis Waller[12] working it up - but its all true and I can tell you it was very thrilling - I do hope they give me an M.C. but they have been very sparing of honours in this show - It would be something to keep and cherish afterwards if I get through and in any case it will always be nice to feel I've been mentioned - the list wont be published I expect for at least six months and I may not live to see it in print and that is why I wanted to tell you all about it myself - but keep it a great secret wont you.

I am practically well now and have been appointed adjutant[13] to the 5th Buffs so join up again in a few days the appointment dates from Jan 8th. when the adjutant was unfortunately killed and as it means £10 a month extra pay it is very nice but this I suppose will cease when I can get to the Dorsets. Best love old girl

from Stan

*****

---

[11] This was the commanding officer of the 37th Dogras, who had been shouting for help in a manner Stanley, (as he explained 58 years later), considered unfitting and ungentlemanly.

[12] This name has not been traced.

[13] Lieut H S Marchant, Adjutant of 5th Buffs, was killed on January 7th 1916. Stanley was appointed Adjutant in his place. (See RSH Moody, op. cit., p.125).

No.16/4

I.E.F. 'D'
Mar 5 1916

Dear old Elsie

Just a line to tell you I am all right except for two frost bitten toes. My wound is not troubling me a bit but I think I shall always be a little lame.

Your last letter was dated Jan 4th. and I have had no parcels at all so some day if only we can get to Kut and things smooth themselves out a little I shall have a big mail bag all to myself. I may not be able to write again for some time as we are just finishing preparations for another big advance[14] - I only hope we shall be successful and that before this reaches you the news of the relief of Kut will be wired across the Empire. Everyone is keen and very anxious and I hope the luck that has been mine all through this fighting will stay with me. I cant remember any dates now my mind is so busy with other things and so I'm so sorry I cant send you a birthday letter but I fancy the day wont be far off[15] when this arrives so heres my most affectionate birthday wishes & greetings. We have lived through very exciting times lately - every day the guns are busy and there has been a lot of night work - sapping and bombing -, Its all very wearing and one needs cast iron nerves I can assure you.

Ive had no home news since Dec 30th. but I fancy the Pater and the girls are carrying on most nobly and bravely - I look forward when these new battles are over and our object is accomplished to a good long rest - I feel Ive earned it! and I long to get away somewhere quiet for a time - well - so long -old girl

Best love & every good wish

from Stan

*****

No. 16/5

I.E.F. 'D'
Mar 28 1916

My dear old Elsie

A few lines to tell you I am safe and sound and fairly well. I cant remember when I wrote last and there is really very little news to tell you for we are not allowed to say very much about the latest happenings in this country. I wonder what the home papers have told you. Thank goodness I came through the last fighting Mar 8 to 10 safely and since then we have been doing a spell in the trenches - it is a most depressing work and there is no rest for the poor adjutant. Now we are under canvas about 4000 yards behind the firing line and it is a real treat to get a shave and a wash and to take ones boots off. We are supposed to be resting but the whole force is busy preparing for the next great effort for Kut - it was a great disappointment to us that we did not get through on the 8th to 10th - it was a very near thing but it was necessary to get far away from the river and we were simply driven back from want of water and from fatigue. I am so sorry to

---

[14] The attack on the Dujailah Redoubt March 8th - 10th.
[15] Elsie's birthday was February 12th. This letter was a bit late!

say my mail has failed me again the last 3 weeks and I miss my letters ever so much but yesterday the parcel you so kindly sent of soap toothpaste tobacco and sweets arrived it came just at the right moment - thank you so much dear - you would have been amused to see me with a bucket of water and my piece of coal tar soap which is the envy of the officers mess - I feel cleaner now than I have for ages and for the time being I believe Ive got rid of most of the fleas and horrid things that have been biting me up lately. Im longing to get some home news again for I'm always wondering what is happening.

It may be some time again before I get a chance of writing but I hope you wont worry about me - if we could only get to Kut I think they would give the Brigade a long rest and possibly send us back to India - we have done more than our share and we are all tired out. My poor old leg gets inflamed and some days I am very lame but I dont want to give up until Kut is relieved - every one of us is wanted for that job. No news yet of the Military Cross but Ive great hopes for a few days ago the boys at Basra Headquarters wired up for my full Christian names - youll also be pleased to hear that the General has recommended me for temporary promotion to Captain so Im hoping in a little while to have 3 stars - it will mean a good deal extra pay and altogether will be very nice - not a word of all this until things are settled! Well cheerio dear old thing - theres a good time coming - or at least I keep on hoping so.

Best love

from Stan

*****

No.16/6

Coluba Hospital, Bombay
June 10 1916

[Note: address c/o Cox & Co. Bombay.]

My dear old Elsie

I hope you wont think it very unkind of me not to have written to you for so long but I daresay you have been able to get news of me through my letters to Elm Grove but these I am afraid have not been very regular either. You will I know be glad to hear dear that I am practically well again now. I have had my Medical Board and tomorrow I set out on my journey north for two months leave (I think I had earned leave back to England but the Board thought the War Office at home would snap me up and not allow me to come East again so they kept me in India!) I shall go via Delhi and have a look at Indias great show place and then on to Meerut where half the old Regiment is stationed and then on to Chakrata (in the lower Himalayas) where the Colonel and Headquarters and the other half of the Regiment are stationed. I shall be able to spend a nice quiet time amongst old friends and shall soon regain my lost strength and the two stone in weight which I have entirely lost. I am afraid I did not write you very much (if at all) during April and the part of May I was at the front. April was a very dreadful month and I shall never forget it as long as I live night and day we were fighting to get to poor old Kut for we knew they were on their last legs - well old thing - we failed and it was the greatest disappointment of my life[16] - I dont think anyone can ever realize how we tried and tried again against every conceivable difficulty - time after time we stood up to be shot at and attempted to storm almost impregnable enemy positions - added to these anxieties we were faced with a terrible cholera epidemic[17] which I suppose people at home will never know about - twenty of my poor regiment went down in 36 hrs and not one recovered - the sights I saw were really heart-breaking - To my great regret our Brigadier General Rice who was a very good friend to me died of cholera a few days before I left the regiment - By the way - old thing - I am Captain now and it was really due to him that I was recommended for my third star. All I want to make me happy is my Military Cross now - I do wonder if they are ever going to give it to me. I have heard once or twice from the Colonel of the Buffs and I am glad to say that he thinks the cholera is dying out but of course the heat and flies and myriad discomforts are very distressing - I was so sorry to leave them all and fought hard against this fever but it conquered me in the end and then jaundice set in and my whole skin went a delicate primrose colour - there are hundreds of cases of jaundice in the Gulf & the medical people say it is all brought on by bad water & food - it is a most depressing thing to get I can tell you.

About the middle of April when my troubles were at their height a most delightful parcel arrived from you - dear old thing - thank you ever so much. I wish I could tell you in words what pleasure it brought me, at that time I had come to my last pipe (which was one of a pair you gave me some time ago) I had unfortunately lost the mouthpiece of this and had made one with a bit of stick and a penknife which wasnt at all satisfactory - Imagine my delight when I discovered a pipe amongst my parcel & the little mascot too was splendid! The first few days of my illness I lived on your cocoa and soup tablets - even after nearly two years of war the Field Ambulances in Mesopotamia have simply nothing in the way of comforts and drugs. I hate to be always grumbling but really it is a disgrace - I only hope France is run better than Mesopotamia (but it surely must be) else we never even deserve to win the war - and what awful lies the newspapers print[18] - why ever cant the British public be told the truth - some day perhaps Ill tell you all I know - but I daresay when peace comes and I am in dear old England once again I shant want to talk about the war at all but just try to forget all this horrid time.

I must be patient until letters from England find me again - it is a long time since I had my last mail - some time in April I think - I do hope you are all well - with best love

from Stan

*****

---

[16] Kut surrendered on April 29th after repeated & vain efforts for its relief.

[17] There were 800 cases of cholera in the Tigris Corps during April & May (Moberly op. cit. vol. III p.9 footnote). Cholera was no respecter of rank.

[18] *Eye Witness* complains 'It is impossible to communicate freely with the outside world. Things were evidently going wrong and this fussy meddling supervision, this constant fear of anything discreditable leaking out, did not increase one's confidence in the Higher Command' (Edmund Candler, op. cit. vol. I, p.65).

1/5 Somerset L.I., Chakrata, Upper Provinces, India
July 8 1916

My dear old Elsie

You will be pleased to know that I am ever so much better and am now right up in the Himalayas with the old Regiment! I have had such a kind welcome from the Colonel[19] down to the smallest private in my old company - they have given me such a swell dinner at the Mess and it is simply glorious being amongst the old Regiment again.

The Colonel says that now he's got me he's going to stick to me and has already applied to Simla[20] for my return - I think I told you that my leave carries me on until Aug. 20th. and I shall not know what is going to happen to me until then. Everyone here thinks this Regiment is going on service to the Gulf in the autumn (the Colonel appears to have had some private information about this) - already all of the officers here have bought a lot of their field service kit - If this is so of course I should like nothing better than to go out again with them but I certainly do not want to loaf about India doing ordinary Regimental duty while there is a war on. The Colonel of the Buffs will be very sick too if I don't go back to my adjutant's job with him - but I shall have to wait and see until my orders come from Simla. I shall have to go before another board of doctors before my leave is up and they may not pass me fit for service again. At present my poor inside is altogether wrong - I suppose it will be some time before I can get over the effects of all the bad food and water I've had to live on for so many months. It is really beautiful up here - 8000 feet above sea level, to get here one has to take a motor ride of 60 miles for we are right in the heart of the Himalayas and in clear days the "everlasting snows" glisten in the distance and make one just look and wonder & think what a marvellous world we live in - I cant walk very far in these hilly parts yet but Frank Calway (with whom I am sharing quarters) lends me his pony and I just hack about enjoying the scenery and fresh air.

Well my dear old thing - it seems a long time since I had any letters from you but I am hoping in a few days, to hear from you direct through Cox - yesterday however a ripping parcel came from you which had been travelling all round the Gulf. It is so kind of you but you must promise me not to send me anything more until I go on service again but save your money for War Loan - the knife is just what I wanted & the diary too & the lighter & baccy all splendid - really it is too good of you old pal and I dont deserve it in the least.

To my surprise I had a wire from Harold yesterday saying that he was at Mhow at the Staff School - it is a long way from here but I quite hope we should be able to meet before he goes back to Burma.

The Mesopotamian campaign seems at a standstill just now - the weather is so awful that I think our force is quite unable to do much - I suppose they will wait until September. I saw the Russians who joined up with us about the middle of

---

[19] Lt-Col Cooke-Hurle - see note 1915/13.
[20] See note 1915/37.

May and it was all very interesting[21] - I noted that they are trying to fix the blame of the foolhardy Baghdad advance on to someones shoulders and personally I do not see how Sir John Nixon can explain away his entire lack of judgement! I am wondering if Leslie and Bert[22] will have to join the colours and what the girls will do then it is very sad and all this upsetting of homes and peoples lives but it simply must be done if we are ever going to end this war successfuly.

I am anxious to hear how the Pater is getting on now & hope everything goes all right at Elm Grove - he is enjoying the garden I expect & he always feels better in the warm weather

[unsigned]

*****

No. 16/8

Charleville Hotel, Mussoorie, C/o Cox & Co, Bombay
Aug. 4th 1916

My dear old Elsie

I have just returned from the Intercession Service[23] at the Church - it has all been very impressive and the singing was led by the splendid band of the 7th. Hussars.

I suppose there are similar services today all over dear old England - it is hard to realize that this horrid old war has been raging for two whole years and at present I see no prospect of peace for many months to come. I must say it all makes me feel very sad and very homesick but I suppose it's ones duty to keep smiling & present a bold front to the world, weve simply got to win this war and we shall need even yet all the smiles and bravery of Englishmen - and Englishwomen - too to accomplish it. I hate writing about the war but its hard to forget it and at the back of my mind always there is Mesopotamia and all we went through in those months of struggle to relieve Kut but Ill try to write you of other things. Many thanks dear old thing for all your letters and Tatlers etc. - I am hearing from you regularly again now and besides I am getting a good many through from the Gulf - last week I actually got a letter and Tatler dated Nov. 24th. last year, these had obviously been in the Kut mail bags. I hope you have received the letters Ive written you since I came back to India but Im afraid Im an uncertain letter writer - I always was wasnt I? But I love your letters and they mean such a lot to me - sometimes I think I dont deserve all the love and thought you give me.

Today I have sent you by registered post a little lot of twelve skins - they are the skins of the Himalayan snow fox[24] - I want you to have them made up when you feel inclined into a muff and stole thing but you must please let me pay for

---

[21] On May 20th a Russian Cossack patrol of 113 officers & men arrived at Ali Gharbi, after a march of 200 miles. They stayed a fortnight; their officers were awarded British Military Crosses (Moberly, op. cit. vol. III p.13).

[22] Leslie Hyde & Bert How, brothers-in-law to Stanley. Leslie was employed making munitions in Manchester.

[23] On the second anniversary of the outbreak of the war.

[24] Elsie never had these furs made up, but they survive in 1998 as collar and cuffs on her daughter's coat.

doing them up - probably you would find someone in Cheltenham to do this. These skins are scarce now so I hope youll like 'em and I shall look forward to seeing you wearing them (not next winter I fear). You will be glad to hear I am ever so much stronger than when I last wrote and Im looking ever so fat and fit now my wound doesn't trouble me at all but my inside is still quite hopeless - the doctor here says I must expect this for some time - the funny part about it is that this trouble doesn't make me feel ill at all now and of course I am bound to be passed fit for service when I come up for my final Board in about 10 days time. I am still at Mussoorie but must leave for Chakrata in 3 days time - Capt Body left about 10 days ago and is I expect already at Basra but he left his wife here and a week ago Capt. Major & Lieut. Moore[25] of the Somersets turned up from Meerut and persuaded me to stay on with them for a bit. I hope to see Harold if I go off to Mespot again from Bombay - my address will be

> Capt E.S.Goodland
> 1/5 Buffs
> Mesopotamia Expeditionary Force
> c/o India Office, London

it is better to drop the Somerset L.I. as it is confusing and we are no longer I.E.F.'D' but M.E.F. I imagine you are on holiday now and hope you will have ever such a nice time and good weather- you deserve a long rest & change I am sure. This is a very jolly place and there is always plenty to do and everyone seems in the right holiday mood - I will tell you what Ive been doing in my next - the mail goes out almost immediately and I dont want to miss it. Many thanks again dear for all your letters and papers - with best love and good wishes for your holiday

from Stan

*****

No. 16/9

Charleville Hotel, Mussoorie
Aug 11th 1916

My dear old Elsie

I forgot to tell you last mail that in that box I have sent you I have put in a few wooden toys that the natives make and paint and also a little round hat which the rich Indian children wear - I thought these would please your little family. I am still at Mussoorie because I have been ordered to have my Board here tomorrow the 12th - instead of at Chakrata - besides I am under the medical people here and am having medicine and special diet which is a great nuisance - they ought to give me some more leave but I suppose they won't for I look so sunburnt and fit. I shall send a cable home when I get my orders so you will probably hear of my destination.

I am thinking of you on holiday now and hope you are getting good weather and a real rest but expect Ronald will be taking up a lot of your time. Your letters

---

[25] Capt Major sailed for India with the Regiment in 1914. He died in the battle for El Jib in Palestine. The two Moore brothers (Thomas & RB) were also in the Regiment from 1914. They both survived the war (*BoR* pp.xiii, 13, 73). They were brothers of Mary, wife of Capt later Lt-Col FD Urwick.

come regularly now thank goodness & the Tatlers too - also the old ones keep dribbling in - some written last year - I think I should get most of my mail in time - 3 parcels have reached me so there's 2 more somewhere to look forward to - tis good of you old thing - the letter of Mar 12th which you mention hasn't come yet! I hope to send you some snaps soon - Mrs.Body[26] is keen on her camera and has taken several when we have been out picnicing - we had a grand time yesterday climbing another mountain - in the woods coming home we met a whole school of monkeys - they are a big kind with grey blue hair - apes I suppose they were and it was most amusing to see them playing about in their natural haunts! The war in the West is hell now[27] and the casualties heart-breaking but I believe we are steadily doing well and when we get the enemy's third line we shall surely get on faster - one has to be so very patient! The Mesopotamian enquiry sickens me - so many lies are told and so much hushed up - I wish I could write a letter to the Times about it all! The despatches for January still linger in the printers hands I suppose - I sometimes think the awards will never go through - well so long dear old girl - don't worry about me for I'm all right and I'll turn up smiling in dear old Blighty[28] some day

Best love

from Stan

*****

No. 16/10

postmarked 10 Aug. Charleville
[This is a post card of the Savoy Hotel, Mussoorie, but with no message. It appears to have been the label for the parcel referred to in the previous letter 16/9.]

*****

No. 16/11

Chakrata, India
Aug 24 1916

My dear old Elsie

You will see by my address that I am with the old Regiment again at Chakrata - the Medical Board at Mussoorie passed me fit for active service last Saturday and now I am waiting my orders from Simla - these may come at any moment. As a matter of fact my leave was over on the 20th. so I am, having a few extra days holiday. My own Colonel here is doing every thing he can to keep me and he says that if I am ordered to Mespot again he will tell the authorities that I'm not fit to go and demand another Board - but I don't think he can do this - I feel very well - dear- and can do quite a lot of walking and heavy exercise but my poor inside is still all wrong - I told the Board this but I look so fit that they were almost bound to pass me and I've got back all my lost weight too. I shall be glad when it's all

---

[26] Wife of Capt Body (see 1916 Introduction, note 4).

[27] Battle of the Somme, July 1st - Nov 18th.

[28] Army word meaning England, Home. Corruption of Hindi from the Arabic 'bilayati' meaning 'European, foreign.'

settled and if I am ordered back to that godforsaken country of course I'll go very cheerfully. I'm so glad I stayed on at Mussoorie for it is deadly dull here in this very small station - all my pals are busy through the day and I'm left all on my lonesome - I felt I was entitled to a real good time and towards the end of my visit I got to know a very jolly crowd of people and I thoroughly enjoyed myself. I've got awfully keen on dancing again - old girl - fancy at my time of life too - I learnt all the Boston steps and the one step[29] steps and when this old war is over we will take the floor together won't we? The last night I was there we gave a grand concert at the Hotel and got nearly £50 for Mespot - I will enclose a programme[30] - it was a great success and it was a splendid audience - the little play I had done in England several times with Mrs. Sheen so we soon worked it up and Mrs. Jesse who acted with me hand painted all the programmes and we got 2/6 each for them. In the troupe I was dressed as a 'Jack Tar' and looked very funny too. It was a glorious motor ride on my way back from Mussoorie - 60 miles of Himalayan country - the heavy monsoon rains had simply ruined the roads in several places and little streams we had to cross were big rivers then and three times we had to be pulled out by gangs of coolies - I wished I'd got my camera! The home news keeps good and I suppose Do and Gretchen[31] are at Elm Grove at present - I have thought of you on holiday and hope you have had a good time and real rest - I must write to the Pater now so goodbye - with best love

from Stan

*****

No. 16/12

Somerset L.I. Chakrata, India
Aug 30 1916

My dear old Elsie

Just a short letter this mail to tell you I am still enjoying a thoroughly lazy time with the old Regiment at Chakrata - my leave was over on the 20th so already I have had ten extra days holiday and Simla seems in no hurry to send me my posting orders - it is really a very good thing for it gives me a chance of getting stronger for my poor old 'tummy' is still far from well - I am staying with Frank Calway and he has taken a day or two off and we've been long tramps in the hills - we've had a good deal of monsoon rain but it is really beautiful and very wild and romantic - the day before yesterday we had quite a big earthquake - I was writing at my table at the time and it was an extraordinary sensation - the table began to rock and sway about and for a moment I thought I was ill but soon realized when trees and bungalows began to collapse that it was the old earth having a quake! Fortunately no one was hurt much! Since I last wrote to you another of your lovely parcels has turned up with all sorts of good things in it - Bivouac Cocoa - tobacco chocolate & sweets - Many thanks dear old girl - I think it is simply splendid of you - Last night at Mess we were all very excited for a wire came saying Roumania had joined[32] in with the Allies - that's the best news we've

---

[29] Dance steps fashionable at the time.

[30] The programme survives: see plate, section I p.8.

[31] Stanley's sisters - see notes 1914/3 & 4.

[32] Roumania declared war on Germany and Austria -Hungary in 1916, was defeated and Bucharest occupied December 6th 1916.

had for ages and I wonder if after all my dream will be realized and that all the armies in and around the Balkans will soon sweep up through the plains of Austria Hungary -one thing is pretty certain - Turkey must quickly be cut off from Europe and go down on her knees suing for peace! I wonder - in the meantime it must be simply Hell in France! So long dear girl - keep well - with best love

from Stan

*****

No. 16/13

1/5 Somerset L.I., Chakrata, U.P. India
Sept. 7 1916

My dear old Elsie

Just a few lines this mail to tell you I have been ordered to rejoin the jolly old Somersets at Chakrata - we stay here until Oct 9th when we set out on the 100 mile march to the railway and travel down to Meerut - On about Nov 15th we go out into camp for the annual manoeuvres for a month and this will take us on til nearly Xmas unless anything unforeseen happens. I am quite sorry to sever connection with the Buffs for I'd made a lot of friendships in that Regiment and having gone through so much with them I was naturally very attached to 'em- however many things may happen during the next few months which seem to me to be the most exciting and momentous ones in our dear old country. Many thanks dear girl for your last letters and the Eve book[33] which I'm never tired of looking at and which gives me such pleasure. I'm gradually getting better and I'm sure I look awfully well and it really is nice to be back amongst the men I know so well - we are asked to send a draft to the Gulf of 100 men and these go off in 3 days time[34] - the Colonel has given me the job of getting them ready and of course I'm liking it very much and shall be longing to go off with them when the time comes. So long - dear old girl - I hope you have had a real good holiday

With best love & cheerio from Stan

*****

No. 16/14

1/5 Somerset L.I., Chakrata
Sept 14th 1916

My dear old Elsie

I got your sad little letter[35] of August 14th last mail but the Tatler hasn't come yet so I have not been able to read 'Silent Friends.'[36] Anyway I am so sorry dear old girl to have made you feel so miserable - I thought I'd been writing to you almost every mail since I came out of hospital and can't help feeling some of my letters have gone astray. I was always a little uncertain in my writing wasn't I? but for goodness sake don't think I've altered in the slightest for I'm always

---

[33] May be a collected 'Letters of Eve' from *The Tatler*.

[34] This draft left Meerut on October 20th and reinforced the 1/4 Somersets in Mesopotamia.

[35] This is the only hint of the strain which a long and anxious separation imposed on those engaged in war.

[36] Feature in *The Tatler*.

thinking of you and thanking you for all your letters & papers & parcels and so long as I live I shall feel ever so grateful to you - I thought I'd just send your letter back but perhaps you were feeling a little seedy and depressed when you wrote it so I'll tear it up and forget all about it for it made me very unhappy to feel I'd disappointed you and made you miserable.

I'm writing in pencil for Frank Calway and I are changing houses to day and are all packed up - I hear we are likely to stay at Chakrata until almost the end of October now and we are going to live together in a topping little bungalow with a view of the mountains & snows which is simply magnificent - I feel I shall never be able to properly describe all the things I've seen since I last saw you! I have been working hard at the language lately with a native teacher and am just able to speak it now - I thought it would be useful if I was ever offered a staff job and in any case it's nice to know something of what is said by the natives around me. Last night I dreamt the war suddenly ended and that we were all together again at Elm Grove for next Xmas - I wish I could really think so. Anyway when peace does come and I come home do try to be down at Taunton to meet me - promise? - After all the monsoon rains the hills are gorgeous now - they are covered with wild dahlias - orchids and convolvulus of every colour. Best love - dear girl - and keep smiling

from Stan

*****

No. 16/15

1/5 Somerset L.I. Chakrata, Upper India
Sept. 22nd 1916

My dear old Elsie

It's my birthday today and I can't remember if I'm 33 or 34![37] Frank Calway kindly says I'm 34 but it doesn't matter much does it - I feel younger than when I left England and if only I could get my 'innards' right I should be as fit as ever.

My poor old leg hurts like anything on wet days but I'm not a bit lame now and can run about at tennis and do long route marches without any trouble - Many thanks dear old girl for your last letter (Aug. 22nd) with birthday wishes - I wonder if by this time next year this horrid war will be over but I suppose that is too much to hope for - I'm trying to get reconciled to the feeling that it will be 1918 before I see you and dear old England again! I'm looking forward to meeting Harold about Oct 2nd - he is coming to Meerut on his way to Calcutta and Burma and I've got five days leave to go down to him and then have to return here - it will be so nice to see him again and we shall have simply heaps to talk about. It is difficult to get photos done in this country but in a week or so I really hope to send you a few snapshots. I almost despair of ever getting that M.C. they are so long in publishing despatches aren't they but I haven't quite given up hope yet! I saw one of the Mundens was killed - I think it must be Dr. Mundens

---

[37] He was born in 1883, therefore was 33 on September 22nd 1916.

younger brother[38] - Aren't the casualty lists heartbreaking now? Cheerio and my best love

from Stan

Postscript:
Many thanks dear for the 'Eve' book - it is lovely & I'm always looking at it - the other fellows in the Mess love it too - Stan.

*****

No. 16/16

Somerset L.I. Chakrata
Sept. 28 1916

My dear old Elsie

I wonder where you will be when this reaches you? On holiday I hope for I'm sure you have earned a good rest - I imagined you were away last August but suppose that fell through. Many thanks dear for your last letter & Tatler (Aug 29th) - I can't think why you haven't heard from me for I'm sure I wrote you several times from Mussoorie - some of my letters from home have been lost lately too! The best news I've got this mail is that Harold is coming up here to stay with me in about 10 days time - I am looking forward so much to seeing him again - he's got a fortnights leave and is going to have a look round Agra & Delhi on his way up. It is very quiet here but so beautiful that one is never dull - I am writing in my bungalow verandah now and I've got a magnificent view of the mountains & snows - I'm sure Harold will enjoy it & we'll go off for long walks. The Colonel & his wife have gone down to Meerut now and I'm keeping her dog for her - it is a beautiful setter - reddy brown colour and he is such a companion. When you get this we shall probably be on our long march down to the Plains - I shall enjoy this I'm sure - I hear there's going to be a push in Mespot early in November and I do hope they'll send a large enough force to get to Baghdad this time - My old pal Thomas Moore is getting married next week - his fiancee is coming out from Cheltenham & he's marrying her at Bombay - Here's my best love & a cheero

from Stan

*****

No. 16/17

1/5 Somerset L.I. Chakrata, Upper Provinces, India
Oct 5th 1916

My dear old Elsie

Since last I wrote I've had a couple of days in bed with my old malaria fever again - I haven't mentioned it in my home letters for they would probably think more of it than necessary and I suppose I shall always be subject to attacks while I'm in the East. I'm better today but a bit shaky and I've got to drink a lot of milk which I loathe. I am expecting Harold to turn up either to day or tomorrow and

---

[38] This name has not been traced.

61

we are sure to have a good time together[39] - the last few days we've had torrential rains and I hear parts of the road have been washed away but I'm sure he'll get up somehow - it is 60 miles from the nearest railway station to Chakrata!

Now we shall be getting ready for our exit and march down in two weeks time - it will all be very jolly and we are likely to have perfect weather. The home news seems very good and I get wonderful letters each month from the Pater - the Babe has had a good holiday in the Mumbles. The war news keeps good too and the new armies seem to be fighting magnificently - Well cheero - old girl - many thanks for your last letter & Tatler

with best love

from Stan

*****

No.16/18

1/5 Soms L.I.Meerut
Nov. 3 1916

My dear old Elsie

Many thanks dear for your welcome letter of Octb 3rd. and also for a simply splendid pipe which came during the week. I think it's quite the best I've ever possessed & very expensive too - couldn't resist the temptation of starting it at once & already it's getting so nicely coloured - many thanks again & again. I am thinking of you now at home on holiday but I fear by this time you are nearly due to return to Minch. I do hope you have had ever such a good time and fine weather.

We are settling down in our new station very nicely & already are making friends - the 7th. Hussars are here too and you know the swagger & smartness of a British Cavalry Regt. don't you? but they are all very nice & I think we shall have many good times. At present we are busy getting ready for Camp - we march out on the 13th. and are going 14 miles south of Delhi - we shall march through that old city and probably spend a night in the old Fort. Frank Calway is away for 3 weeks on a course and I am acting Adjutant so I've got a busy time as he does not join us again until after we get into camp. We have such a nice Mess here and are a very happy family & we are expecting 10 new officers out from home next week. My pal T. Moore brought his bride back last night & there was great jubilation - Best love dear old girl & cheero

from Stan

*****

---

[39] There is no surviving letter between October 5th and November 3rd. So it is not certain whether Stanley's brother Harold reached Chakrata to visit him after so much anticipation. But see letter 16/20: Harold had been in hospital.

My dear old Elsie

Just a few lines of greeting from Delhi - I've been on the long march for nearly a week and I'm sorry I missed writing you last mail - I hope to write a long letter when we reach our camp in two days time. You will be interested to hear the Regiment is ordered up to the Frontier after camp - that is just about Xmas so please address letters at present c/o Cox & Co Bombay. You need not be very alarmed as at present there is not much trouble up there and I believe our Division is only to be in reserve somewhere up near the Indus. It is bitterly cold up there for 3 months and I've been extravagant enough to buy a warm sleeping bag. I can't get a good pair of mittens in this country and if you would be so kind as to send me out some it would be so nice of you. You always tell me to let you know of anything.

I am having a very busy time as Adjutant but I ride a horse now which saves my poor old leg the long marches - I'm very well & enjoying it so much - it makes me quite thrill with excitement to be encamped neath the walls of the historic Fort at Delhi - Best love dear old girl

from Stan

*****

No. 16/20

Tughlakabad Camp, Nr.Delhi
Nov. 24 1916

My dear old Elsie

I've just been told the Xmas mail goes out tonight so I thought I simply must write to you. Fancy Xmas being in sight again - it really seems only the other day I was eating my dinner of bully beef and biscuits in a dug out in Mespot - how time flies. Its awfully difficult to know what wishes to send ones pals at home but you will understand my feelings and I shall be thinking of you at any rate we can all most sincerely wish that this old war would soon fight itself out and I expect that is the wish which will predominate everything else. Peace and a safe and speedy homecoming for the fighting men. Your last letter came yesterday forwarded from Chakrata - Many thanks dear for your congrats on my 'mention' - It's very nice to have got some little honour out of the war - sometimes I feel that they won't give me any further award and I suppose I ought to be quite satisfied - but Lloyd George said about 3 weeks ago that the list of awards for Mespot would be published shortly and until this appears I shan't altogether give up hope! We are having a gorgeous time - plenty of hard training and a whole lot of night work - Lord Radnor[40] is our Brigadier and is a real good soldier.

---

[40] Jacob Pleydell-Bouverie, 6th Earl of Radnor, 1868-1930. MP for Wilton Division of Wiltshire, 1892-1900 Lt-Col and Brevet Colonel, CO 4th Battalion Wiltshire Regiment. Served in South Africa 1900, India 1914-1917, Brig-General Dehra Dun Brigade 1915-1917 (*Who was Who* Vol III).

There is very little further news about our move to the Frontier except that advance party has already gone off to make preparations for us - it looks as if we are really going but I daresay we shall hear more about it next week when the Viceroy[41] and the new Commander in Chief[42] come to see us. I've had a busy time as Adjutant but now Frank Calway is back and I'm with my company again it was very interesting marching down and the men simply loved Delhi - we entered through the Cashmere Gate and came out through the Lahore Gate - the museums in the Fort are full of the most thrilling relics of the great Mutiny - very near our camping ground are the ruins of one of the 7 old cities of Delhi - in fact the whole country is a mass of old mosques and ruins. I've had several letters from Harold lately - he has had a turn in hospital with a poisoned knee but seems better now - he simply loves his staff job and of course is wildly excited at the thought of having Alice out with him and it will be awfully nice for them both. I'm so glad you got your holiday at last and I hope you have returned to Minch feeling all the better for the change - I'm sorry to hear you keep so thin and you really must try to get fattened up for Xmas.

I hardly know how to write to the dear old Pater for Xmas - and I'm afraid it will be full of the saddest possible memories for him but he bears up wonderfully and seems to keep well.

Heres my best love and warmest thoughts & wishes for Xmas

from Stan

*****

No.16/21

Tughlakabad Camp, Delhi
Dec 2 1916

My dear old Elsie

Only a moment this mail to send you a line to thank you ever so much for your last letter written from Hale[43] - you seem to have had a real busy holiday but I'm sure the change must have done you good. We are very busy and training strenuously - very often night and day - we are all very fit and must be hard as nails - I'm bound to say I like camp life much better than barracks. We go to the Frontier on Jan 15 - so that will give us about 2 weeks in Meerut to pack up and make other arrangements - best love dear old girl and a New Year kiss from

Stan

*****

---

[41] Viscount Chelmsford, see note 1915/10.
[42] Gen. CC Munro, in post 1916-1920.
[43] Home of Elsie's family, near Altrincham, Cheshire.

No.16/22

My dear old Elsie

I'm so sorry I've been writing such bad letters lately but I really have had no time and this mail must be a short one too - I will try to write a long letter sometime during the Xmas holiday.

We've got back to Meerut quite safely but are living in state of readiness to go to the Frontier any day. The Colonel has told me he wants me to take on an advance party of 100 men so I shall in all probability go in 10 days or so before the Regiment leaves Meerut.

Many thanks dear for all your letters and papers it is so good of you. I shall be thinking of you during Xmas. I shall have a quiet time - shall have midday dinner with the men of my Company and in the evening I am dining with Mrs. Urwick[44] one of the ladies of the Regiment. Excuse haste - best love and all good wishes

from Stan

*****

---

[44] Wife of Captain (later Lt-Col) Urwick of whom much will be heard.

CHAPTER FOUR

1917

The Background.

Throughout the First World War the Government of India had reason to fear the outbreak of internal disorder and the conflicts for which the North-West Frontier was notorious. There was substance in the reports from Persia and Afghanistan of the activities of German and Turkish agents whose influence percolated to the Punjab. The pre-war Indian army had been professionally skilled at meeting such threats and the Territorial battalions sent out to replace the Regulars trained hard to reach the same standard of proficiency. An example of operations on the North-West Frontier occurred in November 1916 when 6000 men of the Mohmend tribes were dispersed only after the deployment of two infantry brigades of the 1st Peshawar Division backed up by supporting troops, armoured cars and aeroplanes.[1]

In the two-way traffic of men and materials between India and the United Kingdom Egypt played a vital rôle. Since 1882 the British had governed Egypt through an administrative structure which controlled without abolishing the authority of the Khedive and his ministers. On August 5th 1914 the Egyptian Government was required to announce that Great Britain's enemies were also Egypt's enemies; when war was declared on Turkey martial law was proclaimed and in December 1914 Egypt became a British Protectorate, enabling recruitment to the Egyptian Labour Corps to become increasingly energetic, amounting to virtual conscription in some rural areas. The Turks hoped that they could stir up trouble by declaring a Holy War against the British, though only the Senussi of the oases on the fringe of the Western Desert responded, their rebellion being suppressed early in 1917. When Turkish armies on three occasions crossed the province of Sinai and approached the Suez Canal the Egyptians of the Nile Valley did not stir.

In the first two years of the First World War Egypt was the chief Imperial staging post from which troops were despatched to the Western Front, the Dardanelles, Salonika, Mesopotamia and India. The third Turkish attack, delivered by a force of 16,000 men including some German and Austrian artillerymen and machine-gunners, was turned back in the sharply fought battle of Romani, 15 miles east of the Canal, in August 1916. This incident convinced the War Office of the need to put the security of the Canal beyond doubt, to be achieved by the recovery of the Sinai coastal strip up to the Palestine border. Correctly assuming that a British army was not as well adapted to desert operations as were the Turks the Egyptian Expeditionary Force began to construct a standard gauge railway, eventually 150 miles long, and a 12-inch pipeline carrying water, suitably filtered, from the Nile. At the end of 1916 the Government indicated that, though British

---

[1] Moberly, op. cit., vol. III, p.55.

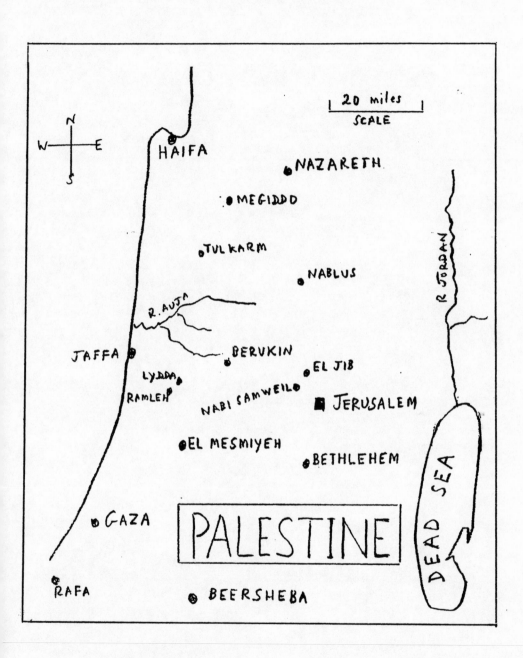

and French offensives on the Western Front were the top priority for the Spring of 1917, it envisaged a major campaign in Palestine in the Autumn. Meanwhile the EEF must do its best to distract Turkish attention from Mesopotamia, where General Maude's plans to recover Kut and capture Baghdad were unfolding.

The EEF crossed the Egypt-Palestine border in January 1917 and in March and April made two attempts to take Gaza by storm; the first, with the advantage of surprise, was nearly successful but the second was foiled by the tenacity of the Turkish soldiers who by then were well dug in. The EEF needed reinforcements and a new leader. In late June General Allenby, 'The Bull', formerly commander of the Third Army in France, arrived in Egypt, having been told by Lloyd George that Jerusalem was wanted "as a Christmas present for the British nation."[2] Allenby's frequent visits to the front line and his removal of Headquarters from Cairo to a point only twenty miles from Gaza speedily restored the confidence of a demoralised army. He demanded, and obtained, reinforcements, some from Salonika; those from India included infantry battalions which, with other units, were brigaded into the 75th Division. Meanwhile the Turkish Government, encouraged by the collapse of Rumania and the faltering efforts of the Russians on the Caucasus front devised the 'Yilderim' project, which with German assistance, would achieve the recapture of Baghdad and the defeat of British ambitions in Palestine. The Germans provided 6500 men including three infantry battalions, artillery batteries, machine gun companies, four squadrons of aeroplanes and the distinguished staff officer General von Falkenhayn. Their presence ensured that when Allenby was ready any attack would be sternly contested.

Allenby won the Third Battle of Gaza in early November by using his superiority in cavalry to turn the left flank of the Turkish position at Beersheba, about 30 miles from the sea. From October 27th the Gaza stronghold was subjected to military and naval bombardments, successfully deluding the enemy into expecting a third frontal assault on the town. On October 31st the operation began which won control of Beersheba, but difficulties with the water supply and strong Turkish reaction led to six more days of heavy fighting before the enemy was forced to pull out of Gaza on the night of November 6th/7th. In the next ten days the British advanced fifty miles along the coastal plain reaching Jaffa and, inland, the foot of the Judaean hills. The Turks avoided disaster by fighting rearguard actions but they lost much equipment and 10,000 men taken prisoner.

Determined to press his disorganised enemy hard, Allenby turned East into the hills on November 18th, as the winter rains set in. His line of supply could support just two infantry divisions - the 52nd and 75th - and a Yeomanry division, covered only by the mountain guns of mule and camel batteries. Aware of the potentially adverse propaganda the enemy might make of a destructive battle for the Holy City Allenby intended to cut off von Falkenhayn by capturing the villages commanding the road which runs north from Jerusalem to Nablus. This manoeuvre involved a march over precipitous, stony and trackless country, with the nights bitterly cold for troops still in their desert kit. Despite their gallantry the men of the 52nd and 75th Divisions had neither the numbers not the fire power to force their way through to the Nablus road, though they gained and held Nabi

---

2 AP Wavell, *Allenby: a Study in Greatness*, Harrap, 1940, p.186.

Samweil on a high ridge only five miles to the North-West of Jerusalem, the traditional point from which pilgrims and crusaders had their first view of the city. On November 24th Allenby called a halt and for the next fortnight re-grouped his command, making the tracks usable for wheeled traffic and bringing up divisions which had been rested since the Gaza - Beersheba battle. With these the second attack on Jerusalem succeeded in breaking through enough of its outlying western defences to persuade von Falkenhayn and the Turks to evacuate the city on December 9th. Allenby had delivered Lloyd George and the British nation their early Christmas present, yet his army still had work to do. Von Falkenhayn's Turks made several fierce efforts to recapture Jerusalem but by the year's end the villages which had remained beyond Allenby's grasp in November were firmly in British hands and Jerusalem was secure. At the coast the front line was pushed far enough north of Jaffa to make it safe from counter-attack. In the wettest season in living memory British, Turks and Germans went, briefly, into winter quarters.

Stanley Goodland in 1917: India, Egypt & Palestine.

Alone among the officers of the 1/5 Somersets Stanley Goodland had seen front-line service and had been decorated for his bravery. Evidently thinking highly of him, his Commanding Officer recommended Stanley as a worthy candidate for a Regular Army captaincy but he did not wish his name to be put forward. Meanwhile Lt-Col Cooke-Hurle tested Stanley's potential as a prospective Adjutant by putting him in charge of the advance party which prepared a camp for the Battalion in the wilds of the North West frontier.

After two and a half years of soldiering in India, during which hard training and close comradeship had honed its military efficiency the 1/5 Somerset Light Infantry was summoned to play its part in the Egyptian Expeditionary Force. On arrival in Egypt the Battalion was posted to the newly created 75th Division and, with the 3/3 Gurkhas and two more territorial units, the 1/4 Wiltshires and the 2/4 Hampshires became part of the 233rd Brigade, commanded by Brigadier-General the Hon EM Colston, DSO, MVO.[3] In 1930 the Brigadier, asked to contribute a forword to the *Book of Remembrance*, recalled his first impression of the 1/5 Somersets, who had disembarked at Suez on the morning of May 11th. That night he and his staff were waiting at a siding near Cairo. 'Punctual to the moment, like a snake the huge troop train glided in; one whistle and the war- strength Battalion detrained and in ten minutes, headed by their bugles and band they marched off. The Adjutant turned and said: "As good as a Regular Battalion. You are lucky, Sir." I echoed his sentiments . . . that night was the beginning of a friendship which was to outlive the War.'[4]

Three weeks of re-equipping and training preceded the rail journey of the 233rd Brigade to El Arish and on to Rafa, on the Egypt - Palestine border. By early September the Somersets were in the front line South East of Gaza where the width of no man's land - 2000 yards - determined the style of warfare, which was confined to night patrols and the exchange of artillery fire. On October 6th the

---

[3] 1880-1944. Grenadier Guardsman: succeeded as 2nd (& last) Baron Roundway, 1925.
[4] *BoR*, p.7.

68

night raid on the Turkish outpost in the 'Old British Trenches' was a spectacular event which brought renown to the 1/5 Somersets who succeeded where other units in this part of the front had failed.

This 'stunt' had been meticulously planned at Brigade, Battalion and Company level. It was predictable that Stanley Goodland, with his campaign experience in Mesopotamia, would be given command of the raiding party. In their eagerness to use the bayonet his men omitted to capture any prisoners but the congratulations from higher command showed that this short and sharp operation boosted morale in the Egyptian Expeditionary Force. Lt-Col Cooke-Hurle's report to Brigade praised 'Captain E.S. Goodland MC who commanded the assaulting party [and who] is a fine leader of men. I attribute the smoothness of the running of the raid to be due to a great extent to him.'[5]

After the raid Stanley was given a week's leave in Cairo, enjoyed in the company of Lt Harry Milsom. Soon after his return to the Battalion Stanley became Adjutant, succeeding Captain Frank Calway who had received a staff appointment. For the events of November 1917, during which the 1/5 Somersets faced their severest ordeals, there are several documentary sources. As Adjutant Stanley Goodland wrote the daily entries in the Battalion War Diary which supplements his letters to Elsie and the account he wrote to his father printed in the *Somerset County Gazette* of January 26th 1918. Lt Harry Milsom's uninhibited story of the campaign up to the attack on El Jib, in which he was severely wounded, provides further information. So does the privately printed pamphlet entitled 'Some Fighting in Palestine in 1917' by A Major (Act Lt-Col.) DSO, that is, Frank Urwick who commanded the Battalion in the absence of Lt-Col Cooke-Hurle, who was in hospital.[6] These narratives speak for themselves of the triumphs and tragedies of a Battalion which, as Stanley wrote in the War Diary summing up the events of November, earned for the Regiment 'an enviable reputation in the E[gypt] E[xpeditionary] F[orce].'[7]

The 75th Division did not take part in the entering of Jerusalem but won the right to wear a flash depicting a key because its brave advance into the Judaean Hills and the capture of Nabi Samweil unlocked the door to the Holy City. The depleted 1/5 Somersets spent most of December in the Ramleh area of the Judaean foothills, including eight days at Surafend, that 'nest of thieves.'[8] They moved up to the front line on Boxing Day but their main enemy over the Christmas and New Year season was the miserable cold and mud of an unprecedentedly wet Palestinian winter.

---

[5] Insertion in War Diary, 1/5 Bn SLI. PRO WO 95/4690.
[6] see Appendix.
[7] PRO WO 95/4690.
[8] Cyril Falls: *Armageddon*, 1918, Weidenfeld & Nicolson, 1964, p.175.

The Letters Written in 1917

No. 17/1

1/5 Somerset L.I., Meerut
Jan 4 1917

My dear old Elsie

You will see by my address that we are still at Meerut - all packed up - and waiting the order to go further north. I think perhaps I told you that I am to go ahead of the Regiment with an advance party of 100 men and as we shall probably get 10 days start I am expecting to move any day.

Of course now everything else in my mind is eclipsed by the announcement of my Military[9] - the cable from the Pater (it hasn't appeared in the Indian papers yet) arrived one evening just as we were going into Mess - everyone went mad with excitement and it was a very merry night I can tell you. Well - my dear old girl - thanks so much for keeping my secret - it's been a long long time of waiting - practically a year and many times lately I've given up hope even of getting it. It's made the events of that awful Janry 1916 come back very vividly to my mind and it really is a perfect miracle that I'm still alive and well. The Colonel is delighted and I've had congratulations on all sides - I'm glad to have been able to bring a little honour to the jolly old Regiment and it pleases me beyond anything to feel how delighted the old Pater must be. I only hope he is better now! Ever so many thanks dear girl for your Xmas letter & papers & parcel - the latter arrived actually on Xmas morning - it is so kind of you & I'm enjoying the cigarettes so much - the little dominoes are sweet & everything else simply topping. Considering all things we had quite a good Xmas - 3 or 4 of our officers have their wives out here and they gave all sorts of gay parties. On Xmas morning I went to Church Parade and then back to see the men sit down to a tremendous spread - of turkeys geese ducks ham beef plum pudding etc etc - all very small and poor things that would make our English birds blush for same [shame] but it was all very jovial and nice - lots of singing - lots of toasts - lots of soldiers talk which I simply love. I've been thinking of you and all the people at home - thinking of poor Mother & it's so difficult & almost impossible to quite realize that she isn't at Elm Grove waiting for the end of the war and waiting til we come home. I expect you have had a busy time with the children and I hope you have had a happy time - I can't tell you what's going to happen to us on the Frontier. In any case there won't be any trouble until about March when the hillmen have no work to do and no crops to worry about - it's at those times that they come down & make trouble.

We shall be under canvas or in blockhouses or dugouts & the cold for the next few weeks will be intense - After March it gets so hot that we shall have to be sent

---

[9] 'The London Gazette announced that Lieutenant, temporary Captain, Edward Stanley Goodland, (Somerset Light Infantry) had been awarded the Military Cross. Captain Goodland is the well known Somerset cricketer. He is the son of Mr EC Goodland and a member of the firm of Franklin, Hare & Goodland, jewellers, etc., of Taunton. He was wounded during the advance on Kut some months ago.'(*Somerset County Gazette*, December 30th 1916).

somewhere where we can get more shelter than canvas. I'll let you know my movements but of course I'm not allowed to tell you very much.

Again many thanks dear old girl for your letters and gifts - with best wishes for the New Year and lots of love

from Stan

*****

No. 17/2

1/5 Somerset L.I., Meerut
Jan 12 1917

My dear old Elsie

I've got my orders at last and early tomorrow I'm off to the Frontier with an Advance Party - Today we are all very busy making the final plans.

It will be bitterly cold for the next few weeks under canvas but I've treated myself to a nice warm sleeping bag and I've got those lovely bed stockings which Mrs. Hyde gave me on Salisbury Plain - I hope next mail to be able to write and tell you my first impressions but we are told that we shan't be allowed to say very much as to what goes on. It is a long train journey but through interesting country so the time will pass pleasantly enough. Thank you dear old girl for your last letter - we shall look forward to our mail more than ever now we are going right away from civilization. Today a wire came from Harold saying that Alice had rejoined him safely and well - so that's good news for he has been frightfully anxious during her voyage out. We still have celebrations in the Mess of my Military Cross and you can realize how proud I am of the ribbon I am now allowed to wear - since I last wrote I had to go up to the Brigade General and the Divisional General to be congratulated - I have packed up a little Cashmere scarf to day for your birthday and hope it will reach you safely - goodness knows when I should have another opportunity of sending off a parcel - it brings with it loving birthday wishes - I've also included two collar badges. These are the ones I wore all through Mespot, and I want you & Gretchen to have one each - please send her one won't you?

They make up into quite a nice brooch and you can get some Regimental ribbon from Browns of Taunton - colours green and blue with a thin gold stripe - very pretty I think - I'll try to draw a little sketch of how it should go. You will want to have a metal brooch pin soldered on the back.

The news from Home seems better and I do hope the old Pater will soon be his wonderful old self. I've sent your mother a few lines this mail - it was awfully kind of her to send me out Punch's Almanac.

With best love

from Stan

*****

71

No. 17/3

Burhan Camp, Nr. Attock,[10] North West Frontier, India
Janry 18 1917

[Note: the envelope of this letter is printed O.H.M.S. and '16th Indian Division']

My dear old Elsie

Here I am in camp once again and quite safe and well. I was sent off from Meerut at very short notice with 100 men and we are busy making all the preparations to receive the Regiment which is arriving on the 27th. inst. Weve got our hands full for besides fetching 300 large tents there are cook houses & washhouses and mess kitchens to be built besides roads and drains to dig I was sorry to leave Meerut where we had many good times and made lots of friends and this is a very desolate spot to be sent to - however its more like real soldiering & theres always the danger and a certain amount of excitement which appeals to me more than ordinary barrack life. Its almost impossible to describe this spot - it looks as if there had been a huge earthquake for the ground is all broken and churned up - theres hardly a tree or any green thing to be seen - we are surrounded by mountains all covered in snow & it freezes hard every night - so you can imagine how cold it is living entirely under canvas Theres absolutely nothing to do so we can give our minds entirely to soldiering, and it isnt completely safe to wander very far from camp

The whole neighbourhood is haunted by Pathan rifle thieves - very desperate men who get a big price for a rifle if they can get one back across the frontier I havent had my last two mails & suppose they will be a bit uncertain until we are a bit more settled and of course I am very anxious to get the latest news of the poor old Pater I feel frightfully lonely up here & shall be so glad when the Regiment arrives- we are such a happy crowd when we are altogether - hope you are fit - best love dear old girl

from Stan

I hadnt time after all to post the parcel at Meerut so will do so first opportunity.

*****

No. 17/4

Camp Burhan, Nr.Attock, North West Frontier
Janry 25 1917

My dear old Elsie

Many thanks dear old girl for your letter of the Dec.19th which reached me only today - goodness knows why it has taken so long in coming - I hope you have been getting my letters lately too - Im sorry I could not write much while in camp at Tughlakabad[11] - but I think I sent you a line most mails since. We are getting on very well with our camp here and when the Regiment arrives in a few days time I think we should be practically ready to receive them and to make them comfortable - Our Quartermaster has to remain at Meerut to hand over and will not join us for two weeks or so - the Colonel writes to say I am to act as

---

[10] Attock lies between Peshawar and Rawalpindi.
[11] The ruins of Tughlakabad, one of the seven cities of Delhi : see also Letters 16/20 & 21

Quartermaster until he rejoins so I should have a busy time feeding over 900 hungry mouths & clothing them & making them comfortable! Ive had no chance of doing any exploring since I last wrote - it isnt safe to wander far without an escort and weve all been very busy. As a Major on the Staff said when we first arrived "theres damn all to do up here except soldiering" and Im sure hes quite right. There's very little shooting even - the other evening I shot a hyena but there are no birds at all - sometimes a flock of geese come over but they fly so high and so fast that they defeat me altogether. They are equipping this Division regardless of expense and I fancy it must mean that when we have all been training together for some little time that we shall see service somewhere - they are completing us in transport - field ambulances all the newest Maxim & Lewis Guns - bombs in fact every thing necessary for service - If we do go I hope it will be anywhere but Mespot.

Since I last wrote you I have passed the anniversary of my wound and my Military Cross - It seems only yesterday I was passing through those awful times and everyday I go through the different thrilling events in my mind. Ive had several letters lately from old friends in the Buffs - they are still fighting and on Jan 11 and 12th lost a good many casualties - they have had a very very hard time indeed and must be absolutely done up by this time.[12]

Its awfully lonely here and I shall be so glad when the Regiment comes - we are such a cheery Mess when we all get together - Banes Walker[13] - Milsom[14] and the two Moores are the only subalterns left of the old crowd who came out in the Kenilworth Castle and we are all the greatest of pals - all the others - about 16 - have dwindled away - most of them have got jobs in the Indian Army with the intention of sticking to soldiering after the War.

Todays mail also brought a few lines from the Babe[15] with quite a cheerful report of the dear old Pater - he seems really wonderful and has quite rallied again. Before next mail I hope to get your promised parcel off - the post office is two miles away and I havent had a chance of going down yet.

Many thanks dear girl for the Tatler - I shall enjoy the two letters more than ever now we are so far away from civilization. The married men of the Regiment are of course frightfully sick because no ladies are allowed so far north as this - they are staying at Meerut for the present.

Well cheero dear old thing - heres my love to you & the best of good wishes

from Stan

*****

---

[12] The Buffs were involved in the campaign to recapture Kut.
[13] Gerald Banes Walker of North Petherton, Bridgwater, Somerset. He, Harry Milsom and Stanley were close friends and colleagues. They are mentioned several times in subsequent letters.
[14] Harry Milsom (1889-1970) MA Cantab. Ranching in British Columbia before the War. Assistant Secretary of the [Royal] London Hospital, Whitechapel, 1919-1930. Secretary, 1930-1939.
[15] See note 1914/2.

No. 17/5

Pir Gumat Shah, Attock District, North West Frontier, India
Feb 1st 1917

My dear old Elsie

I was so very sorry to hear in your last letter that you were in bed with 'flu and feeling so dreadfully seedy - I do hope you have got over it long ago and that you are your cheery self again.

Its a beastly thing to get but the weather at home seems to have been very severe and I dont wonder at people feeling ill. Do take care of yourself - goodness knows how your little family gets on when you arnt well. Mrs.Brown started the letter quite well - why didnt you let her carry on a little more! Anyway I hope to come to see them all one day in the dim future - and this reminds me of some news which I hope will pass the Censor all right - weve heard on very high authority that many British Regiments are going to be sent to Europe in April - ourselves included. They are sending a whole lot of Garrison Battalions into this country now to take our place and everything seems to point to our going somewhere - Especially as the Frontier seems so quiet just now. We may go to Egypt and then Salonika[16] or to England to refit for France - the latter I hope and trust. It seems quite certain that every white man possible will be wanted for the great push this coming summer. And so dear girl, you may see me sooner than ever you expected but you musnt count too much upon it for all orders change about a good deal.

Another thing I must tell you is that the Colonel has been asked by the War Office if he has any officers he can recommend for commissions as Captains in the Regular Army - the Colonel has very nicely selected me as the only one suitable in the Regt and of course I feel very flattered. Of course I dont want to leave the old Battalion again and the CO doesnt want to lose me but he says he feels that it his duty to put up my name if I am willing. I should probably have to stay in the Army a few months after peace is declared and perhaps this would suit me quite well for it will take the country some little time to settle down and for business to find its footing again. Anyhow the Colonel has given me a little time to think things over. If I got into the Regular Army I should certainly be sent home even if the Somersets remained in India.[17] Since I last wrote the Regiment has arrived and we are quite comfortably settled down - every one was very pleased with all our arrangements and really the men I had with me worked splendidly. Im still Quartermaster and have plenty to do all day long - its been bitterly cold and theres lots more snow on the mountains which look simply glorious in the sunshine. Many thanks dear girl for the lovely mittens and tie - it was so nice of you and I wear the mittens every day and they are such a comfort to me - everyone in the mess is frightfully envious [jealous deleted] of them.

I am afraid that the Pater has had a very nasty turn and that Dr. Iles says a similar stroke may be fatal - of course he is getting a very old man now but I do hope he will live to see us home again and peace declared. I sometimes wonder

---

[16] British and French forces were sent to Salonika in late 1915 to support Serbia, their ally, against Bulgaria which came in on the side of the Central Powers.

[17] Stanley did not take up the offer.

if the Babe is equal to her most difficult task? Many thanks again dear for the mittens & tie and hopes that you are well again - with much love

from Stan

*****

No. 17/6

1/5 Somerset L.I., Pir Gumat Shah, India N.W.
Feb 8 1917

[Letter addressed to 'Highcroft' [18]]

My dear old Elsie

Very many thanks dear for your last letter dated Jan 9th and I am so glad you are getting over your 'flue' and are beginning to feel stronger - you must have had a very nasty illness and I hope you are getting a little Spring weather now & sunshine to help you get quite well. By this time I expect you will have moved into 'Highcroft' and I hope you are very comfortably settled - it is such a business to change houses as a rule. I havent much news this mail - we have had no orders yet regarding our future except that we break up this camp on March 17th and go somewhere. They will probably only give us a few days notice - we may go into blockhouses for the hot weather - or go to some Himalayan Hill station or there is the great chance still of going home. Im still Quartermaster of the Regiment and shall be glad to hand over in a few days - its a worrying job and I hate so much office work - Id much rather be out amongst my men.

Ive had several letters from Alice who seems much impressed by Burma and she is of course delightfully happy. Harold is lucky to be stationed in such a nice place as Maymyo & to have such a good job. We get papers 3 days late here and are at present wondering & wondering if America really intends to declare war on Germany.[19] Best love dear old girl - and do keep well now
from Stan

*****

No. 17/7

Attock, India
Feb. 15 1917

My dear old Elsie

I've been out in a blockhouse on the front line since last I wrote to you with a detachment of 70 men of my Company - I hear the post goes in a few minutes so I thought I must send you a few lines. It's been a very exciting week for me and now we are all dead tired and looking forward to a good days rest! I'm not allowed to say what's happening out here but things are fairly peaceful and at any rate the Frontier is so well guarded just now that there isn't much danger - We still hear very strong rumours that we are soon to go home and I really think you will see me before many weeks are over. The mail boats are very uncertain now and I haven't had a letter from you for two weeks - I suppose the submarines are so busy in the Mediterranean now that mails will be delayed. I do hope you are much

---

[18] The Brown family had moved to another house in Minchinhampton.
[19] The USA declared war on Germany on April 6th 1917.

75

better now & entirely lost your 'flu. Very little news here - I'm afraid my letters are very dull - but our lives now are simply spent in soldiering & soldiering all day long. I'm always thinking of you & dear old England

With best love

from Stan

*****

No. 17/8

Feb 22 1917

My dear old Elsie

We've had no English mail for the last 3 weeks & consequently are very fed up - I suppose the submarines have been too busy or perhaps the mail boats are being sent round the Cape. We are all hoping 3 letters will come all together. I am wondering how you are now - in your last letter you told me that you were just recovering from a nasty touch of 'flu - I do hope you are quite fit again & I shall be so anxious to know. We are still in camp and very little exciting happens - we've got a very energetic General who makes us do plenty of hard work but we don't mind that because theres absolutely nothing else to do - On March 2nd the whole Division is going out on a reconnaissance over the Frontier and we are busy making all the preparations - we shall be away from this spot for 15 days about - it is very likely that we shall not be able to get any letters posted so you will know if you dont hear from me - there are of course no roads where we are going so we have to take camels to carry all our stores and kit. Nothing more has come to hand yet about our future but we think we shall get news before many days are over & everyone seems confident we are going to be sent away from India at the end of March or the beginning of April! Best love dear old girl

from Stan

*****

No. 17/9

1/5 Somerset L.I., Pir Gumat Shah
Mar 1 1917

My dear old Elsie

We've got our orders at last and are to embark on March 30th. We do not know our destination yet and it is quite likely we shall sail under sealed orders - Of course we are wildly speculating - some favour Salonika -some Egypt & Palestine - but most favour home & France via the Cape.

Naturally every man is frightfully excited and now we are all busy with the necessary preparations - Tomorrow we go off for our trek and shall not return until March 17th but it is quite possible that this programme may be modified or as far as this Regiment is concerned cancelled altogether.

Since I last wrote I have been down to Rawalpindi to get stores and ammunition - I was away 5 days and enjoyed seeing a little civilization once again - Last mail brought two welcome letters & papers from you- many thanks dear old girl - I'm so glad you are better and I hope by this time you are settled comfortably in your new house. Perhaps it will be best to address me now c/o G.P.O.

London - but please put the name of the Regiment clearly (1/5 Somerset Light Infantry).

I am hoping to see you once again before many weeks are over - Cheero until then

best love from Stan

*****

No 17/10

N.W. Frontier, India
Mar 7 1917

My dear old Elsie

Just a hurried line to tell you I am all right - we are now on trek right out in the blue and nothing very exciting has happened yet - we have had a little trouble with some of the Pathan tribes and they've stolen our things and cut our telephone wires - otherwise it is very peaceful

Our latest orders are that we sail from Bombay on March 27th but we dont know our destination yet except that everything points to it being Europe

By the way your parcel has been sent off at last - it will be very late for your birthday and Im very sorry but it couldnt be helped. Our Adjutant and Quartermaster are so busy with detail for our embarkation that they have remained in camp at Pir Gumat Shah and as I am doing both duties on trek I am a busy man these days   The news from Mespot is most cheering & Im following it all with the greatest interest - but Im afraid our casualties are very heavy. I hope the weather at home is better now and that you are now comfortably settled in your new house - you seem to have had a very severe winter

Best love dear girl & cheero!

from Stan

*****

No. 17/11

1/5 Somerset L.I., North West Frontier
March 15 1917

My dear Old Elsie

I was very disappointed not to get a letter from you last mail but everything in the way of mail boats is so very uncertain now and I suppose we ought to be thankful things are no worse! The past few days we have lived in a sand storm - it is the first sign that the hot weather is at hand but it is very uncomfortable- we have lived in sand and dust and goodness knows how we have managed to keep so well - we haven't seen the sky for days! Our future is all we care and worry about now - we are all so desperately keen on getting home to dear old England that I'm afraid we sometimes overlook the tokens of service on other fronts and I must say I am almost inclined to think that Egypt is to be our destination!

It's too bad of them to keep the secret so long but I suppose it's very necessary - India is full of spies and German Agents - we are leaving here for Bombay on the 26th - it will be a long and trying journey and very hot down south.

77

Isn't it glorious news from Mespot[20] at last. I only hope we shall not be trapped again but I think our Generals out there have learnt their lesson from Sir J Nixons blunder in 1915. I'll write again before leaving India & if possible I'll cable home so you will here (sic) where I am bound for. Cheero! dear old pal - best love

from Stan

*****

No. 17/12

Rawal Pindi Club, Rawal Pindi
March 22nd

My dear old Elsie

No English mail has come again and I'm very disappointed - it's absolutely rotten to get no letters! I am at Rawal Pindi again to day on duty - and return to our old camp late tonight. I wonder if you have received my recent letters telling you we are under orders to leave India? We start our long train journey on Sunday and we go first of all right down to Poona which is nearly two thousand miles - we rest at Poona and when our transport is quite ready we shall be near Bombay and can go right on to the docks.

It's a long and tiring journey and we are going in two trains and even now we don't know in the least our destination and it's quite likely they won't tell us until we are well out to sea.

The ladies of our Regiment are being sent home by the India Govnt. and left Bombay yesterday - they will have a long trip round the Cape.

Isn't this war news splendid[21] - at this rate the Germans will soon be out of Belgium & France.

I shall send a cable home when I know something definite so you will probably hear about me. This will I expect be the last letter I shall be able to send you for sometime. The parcel you mention you have so kindly sent me hasn't turned up yet but I hope to get it before leaving - many thanks dear old girl. With best love - hoping to hear from you soon & that you are all right - cheero

from Stan

*****

---

[20] Kut was recaptured on February 24th 1917, and Baghdad taken on March 11th.
[21] German strategic withdrawal to the Hindenburg Line, March 1917.

No. 17/13

My dear old Elsie

Here we are at Poona quite safely at last, it has been a long and tiring journey from the Frontier - down here the hot weather is at its height and my dear it is terribly hot and as we are under canvas in a temporary camp on the Race-course, it is most unpleasant.

But we are now only 6 hours journey from Bombay - so it will not take long to get us on board our ship when once we get our sailing orders - Even now we have not been told any news of our destination but of course we all still go on hoping for Blighty . The home mails have been dreadfully uncertain lately and I've had very few letters from you - it always is such a disappointment - I hope mine have reached you for I've written every week for a long time. Fancy it's Easter in a few days! the months and seasons go quickly on & the old war runs its course - what does this wonderful advance in France mean - is it too good to be true that it's the beginning of the end. It seems strange to be in Poona once again & I'm wondering if I shall find any old friends. I hope you are very fit dear old girl And settled in your new house by this time - Best love dear

from Stan

*****

No. 17/14

1/5 Somerset L.I., Poona
April 12 1917

My dear old Elsie

Ever so many thanks dear for your last letter (Mar 7) and also for a lovely box of 'comforts' which reached me quite safely. I've been suffering the last few days from the effects of inoculation for enteric fever and have had a horrid time - but I've enjoyed soup made out of the tablets you sent me and for a couple of days or so could eat nothing else - many thanks again dear old girl - and also for all the other useful and welcome things. Even yet no news of our going has come in - we are still hoping and betting on 'Blighty' and are almost sure to be off in a few days time. I think I must have missed at least two of your letters lately and the post has been very uncertain - I gather you are settled into your new house and I hope the weather is better for you at last - We spent a very funny Easter - busy the whole time with our plans for embarking and no hot-cross buns of course! The war news at last seems almost too good to be true and America has really joined in at last - I sometimes wonder if the whole thing won't be over before we get to France! I know you'll be glad to hear I've got my Captaincy in this Regiment at last - I may finish up a Major yet eh. I hope you are very fit dear and I'm ever so glad you are still so happy at Minch. Best love dear girl

from Stan

*****

No.17/15

[Envelope stamped 'passed by censor No 3009']

My dear old Elsie

Before leaving Bombay I sent a cable to Elm Grove saying I was sailing - I hope the censor sent it off all right and that Greta has let you know. It is just possible we may put in at Aden tomorrow for new stores of fresh meat water and ice and so I am hoping to post these few lines on to you. Unfortunately I can[t] tell you our destination even yet but we gathered unofficially at Bombay that we are bound for Egypt and after re-equipping at Suez Alexandria or El Arish we are to join up with the forces operating at the bottom of Palestine. Of course all these plans may be moonshine and some of us are still hoping that we are on our way to old England Its rather exciting this uncertainty but we should probably get our definite orders at Suez and of course I shall write to you at once. I believe the British need reinforcements in Palestine - if you take a look at the map you will find a place called Gaza on the coast - the Turks have got a strong position there stretching inland 40 miles to Beer Sheba. Up to now we are having a fairly good voyage - it is rather a tub of a boat - very different to the Kenilworth Castle - and the Indian Ocean has some days been very rough but I suppose Im a better sailor than I was in the old days. We are one of a convoy and of course our wonderful Navy is escorting us for there are enemy raiders about[23] - day and night we have to wear or carry lifebelts and we are always practising the alarm and every man knows his particular job. We have now been at sea just over a week and I expect it will be another week before we get to Suez for we have to take time from the slowest ship in the convoy and consequently can only do about 10 knots an hour. I think every man was glad to leave India at last and of course everyone is in the highest spirits at the prospect of striking a blow for old England before the war ends - we had a great send off from Bombay and I am sure none of us will ever forget it. The Colonels wife and the other ladies of the Regiment - who have been bricks to us since weve been in India - came to see us off —they hope to get home by mail boat soon.

There were some hundreds of the Bombay garrison at the Docks and of course thousands of envious natives - Our bugles sounded the Advance and the Band played the Regimental March - the men were singing and cheering. Ive been at sea 9 days now and have had absolutely no news - we hope to hear all that's been going on when we reach Aden. I hope you are very fit dear old girl - I shall write to you as often as I can - Best love

from Stan

---

[22] Troopship *Chakdara*: British India Steam Navigation Co., passenger vessel, 1,581 tons, built 1914 at Leith.

[23] The German raider *Wolf* left Germany November 30th 1916. In January & February *Wolf* laid mines off Cape Agulhas, Bombay and Colombo. Then *Wolf* went East and in May 1917 was refitted at Sunday Is, in the Kermadec Group, NE of New Zealand. She laid mines in the Cook & Bass Straits and off the Anamba Is, near Singapore. She then returned to the Indian Ocean and home to Germany in February 1918. (Halpern, op. cit. pp. 372-3.)

No. 17/16

My dear old Elsie

Very many thanks dear for a letter that came today via G.P.O. London and dated April 1st. We are of course very disappointed we arent coming home so I think my best address is Egyptian Expeditionary Force. I hope the letter I posted at Aden has reached your safely - we stayed there a few hours and I went on shore to do some shopping - Do you remember I bought you some ostrich feathers[24] at Aden going out - well dear they were pinched from my kit which I left in India while I was in the Gulf and so I got some more for you the other day - these I shall try to post to you in a day or two - I wonder if you will ever wear them. I hope so - after the war at any rate. We arrived at Suez without adventure and came on by train to this camp.[25] We are quite near Cairo now and are busy getting our outfit of stores and equipment - In a short time we shall be in the firing line and you will know which front we are bound for - the Censorship is very strict in this country and Im sorry I cant send you any particulars at present. Egypt is quite a paradise compared to India - the climate is ever so much cooler the people whiter and cleaner and everything seems more Western and civilized. We are seeing a lot of this wonderful world eh? In a day or two I mean to go in to Cairo and of course I shall go down to see the jolly old Pyramids & the Sphinx - there is a large French element here and the language is spoken very much - it is such a change to see some really nice shops and smart people again. When war is over I should like to take a tour through all the places Ive been to - with just one or two particular pals - would you come dear? Im afraid some of your recent letters to me - and mine to you have gone to the bottom of the sea -

It is very sad but I think we shall very soon discover a way to cope with enemy submarines. I shall write you whenever I can and shall look forward more than ever to your letters - With best love dear girl and thoughts always

from Stan

*****

No. 17/17

My dear old Elsie

Just a line by this mail to let you know that I am very well and safe & sound. I wish I could tell you all about our interesting work but unfortunately the censorship is very strict and I have to be very careful.

We are getting on very quickly and well with all our arrangements and the men are splendid - I feel sure the Regiment will do well when we get into closer touch with the enemy.

---

[24] See note 1914/15.
[25] 'This camp,' Helmieh, near Cairo (War Diary, PRO WO 95/4690).

I sent off the ostrich feathers dear girl and I hope they wont get submarined and Ive also sent a packet of postcard views of Cairo and district these will give you some little idea of a very wonderful city - Since I last wrote to you Ive been to have a look at the Pyramids and Sphinx which are really marvellous and now Im looking forward to having a tour of all the museums tombs and mosques. Weve had a great discussion in the Mess as to what are the seven wonders of the world and strange to say not one of us can remember them all - I think we've got 4 all right - I wonder if you can remember them dear girl? We thought at first that Egypt had a perfect climate but a few days ago we had an awful sand-storm which lasted two days - I[t] was one of my very worst experiences since leaving home - there always seem something to mar the beauties and wonders of the East. Goodnight - dear old girl - with best love

from Stan

*****

No. 17/18

May 31st. 1917
[no address, but certainly Helmieh.[26]]
[On envelope: 'passed by censor No 3983']

Heres another few lines to tell you this is the last time I shall write to you from this camp for in a few hours from now we shall be on the move again en route for the front line.

I'm not allowed to tell you our exact destination at present but it isnt far from Beersheba and you can easily find this on the map so you will have a very good idea. We have worked night and day since last I wrote and now I think we shall set out quite completely equipped and a very fine Regiment indeed. I shall write you as often as I can but there may be some little delay for a bit. Many thanks dear for a photo you sent me of Highcroft, it looks a delightful place and I'm sure you'll simply love these next few months especially if you get some really nice summer weather. I forgot to tell you that when I was at the Pyramids I got a little old bead necklace with charms and amulets on it - these are supposed to have been dug up out of the tombs and may possibly have adorned some ancient Egyptian Princess in days gone by. Ive put it in a cigarette tin and posted it to you and I hope it and the feathers wont get submarined well goodbye dear girl I shall always be thinking of you & looking out for your letters - dont worry about my safety - if I can ward off this fever I shall get through all right

Best love dear girl
from Stan

*****

---

[26] The Regiment left Helmieh Camp for El Arish on June 3rd 1917 (War Diary, PRO WO 95/4690).

No. 17/19
Receipt and Warranty
[This small sheet is a printed form whose blank spaces have been filled in by a 'Dealer of antiquities' with an unreadable signature. See plate, section II, p.2.]

30th May 1917
Cairo

I undertake to refund the sum of P.T. <u>125</u> [?<u>725</u>] paid to me by Mr <u>Capt.</u> <u>Goodland</u> for <u>Necklice</u> of the <u>18th</u> Dy [dynasty] about 1700 B.C. If any of the Egyptologist of the British musim or Cairo musim stated that it is not real old one.

*****

No. 17/20

June 9 1917
no address.

My dear old Elsie

Heres a few lines of greeting from 'somewhere in Palestine' for we left our camp in Cairo a week ago and are now at an advanced base. It was an uneventful journey but of course very interesting and I think the building of 200 or so miles of railroad[27] right across the sandy desert with no fresh water is an achievement with which the nation may well be proud - At present we are living among a sea of sand-hills - fine almost white sand - there are no roads and one simply flounders about and of course its very hard going especially for the poor transport animals - It is fortunately much cooler than India but the sand glare is very trying and Ive always got to wear my dark spectacles and the men are issued with these too. We have one great compensation for our petty discomforts and it is that we are only a few hundred miles [?yards] from the sea - and most days we are able to bathe in the clearest - bluest - warmest sea imaginable Nothing very exciting has happened yet except that we get a good deal of attention from enemy aircraft who drop those loathsome bombs but our guns generally chase them away successfully - All day & night long we hear the artillery duels and at night the sky is illuminated by the star shells and flares The men are all very happy and excited about it all - poor devils - they are such boys most of them - and it rather depresses me when I think what is before them - its a great mercy they don't know as much as I do about the cruel heartless side of war There is no news of our immediate future but I fancy we shall be here for some little time but of course its always impossible

---

[27] 'The main single track railway from Qantara had reached Deir al Belah at the date of Sir Edmund Allenby's arrival. It just sufficed, independently of sea transport, to maintain the force before Gaza. As soon as he received instructions to double this line the work was put in hand by Brig. Gen. Sir G Macauley, Director of Railway Transport, and it advanced very quickly. By the end of August, 8 miles from Qantara had been doubled, while bank work and the laying out of sleepers and rails had been completed for approximately another 10 miles... By the end of September the double line was in use beyond Qatiya, a distance of over 30 miles as the track lay. At the end of October, on the eve of the offensive, it was in use up to Bir el Mazar, a distance of 70 miles, a mile a day thus having been laid during the last two months.' (Cyril Falls, *Military Operations Egypt & Palestine from June 1917 to the end of the War*. HMSO 1930, part I p.20).

to foretell - only a few miles further ahead we come into the Holy Land and there we are told are green fields & trees - orange groves and fresh water in abundance - we long for the time we can push on to these luxuries

I am enclosing dear girl one or two snap shots that Banes Walker took when we were at the Sphinx & Pyramids I am on the black camel in case you can't recognise me.

I hope you are fit & well and having real summer weather

Best love dear old pal

from Stan

*****

No. 17/21

June 16 1917
no address but Regimental Badge not excised

My dear old Elsie

Many thanks dear old girl for your last letter (May 23rd) - your letters are the only ones Ive had since leaving India so you can guess how much they are appreciated - I cant think why the Paters letters arent reaching me unless he is still expecting me home. Well dear girl we move tomorrow further up so we are all bustle and excitement again - the move has come rather sooner than we anticipated - so this is the last letter I shall write from this desert of sand. Tomorrow will bring us actually into the Land of Milk and Honey - we shall leave the sands behind us and I hope find green fields & trees. Im afraid we shall be too near old man Turk to bathe very often and we shall miss this luxury ever so much. - we shall have to go dirty thats all for fresh water will be much too precious to wash in very much. We shall have to wait until we can bathe in the jolly old Jordan with a cake of Coal Tar. I will send you a line when ever I can and I hope you wont worry about me. I am ever so fit now with absolutely no fever and Im so happy to be on service with my own old Regiment. I shall always be thinking of you & looking forward to Peace and the re-union in the dear old country with my best love

from Stan

*****

No. 17/22

June 26 1917
no address

My dear old Elsie

I hope you have been getting my letters regularly because I have told you all my movement sometimes I think the Censor may cut out some of the things I write. As it is past history now I think I can tell you that the place we first came to after leaving Cairo was El Arish - we are now about 30 miles further up so if you look at a map of this front you will be able to see where I am and we are actually in Palestine now. Soon after leaving El Arish which is an absolute sandy desert we came across a blade or two of green grass and gradually cultivation increased and now we are on fairly firm ground with grass everywhere but very few trees yet. Only a few miles ahead we are told we get into lovely country and I only hope we shall soon be able to beat back the Turks towards Jerusalem. We are very busy here night and day and altho the sea is quite near we have had no opportunity of bathing yet and so we are all very very dirty. As soon as we arrived at this place we had to take over the outpost duties and Ive been in charge of three posts with my Company.

Nothing much has happen[ed] yet except that we are rather troubled by Arabs just as we were in Mespot - and we have caught seven prisoners up to date which is a start at any rate. Just ahead the guns are firing incessantly and the airmen on both sides are very active. I wish I could tell you more dear girl I am writing this in my little dugout with a couple of blankets shielding me from the sun- it is very burning in the daytime but a delightful climate compared to India and it is very cold when doing patrol duty at night. It must be two weeks since I heard from you & Ive had no letters from home since leaving India I do hope the postal arrangements are going to be kind to us out here and not like Mespot. The railway and water pipe run right up here so we have plenty of stores - Unfortunately we are only allowed one water bottle of water a day & we have to do all our drinking shaving & washing in that! Its three years since I saw you and I do wish it could all finish and we could return to the dear old days of peace - but I suppose we must all be patient - if only Russia[28] hadnt proved so disappointing - it might have been almost over by now. Hope you are very well dear girl, with best love

from Stan

*****

No. 17/23

July 9 1917
no address.

[letter re-addressed to Gwynant, Park Rd., Hale, Cheshire]

My dear old Elsie

Your letters have reached me at last - many thanks dear girl for six of them which arrived a few days ago and gave me the greatest possible pleasure. I am glad the parcels reached you safely as I was afraid they had gone to the bottom of the sea and I hope you will wear that funny old necklace sometimes. If you string them on the strong fine silk used for pearls they should be all right until Barbara has a good pull at them. I am very sorry you have been so unwell but Im thinking of you now on holiday and hoping the change and sea air will do you ever so much good - you will return to Minch quite refreshed - especially if the weather has been fine and warm.

I had 11 letters from the Pater the same day as yours came so have had quite a budget to read and I hope now to hear regularly altho Im told several more Egyptian mail boats have been sunk.

Dont send me the Tatler dear at present - many thanks all the same - I shall miss it especially Eves letters and 'with silent friends' but they dont bother much about papers out here and so many wouldnt reach me it would be waste of money.

---

[28] The Kornilov offensive had failed.

When you think of it however dear girl you might post me a sixpenny novel - say once every six weeks or so - I dont get much time for reading but when I do get a few slack moments its nice to take up something light and frivolous. My outpost work is over for the time being and my company is resting (so called) Its been a strenuous time with a lot of night work and Ive been in the saddle all day long sometimes. Im very well dear - only a little tired - tired of this horrible war and wishing every day that it may soon be all over. General Allenby[29] our new Commander in Chief has been to see us - It has cheered us up and we are full of enthusiasm and we are going to have a great victory here before many weeks are gone by - but how I wish it was a thing already accomplished for I know what mettle the Turk is made of and I fear there'll be much blood shed before we see the gates of the Holy City - however! Goodbye dear old girl - many thanks again for your welcome letters

Best love

from Stan

*****

No. 17/24

August 1st 1917
no address

My dear old Elsie

The posts seem to have gone all wrong again for this is the third week no letter has come from you - perhaps those wretched submarines have been busy - Ive not written for about ten days because Ive been out on outpost duty again but now we are resting and under canvas and I can get back to my little camp bed. There is very little to tell you and there is a good deal of sameness about our days - sometimes however there are raids carried out and there is always a certain amount of artillery fire and air activity - we are all longing to get further on but there are a good many difficulties to overcome first. The other day our General suggested we should get up some Brigade sports while we are resting and so last Saturday we had quite a gala day here in the desert we had managed to bring our band along with us - and they played all afternoon - the Somersets beat the other Regiments of the Brigade in most of the events - weve got a very good tug of war team.

Ive been thinking of you dear girl on holiday and hoping you have had a very good time and real summer weather - you must have enjoyed seeing all your people and friends again. The last batch of home papers gave the report of the Mespot Commission[30] - of course I am greatly interested and I am glad all the horrible

---

[29] Sir Edmund Allenby (1861-1936) assumed command of the Egyptian Expeditionary Force at midnight June 28/29th 1917 at Cairo GHQ and within a week of assuming command had 'departed on a visit to the front, leaving behind a slightly shaken staff' (Wavell, *Allenby*, op. cit. p.188). Later promoted Field Marshal and ennobled as First Viscount Allenby of Megiddo GCB, GCMG, GCVO, KCB, etc, and numerous foreign honours.

[30] Report of Mesopotamia Commission issued June 1917 (Moberly, op. cit. vol. IV, pp.28-31. Chairman of the Commission, Sir George Hamilton, wrote in a letter to *The Times* July 16th 1917 'Our investigation showed that never before had the rank and file of the British and Indian Armies

things (or some of them) have now been exposed to the world. I could add a few more details - but I try to forget all my experiences out there. It seems ages and ages since we left England and here we are at the anniversary of the war again - whenever is it all going to end dear - we have had no news at all lately from the outside world and are very anxious about Russia - I wonder what people at home think about things especially as food seems so scarce and expensive wouldnt it be grand if we could wake up one morning and find Peace in the world once again. I hope dear girl that you are quite quite fit again - Every day I look out for your letters which I hope will soon come -with best love

from Stan

*****

No. 17/25

14 Aug. 1917
no address

My dear old Elsie

Many thanks dear girl for your last letter from Llandidno [sic] and also one which has come today from Leeds. Im so very glad you have had a good holiday and only hope you will return to Minch feeling like a giantess. This is only a very short letter - we live in strenuous times out here just now and Ive very little time for writing - at present I am on special duty detached from the Regiment - we have half the Regiment here and Im adjutant & quartermaster. In a few days we move up further and right into the front trenches - If you dont here regularly from me dear girl dont worry about me I will write when I can

I shall always be thinking of you and if anything happens to me I shall feel right to the end that you thought well of me and that will make me happy. Goodbye dear girl best love

from Stan

*****

No. 17/26

Aug 31 1917
no address

My dear old Elsie

Just a few lines written under difficult circumstances to tell you I am quite safe and well altho Ive gone a bit lame in my poor old wounded leg temporarily.

Weve just finished a very hard spell of soldiering and its taxed the strength of the Regiment very much - I wish I could tell you more details - several long night marches over very heavy going and little sleep - however we are keeping cheerful and the men are really wonderful and it makes me feel so proud to be with them and to be one of them. At present we are in the trenches facing Gaza actually the real front line at last after 3 years strenuous training - it seems strange that after

fought better than in Mesopotamia. On the other hand it was difficult to exaggerate the incompetence shown in the management of their transport, supplies and medical services.' Austen Chamberlain resigned as Secretary of State for India when the report was published.

ll it should be I who should lead the old Taunton & Minehead Company into the trenches for the first time and I feel it a great priveledge for Ive got 250 of the best fellows in the world in my company. I am some way away from Headquarters and I rarely see anyone else outside my company and I havent seen Banes[31] for 2 weeks altho he is only a stones throw away but we are all underground now and I cant leave my post night or day. The Colonel came to see me this morning and to my surprise he offered me the post of permanent adjutant to the Battalion - Frank Calways term of 3 years is up next month and its the custom to make a change and probably Frank will get a staff job Ive got 3 days to think it over and I expect I shall take it especially as the General has already expressed his approval and it means an extra 5 bob a day pay too and besides its looked upon as the star job in the Regiment   My only regret will be that I shall have to leave my company.

Thank you ever so much dear girl for your letters which come quite regularly again now - last week brought me too a lovely little book to read 'Jerry'[32] I havent had a chance to begin it yet but Im sure I shall enjoy it. And today we had our parcels sent up to us and your delightful box of surprises came for me - I cant thank you enough and Ive already started my new pipe all the things you sent are really most useful - it is so sweet of you dear girl. I am sitting in my dug out now and its just 2 o/c in the morning - weve been heavily shelled all night and have had no rest - I cant sleep now for we have an epidemic of fleas & mice in these trenches - last night when I woke up to do duty I was a mass of bites and I think nowhere on my body could you have put a 5 shilling bit without touching a spot - tonight its just as bad - its a horrid war - but thank God we can laugh at our misfortunes altho all night we scratch and curse. I am so glad you had a real good holiday and that you feel so fit after it

Best love dear and again many thanks for the lovely parcel and book

from Stan

*****

No. 17/27

Sept 9 1917
no address

My dear old Elsie

Heres another line to tell you I am quite safe and fit. Ill enclose a snap taken the other day when were out of the old trenches - Im sure I look fat & flourishing enough dont I? Ive very little news to tell you every day here is much the same as the next - We get shelled every morning and evening but weve excellent trenches - two nights ago we had a bad time but my fellows have been splendid - Unfortunately there have been casualties but one must expect that - this week weve had 3 killed and 18 wounded - the people at home Im afraid will realize the 1/5 Somersets are really in service at last when they see the casualty lists come in. Damn this war I say - I hate to think this fine old Regiment of ours must suffer with the rest - I hope next week we shall go out for a rest and if we can only get

---

[31] Captain Gerald Banes Walker, commander of D Company.
[32] Not identified.

down by the sea again we shall be happy. I am as dirty as can be and the fleas have kept on biting and biting. Banes came to see me just now with Milsom - weve had a good pow-wow - poor Banes has just lost some of his best men and is so depressed about it. I think I told you dear girl I am to be Adjutant of the Regiment in a few weeks time Im awfully gratified and the Colonel has been so nice about it. It's a big job on service I know but I shall do my damnedest. My name has gone in to the War Office for its got to go through the Gazette and my appointment will start on Oct 10th for 3 years but of course the war will be over long long before my term is up - lets hope so anyway.[33] Ill send you a snap shot one of my fellows took of me the other day - it surely speaks for itself and I hope you will realize how fit and flourishing I am

Best love dear girl

from Stan

*****

No.17/28

26. 9. 17
no address

[written on page from field service note book]

My dear old Elsie

Very many thanks dear old girl for your birthday letter and especially for the delightful leather cigarette case which reached me quite safely on the 23rd. - only a day after the event so you timed it very cleverly. I shall use the case every day and find it ever so useful - one smokes an awful lot in the trenches and so I now shall always be able to carry about enough to last me ages - it is so sweet of you to send me all these things - it seems only a few days ago all those comforts came from you and the book too which I am enjoying so much! I hope you have been getting my letters all right - I try to write to you each week but it gets more and more difficult - we have been in the trenches a long time now and are badly in need of a rest - I fancy in a weeks time we are being relieved but nothing is definite. Very soon now dear girl there will be news from this front but I said this some time ago didn't I? I wish I could tell you more of what is going on here - how within the next few days I personally am going to attempt the biggest thing in my life[34] - Ive got just over 100 of the picked men in the Regiment to help me through with it and when it is all over I hope to write and tell you all about it. Its the most important thing the Regiment has been ordered to do up to now and I feel ever so proud to be chosen to carry the job out. When that thing is over I shall have to leave my Company - with many regrets - and go down to Headquarters and take over the work of Adjutant - I shall miss being always with the men but I expect I shall always have heaps & heaps to do to occupy my mind. It is getting cooler here especially at nights - it is surprising how many birds one sees now - a month ago there seemed to be no bird life at all here but lately all sorts of familiar birds have turned up and fly about 'No mans Land' - it shows winter is

[33] He served until June 2nd 1920.
[34] Refers to forthcoming night raid.

89

coming along in your part of the world. I keep very well and quite cheerful in spite of a very depressing existence and practically no exercise - Im afraid this is rather a rotten letter but Im awfully tired as I havent been to bed for two nights & it is very late now - so goodbye dear girl and again many many thanks for all your kindness

love from Stan

*****

No. 17/29

7 10 17
no address

[passed by censor No. 3983]

My very dear old Elsie

Just a line to let you know I am quite safe and well - In my last letter I think I told you that I was going to attempt a big thing - It was indiscreet of me perhaps to mention it to you but one gets so pent up with excitement that unless on these occasions one can confide in someone one would simply burst! The great event was a night raid and it came off very successfully last night. I will write you more about it in a day or two - you will be glad to hear the Regiment has received many wires of congratulations today and I personally have had many kind words said to me by the General and my Colonel. The Colonel thinks we are going to be relieved almost immediately for a rest and then he says I am to go to Cairo for a weeks leave and rest. I shall look forward to this. Many thanks dear girl for your letter received yesterday I am glad that the Doctor is back again and Mrs. Brown is better. Best love dear old girl

from Stan

*****

No.17/30
TELEGRAM dated 14 Oct 17

HYDE HIGHCROFT MINCHINHAMPTON =
AM ENJOYING WEEKS LEAVE CAIRO =
GOODLAND =

Sent as weekend telegram, via Eastern Telegraph Company Limited

*****

No.17/31

14/10/17
Turf Club. Cairo

My dear old Elsie

I am enjoying a weeks leave in Cairo and its a really delightful experience after nearly six months of Desert life.

I sent you a wire so that you would know that I am out of range of the shells & bullets for a time and I know you would realize that I'm having a real good time.

90

Milsom is here with me and we are doing ourselves just proud and tucking in like chool boys to all the good things one cant get up in the fighting area - like butter - fish - fruit. We've got a big double room at the famous Shepheards Hotel[35] and its got its own bathroom with one of those white enamel baths & of course we spend hours in the water and it's such a joy to feel really clean again. I found out Karl Jones[36] yesterday and he is coming in to lunch with me this morning and we are going to a most wonderful Zoo later on. Karl looks very well and no one would imagine he has been in hospital nearly six months and I think it will be a long time before he can do any marching or hard soldiering for the muscles of one of his thighs are quite perished a[t] present but he is now passed B3 and will get some clerical job I expect until he gets quite strong. The Regiment came out of the line just before I left but goes back in a day or two - a month in and six days out - it's very wearying work and I long for it all to be over.

Dear girl- you will be pleased to hear that the Regiment got such a lot of kudos out of the Night Raid and did I tell you the C-in-C sent a special wire of congratulation![37] I dream about that night still and I think those of us who were in it will never forget our experiences. I wrote home a long letter to the Pater with a fairly full account of it all but I'm rather afraid the censor will destroy it - I shall be [interested?] to hear if it ever fetches up. We certainly put the fear of God into the old Turk that night and he simply screamed for mercy - Allah! Allah! I can hear them now. When I get back I take over the duties of Adjutant - my appointment has been approved by Headquarters from Oct 10th so now I shall have my hands full. I am looking forward to finding letters from you when I rejoin for it seems some time ago since the last mail came - something went wrong with our mails back in August & early Septbr every one was grousing at home but I hope my letters have reached you better lately.

I hope Mrs. Brown is much better now and that you dear girl are keeping fit - with best love

from Stan

*****

No. 17/32

25 10 17
No address. passed censor No. 3983

My dear old Elsie

Just a hurried line today to let you know that I am back with the Regiment safe & sound again

I had a glorious leave in Cairo with Lieut Milsom - we did very little - scarcely any sight seeing but just enjoying the change and comfort of it all was amazing.

---

[35] Then and for many years the leading hotel in Cairo. It was burnt down during the anti-British riots at the time of the Suez Crisis in 1956. En suite facilities were only to be found in exclusive hotels in 1917.
[36] Karl Jones, engaged to Stanley's youngest sister, Babe, served with the Glamorgan Yeomanry. Invalided from Palestine to Egypt, he later became Chief Cipher Officer, HQ EEF Cairo.
[37] General Allenby .

I found the old Regiment back in the Line again - in another part altogether and we are now almost within speaking distance of the enemy so it is all very exciting all day and night long - I am the Adjutant now and very busy but always enjoy the work - Unfortunately the Colonel is in hospital just now[38] and also quite six or seven of the other officers and a whole lot of men, we really have had a very strenuous time the last two months and the Regiment is beginning to feel it I hope Mrs. Brown is quite well again and your little household normal I found that beautiful leather cigarette case you sent me for my birthday ever so useful dear girl and that pipe you last sent is turning out a real beauty. I will send you some snaps I have just been given - one or two are quite typical of this country - one shows us washing at a trough like a lot of horses when we get out of the trenches. The camel takes our bits and blankets about for us - the most interesting is one of a shell (Turk) which fortunately was a dud! - it pitched as you see it on top of the dug-out where bombs are stored and not more than 10 yds away from me and my Headquarters - it is an 100 lbs shell and if it had exploded goodness knows what would have happened - one wants luck for this game. I will write you as often as I can dear girl but there are great times just ahead of us on this Front and there may be delays but please dont worry about me. Im awfully fit & well - With best love dear girl

from Stan

*****

No. 17/33

Nov. 1st 1917
no address

My dear old Elsie

Very many thanks dear girl for your two nice letters received today. You dont seem to get many of mine - Im sure Ive written you every week for the last two months and I sent you a cable too when I was on leave in Cairo Theres nothing I want for Xmas dear you have sent me so much that you mustnt really spend any more money on me The book Thirtynine Steps[39] came today and Im sure I shall enjoy it when I have time

At present we are all excitement the third great battle of Gaza has already begun - and in a few days time Im sure old England will be ringing with the good news from Palestine. This will probably be the last letter I shall be able to send you dear girl for a little while but I hope you wont worry too much about me Everyone tells me Im a lucky soldier and Ive a sort of feeling that Ill get back safe & sound and well meet again in the glad days which will follow this awful war we [have] been going through some thrilling experiences these past few days and I shall have heaps & heaps new excitements to tell you all about when we do meet again.

---

[38] Lt-Col Cooke-Hurle did not return to the Battalion until December 5th. Therefore command was held by Major Urwick.

[39] The *Thirty-Nine Steps* by John Buchan, published 1915.

We are all full of confidence in our C in C & are looking forward to our advance up through the promised Land Goodbye dear girl   with best love

from Stan

*****

No. 17/34

17 November 1917

This is a printed post card in a standard form: (AFA 2042) Stanley indicates that he is 'quite well.'

*****

No. 17/35

Dec 3 1917
E.E.F

[Passed by censor No.3983]

My dear old Elsie

I hear there is a chance of sending off letters today so I will write you a few hurried lines to tell you I am quite safe and well after many thrilling experiences and to send you my Xmas and New Year greetings - I think the last time I was able to write to you was about Nov 5th the day before we 'went over the top' but I sent a postcard on Nov.17th which I hope you got all right. Well dear girl we have been through another wonderful time and are still in the thick of it but are a badly battered and war worn Regiment now - the men have done simply splendidly but we have suffered heavy casualties and it makes me feel very very sad for all my best pals are either killed or wounded   Poor old Banes was shot through the heart on Nov 22nd and we buried him up in the mountains overlooking Jerusalem where he fell - I was with him when he died.[40]

Milsom is badly wounded and poor old Major[41] and Elliott[42] and Hannaford[43] are all killed - all the other officers except Major Urwick[44] and myself are either wounded or gone down to the Base sick - we two have stuck together the whole time and have had some marvellous escapes - I often wonder now how long my

---

[40] Capt G Banes Walker's grave is in the Jerusalem War Cemetery, plot X, Grave 3. From *Somerset County Gazette* of December 1st 1917: 'Deep sympathy is felt for Mr & Mrs Banes Walker of 'Verriers', North Petherton, in the second bereavement they have sustained during the war by the death of another son, Captain Gerald Banes Walker of the Somerset Light Infantry. [He] was the second son, 28 years old. When war broke out he was occupying a position in a London bank.'
[41] Capt AO Major died November 23rd 1917, buried in the Jerusalem War Cemetery, Plot C, Grave 27.
[42] 2nd Lt HW Elliott died November 13th 1917, during the attack and capture of El Mesmiyeh.
[43] 2nd Lt WA Hannaford died November 23rd 1917, buried in the Jerusalem War Cemetery, Plot G, Grave 21.
[44] Major FD Urwick DSO (1874-1936) served with the 5th Somersets from 1914, when he held the rank of Captain to 1920, rising to the rank of Colonel. He and Stanley were friends and colleagues, particularly after El Jib, when they were the sole survivors of a group who had been together from the start of the war. He was connected with the glove trade in Yeovil. He was the Battalion's Honorary Colonel from 1931 until his death.

luck is going to last   Im afraid there are many anxious homes in Somerset[45] now for the rank and file have suffered heavily but the home people may well be proud of the old Regiment for we have gained nothing but praise on all sides - Goodness knows how much longer its all going to last   We have gained a great victory and we all hope the Turk will soon give in and sue for peace but I suppose Germany wont let him do this and we shall probably have to go on driving the Turk back to his Damascus line. At present we are quite near Jaffa and Ludd - a land of oranges and our bivouac today is in an olive orchard this sounds very peaceful but its anything but that!

I will write you whenever I can dear girl but at present Im afraid my letters will be few and far between. I have had no letters delivered since Nov 1st but our –railway is hastening to catch us up and all will be well soon - No more now dont worry about me Heres my loving greetings and thoughts always

from Stan

*****

No. 17/36

5.12.17

[Passed by censor 3983]
The contents of this envelope is a regimental Christmas Card with no message other than the printed greeting:

A Merry Christmas
and
A Happy New Year

from Stan, E.E.F. 1917-18
*****

No. 17/37

Dec 16 1917
E.E.F.

[Passed by censor No.3983]

My dear old Elsie

Just a few more lines to tell you I am quite safe and well - I was ever so glad to get six letters from you two days ago - These have cheered me up tremendously for lately I have been feeling very sad and sick at heart Since I last wrote you we have had a welcome rest but we are off again tonight into the line and it looks as if we shall spend our Xmas fighting after all We have had no reinforcements yet and Major Urwick and I still carry on as best we can - I spend my days trying to straighten out things and get the office records in order   There are many gaps in the old Regiment which can never be filled again I often think of poor old Banes lying up there under the cold stone of the mountains and I had been looking forward to many happy days with him after the war   Milsom too is so badly wounded that I am afraid he will lose his leg and in any case he wont do any more

---

[45] Total number of deaths of all ranks was 62.

soldiering for many months to come it all makes me curse the war and the devils who brought it on us But it is no use being despondent and fed up for one must think of the men who are left and the work before us but its very hard sometimes and already I am looking forward to some home leave about next April or May

I shall be thinking of you all through Xmas time & only wish I could look in and have a game of ring o roses and blind mans buff with you and your kiddies!

Many thanks dear girl for your letters and with best love and all good wishes

from Stan

*****

No. 17/38

Dec.21 1917
E.E.F.

[postmark dated 23 Dec. passed by censor No. 3983]

My dear old Elsie

Many thanks dear girl for your last letter dated Nov. 20th and the Winters Pie and the little book called The Power House which I hope soon to read

I enjoyed the last book you sent me ever so much - the Thirty-Nine Steps - it is so amusing and Major Urwick loved it too The parcel you speak of hasnt turned up yet and I am looking forward to it so much - nothing gives me more pleasure out here as letters and parcels. Well dear we are up in the line again among the noise and horridness of it all and its more hateful than ever - I think I am getting horribly depressed and not at all Xmasy - the losses of the Regiment get on my mind sometimes and make me very fed up - I think I want a change now and shall try to get a week in Cairo again as soon as things are quieter I have heard from all our wounded officers and they are in hospitals in Cairo and Alexandria Poor Milsom is having a rotten time and I am feeling very anxious about him he is in Alex and perhaps I shall go there for my leave when I can get it I am always thinking of poor old Banes - he was a real white man and you would have loved him

Winter has set in with a vengeance and it pours with rain most days and the wind in these Judean hills is bitterly cold - thank goodness it only lasts about six weeks and then I expect we shall be cursing the heat again. Since we have been so busy fighting we have had very little news from the outside world - but we hear vague rumours of trouble in Italy[46] and still more hopeful rumours of a possible peace - I suppose that's too good to be true.

I think I wont write any more - Im feeling very sad and Im sure you wont enjoy this letter very much

Best love dear girl

from Stan

*****

---

[46] There were serious anti-war riots in August 1917 and in late October the Italian defeat at Caporetto was followed by a change of Government and High Command.

No. 17/39

26.12.17
E.E.F.

[censor stamp illegible]

My dear old Elsie

A few days ago I wrote you a very miserable letter and I have regretted it ever since but I do feel most horribly depressed these days and shall have to pull myself together. We spent Xmas day under most uncomfortable circumstances Two days ago the Turks cleared right away from our front and we imagined we should have a nice peaceful Xmas - but it has simply rained & rained and blown a hurricane - it has really been too wretched for words - we could not get any fires to burn so had no Xmas dinner - today we have moved on again and are just settled in - the sky is just clearing and we long for a fine day tomorrow to dry our soaking blankets I was thinking of you yesterday and wondering what you were doing and wishing to Goodness the damned old war would stop and allow us to get back to our peaceful life of ages ago again,

Best love dear girl and heaps of good wishes for the New Year

from Stan

*****

No.17/40

Empty envelope dated 29 Dec. 17

*****

No.17/41

New Years Eve 1917

[passed by censor no. 3983 E.E.F.]

My dear old Elsie

It is New Years Eve and Im sitting among the rocks of the Judean Hills writing these few lines by the light of my bit of candle. In the red wine of Palestine Major Urwick and I have just drunk to "Absent friends - the West and the Best" and now he is writing to his missis who is in Ceylon. I have very little fresh news since I last wrote - I think I told you what a miserable Xmas we spent - the weather is still very bad but sometimes we get beautifully warm summer days and then we forget all our troubles - I have had no Xmas parcels or letters yet - we are always expecting the mail bags but at present all the transport is wanted for food and ammunition - we are in the line now but I fancy the old Turk is thoroughly demoralised at present so doesnt give much trouble - I wish he would make peace but I suppose Germany wont let him. I often hear from all our wounded officers and some of them will be coming back soon - Poor Milsom is having a bad time still and will probably be sent to England as soon as they are able to move him. Im dreadfully sorry about him.

I wonder how you are spending your New Years Eve and hope you are having a good time I often get letters from Harold - he says he is fed up with his red tape office work in Burma and wants to come out to us but I think he is very unwise

Stanley in Palestine, prior to the attack on Gaza in the autumn of 1917. Perhaps this is the photograph referred to in Letter 17/27; 'I'm sure I look fat and flourishing enough, don't I?'

I undertake ~~to~~ *refund the sum of P.T.* 25 *paid*
to me by M͏ʳ Capt. Goodland
for necklace *of the 1͏ᵗ Dy about* 1700

B.Ç. If any of the Egyptologist of the British musim
or Cairo musim or any other musim stated that it is ᵗnot
real old one.

E. J. Hanna͏ṣ

Dealer of antiquites

OPPOSITE MENA HOUSE HOTEL, AT THE PYRAMIDS

Cairo. 30͏ᵗᵘ May 1917

(above) This delightful receipt refers to
'the little old bead necklace with
charms & amulets on it' mentioned in
Letter 17/18

(below) This is a 'dud' Turkish shell
which landed on the bomb store.
(Letter 17/32) The notice on the sandbags reads 'BOMBS'.

Letter 17/20 refers to a photograph taken of Stanley and Gerald Banes Walker
on camels visiting the Pyramids & the Sphinx. The hats and the strong shadows
make any identification impossible.

'. . . washing at a trough like a lot of horses when we get out of the trenches. The camel takes our bits and blankets about for us. . .   (Letter 17/32)

Defensive position somewhere in Palestine, perhaps Berukin area 1918.

In April 1919 Stanley was sent up the Nile with a very mixed collection of troops to supervise the repair of damaged rail tracks and to make a show of strength in the face of local unrest. These two pictures show their transport on the Nile and some of the destruction. (Letters 19/8–13)

WAR DIARY
or
INTELLIGENCE SUMMARY.

PLACE.	DATE.	HOUR.	SUMMARY OF EVENTS AND INFORMATION.	REMARKS AND REFERENCES TO APPENDICES.
BENI MAZAR	29/4/19		1/5 Somerset Light Infantry. The Beni Mazar was inspected by the G.O.C. Upper Egypt — Major General Sir John Shea K.C.M.G.C.B.D.S.O. The G.O.C. arrived at 10.45 by train from Beni Suef at the usual time. General Salvation arms from Minia. The troops were drawn up in line and the General inspected the men were magnificent by the G.O.C. into the men pleased with their turnout. Afterwards the troops marched past in Companies as the G.O.C. inspected at road left of Minia area.	eng.
	27/4/19		The following villages and various 1/5th S.L.I. and Lieut. Infantry flight 1/5 Somerset L.I. – Tambu Bardunet – El Ashraf — Shulqam – Saquia – El Bahnasa – Ashruba. The troops were marched out and returned to camp at 1700 Return strength Beni Mazar 12 Officers 262 O.R.'s Beni Suef 11 Officers 291 O.R.'s	eng.

Lt. [signature] Comdg 1/5 Somerset L.I.

Confidential Report.

Rank	Present appont.	Whether recommended for advancement	Appt.	Age 35.
Capt. F. S. Goodland I/15 S. L. I.	Adjutant	Yes	Major	Service 4 years 5 months.

Service in Present War.

United Kingdom   Aug. 14th 1914 to Oct. 9th '14.
Overseas – India   Nov 10th 1914 to April 25th '15.
"Transport   May 3rd 1915 to July 5th '16.
"India   July 3rd 1916 to April 26th '17).
"E E F   May 10th '17) to present date.

Remarks.

This officer has done valuable work throughout the war, under all circumstances. He is an ideal adjutant, works untiringly, with great tact. His popularity with all ranks is most marked. He is a natural leader of men. His service in the field has been brilliant as shown in two record. He is devoted to the Battalion.

Tam 18th 19. 9.

Lt. Col. F. F. Cooke-Hurle
Commdg. I/15 S. L. I.

Mentioned in General Aylmer's report. Despatch Oct 1916 Awarded M.C. London Gazette 29.9.'76 dated 22.12.'16 Awarded Croix de Guerre m.s. 17662 dated 16.11.15.

Elsie & Stanley were married on September 18th 1920 at Hale Barns Chapel, near Elsie's home. On her hat are the ostrich feathers which Stanley sent her from Aden; the ones he bought on the outward journey were stolen from his kit when he was serving in Mesopotamia, so he purchased some more on the return voyage. (Letter 17/10)

and I tell him he doesnt know when he is well off and I would gladly change jobs with him and have a bit of comfort again! What do they think at home about the war now? Can it possibly last through another year?

Best love dear girl and all good wishes for the New Year

from Stan

*****

CHAPTER FOUR

1918

The Background.

Allenby's capture of Jaffa and Jerusalem had met the expectations of those like Lloyd George who believed that on the path to eventual victory there must be an alternative to the attritional slaughter of the Western Front; but there were many imponderables in the first months of 1918. Bolshevik Russia was keen to sue for peace, allowing the Germans to transfer armies from the Eastern Front to France and Belgium and it was not yet clear when the arrival of United States' forces would introduce a significant new factor to the Western Front. In March 1918 the Germans struck hard and as soon as the massive scale of this offensive was appreciated Allenby was warned that he might be required to spare some of the Egyptian Expeditionary Force for service in France; in the event two divisions left in April and eleven more British battalions and other units in May, a total of nearly 60,000 men. To replace them Allenby was sent an Indian division from Mesopotamia and many more Indian units recently recruited and lacking in battle experience. Much reorganisation and training was now needed to make the depleted E.E.F. capable of launching a full-scale offensive against a tenacious enemy defending well-prepared positions. Not that Allenby allowed the two Corps of the E.E.F. to remain inactive. In late March and in late April XX Corps launched major raids to cut the railway at Amman and to convince Liman von Sanders - the hero of Gallipoli who had replaced von Falkenhayn - that when Allenby was ready his main thrust would be East of Jordan. Between the two Transjordan raids XXI Corps, whose left flank guarded the coast, planned an operation in the foothills East of Lydda designed to tear a gap in the enemy's defences through which the cavalry would pour encircling his front line and capturing Tul Karm, the headquarters and railhead of the Turkish Eighth Army. The 'Action of Berukin' as the Official History austerely calls it,[1] was fought on April 9th, 10th and 11th. The 75th Division, crossing a wide no-man's land, advanced against an entrenched enemy defending a country of ravines and steep hills. Two German infantry battalions supported by their own artillery, mortars and machine guns, as well as determined Turkish units, contested every metre of ground; any gains were fiercely counter-attacked before they could be consolidated. A few villages and hill tops were taken and held but the looked-for breakthrough did not materialise and the action was called off; the 75th Division had suffered a total of 1500 casualties.[2]

Over the summer, while his army was re-grouping, Allenby matured his grand strategy. Setting his sights on Damascus, Beirut and Aleppo he intended to clear the enemy not only from Palestine but also from Syria. The lesson of the 'Action

---

[1] Guided by Turkish nomenclature: Cyril Falls, op. cit. Part II, p.350.
[2] ibid. p.357.

of Berukin' was learnt; there would be no more attacks involving only one division. Allenby planned to strike the Turks on the coastal plain with such overwhelming force that there could be no doubt of the breakthrough which would enable the cavalry to rush north up the Plain of Sharon, over the range of hills which runs from south-east to north-west and ends at Mount Carmel overlooking Haifa and so down into the Plain of Esdraelon - all this to be accomplished in a ride of at least fifty miles in twenty-four hours. A series of elaborate deceptions confirmed Liman von Sanders in the belief that Allenby would attack in and to the East of the Jordan Valley, but with the concentration of his forces near the coast undetected, the onslaught Allenby launched in the early hours of September 19th, initiating what is officially named the Battle of Megiddo, achieved complete surprise. The following morning von Sanders himself was lucky not to have been made prisoner when, unaware of the depth and speed of the British advance he escaped, in his pyjamas, from his headquarters in Nazareth, on the northern side of the Plain of Esdraelon, which had been entered by a troop of Gloucester Hussars.

In France the Allies had recovered the ground surrendered in the Spring and, as the Germans retreated, reached country behind the front-line areas which had not been devastated by four years of trench warfare. In the Balkans the Bulgarians crumpled on the Salonika front and sued for peace on September 29th. Meanwhile Allenby's cavalry ranged further northwards; Haifa was entered on September 23rd, Damascus a week later, Beirut on October 8th and Aleppo on the 26th. In less than six weeks Allenby's men had advanced 350 miles - many units covering much greater distances - and taken at least 75,000 prisoners. Threatened by invasion from both the South and the Balkans and aware of Germany's imminent collapse, Turkey capitulated on October 30th. The political consequences of Allenby's victory were complex and far-reaching but these were not the concern of the majority of the men under his command, the volunteers and conscripts whose duty had been done and who now longed to return home to India, Australia, the West Indies and the United Kingdom.

Stanley Goodland in 1918: Palestine & Egypt.

From January to April 1918 the 75th Division held its place in the front line due East of Jaffa and North East of Lydda (Ludd). Each infantry battalion took its turn at the front, where no man's land was wide and activity was confined to patrolling. The 1/5 Somersets gradually returned to full strength, though there were gaps which reinforcements and the returning wounded, now restored to health, could not fill. Stanley Goodland felt deeply the loss of his friends Gerald Banes Walker, killed in the battle for El Jib, and Harry Milsom, wounded and invalided home.

The visit of H.R.H. the Duke of Connaught provided a welcome exception to the routine of divisional duties. Stanley commanded the one hundred strong Guard of Honour at the parade on March 16th at Ramleh (now Ramla). The Duke presented medals to officers and men of the 1/5 Somersets. Major Frank Urwick received the DSO for his distinguished leadership at El Mesmiyeh in November. Captains Goodland and Timms received their MCs, RSM Windows was presented with the Distinguished Conduct Medal, Sgt Collard with the Military Medal and Bar, and Privates Cridland, Greedy, Petvin and Rowsell with Military Medals.[3]

The 1/5 Somersets were heavily involved in the 'Action of Berukin,' which began on April 9th. By 0530 hrs no 4 Company had achieved its objective, the occupation of Rafat and by 0730 nos 1 & 3 Companies had seized the ridge between Rafat and Arara. Arara is 'a rugged hill, devoid of all vegetation . . . it stands out a landmark for miles around, and was a position of great natural strength.' 'The prominent ridge [is] fashioned principally from solid rock interspersed with enormous boulders.' The ridge was taken 'in the face of heavy M.G. fire, a hostile M.G. being captured by 2/Lt Franks and used to repel a counter-attack.'[4] Attempts to capture the South-East peak of Arara were frustrated by the fire of three machine guns on the North-West peak and by enfilading fire from the right. Casualties were heavy. Two subalterns were killed, as were five other ranks. Among the wounded were six officers and seventy-five men.[5] Elsewhere along the 75th Division front there were similar stories of merely limited objectives obtained, frequent counter-attacks by a stubborn defence which included two battalions of the German 'Pasha II' contingent and severe losses inflicted by well-directed machine gun, mortar and artillery fire.

When the battle was resumed early on April 10th the enemy had been reinforced and had at least six machine guns in position making the Rafat-Arara ridge untenable, so a withdrawal was made that night. On the 11th the Corps Commander, Lt Gen. Bulfin and his Chief of Staff visited the 75th Division and, having seen for themselves that no immediate breakthrough was possible ordered further offensive operations to be postponed.[6]

The British possession of Rafat, El Kefr and Berukin was still bitterly disputed and desultory fighting continued until September. Through the scorching summer the Somersets were either holding the forward outposts or were bivouacked in 'rest' areas, from which large working parties were employed in road building and the construction of a second line of defence. Artillery bombardment caused casualties. For instance at El Kefr on April 30th three men were killed and three more wounded; two more were wounded when the same village was shelled on May 27th. Night patrols were sent out, some leaving propaganda material in places the enemy was known to visit. In July the Battalion was at Deir Ballut where, on the 13th, when Stanley was temporarily in command, an estimated 600 shells were directed onto the area it occupied but the enemy's attack on Rafat from Arara failed because 'they were prevented by our artillery from reaching the wire'.[7] In late August the Battalion occupied the Berukin area, remaining there until September 12th, a week before Allenby's offensive began.

---

[3] *BoR*, p.58.

[4] 2/Lt Franks was awarded the MC. Bn War Diary 22/5/18.

[5] At some stage of this campaign Major Urwick suffered a shrapnel wound. Bn War Diary for 9/4/18, PRO WO 95 4690.

[6] Falls, op. cit. part II, p.356.

[7] Bn War Diary 13/7/18.

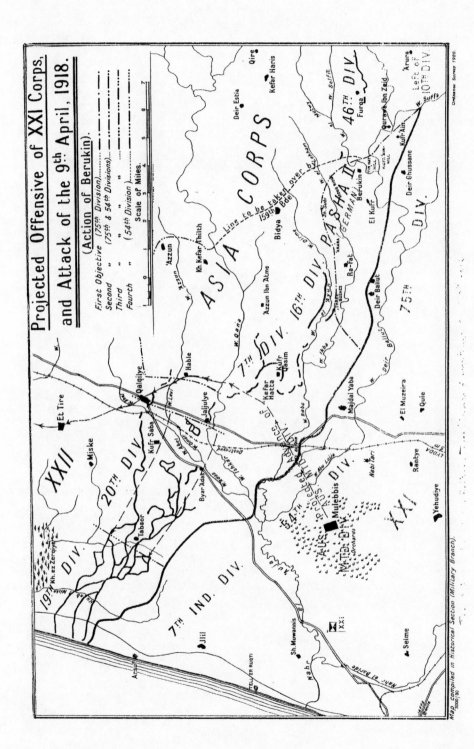

Projected Offensive of XXI Corps,
and Attack of the 9th April, 1918.
(Action of Berukin).

First Objective (75th Division)........
Second   "   (75th & 54th Divisions)........
Third   "   (54th Division)........
Fourth   "   (54th Division)........

Scale of Miles.
0   1   2   3   4   5   6   7

Ordnance Survey 1926.

Map compiled in Historical Section (Military Branch).

Stanley's surviving letters provide only a sketchy account of these months of hard campaigning. German and Austrian submarines continued to sink Allied ships in the Mediterranean till the end of the war; letters were damaged or lost.[8] There is no reference in the War Diary to Stanley's reconnaissance work in August but he must have been minutely examining the area in which the 233rd Infantry Brigade would be deployed in the operations on Z Day, September 19th.

Marching only by night, forbidden to light fires, moving to concealed bivouacs in orange groves, the Battalion prepared for Allenby's greatest 'stunt'. Two Companies were attached to the 234th Infantry Brigade with the specific task of capturing an advanced Turkish outpost covering Tabsor, about five miles inland from the coast. This mission was speedily accomplished without loss, though two men were killed and five wounded later in the day. By nightfall the re-united Battalion had advanced five miles and become part of Corps reserve.

While the British and Imperial cavalry surged North following Allenby's spectacular breakthrough the men of the 233rd Infantry Brigade were engaged in maintaining the railway and roads in the Kalkilieh (Qalqilye) area. The most common War Diary entry for October is: 'The Battalion continued training and bathing'. Stanley Goodland's departure for temporary duty on the Divisional staff is duly noted, as is his return on November 9th, by which time the Battalion had moved South to Hadithe where it had spent the bedraggled Christmas of 1917.[9] Here the news was received by wire of the German Armistice of November 11th. A party of five officers and fifteen other ranks went to Rafat-Arara to make a cemetery for those killed in the battle there. Sickness was prevalent. The Roll of Honour prints the names of twelve private soldiers who died in the last three months of 1918.[10]

On December 6th the Battalion was transported by train to Kantara, in the Canal Zone near to Port Said. It was one stage towards home but for Stanley, the Adjutant, the processing of demobilisation papers made for a busy Christmas.

---

[8] 28 German U-Boats were still operating in the Mediterranean in August 1918: see Halpern, op. cit. p.400.
[9] see his letters, 18/22, 18/23 and 18/24.
[10] *BoR*, pp. v-ix.

The Letters Written in 1918

No 18/1

Jan 11 1917 [sic]
EEF

My dear old Elsie,

Every day we look out for our mails but nothing ever comes, and I haven't had any letters for ages. The truth is we are having some very severe weather and torrents of rain - I think our old railway has been washed away in places and youve no idea how difficult it is to get limbers and animals along in bad weather in a country without roads - it is as much as the supply people can do just to get our rations up and until better times come I guess we shall have to wait for our letters. I have written you several letters quite recently and I hope some of them reach you - they have been rather sad affairs Im afraid but Im feeling a bit more cheerful now - things are straightening out a bit in the Regiment now and we're getting a few officers and men so that makes me happier. Major Urwick as been given the D.S.O. - isnt that great news and a fine honour no[t] only for himself but for the Regiment as well - he is a very proud man of course - Major Watson[11] and Duke[12] who went home on leave in Sept. are in the country again and as soon as they rejoin Major Urwick and I are going down to Cairo for a weeks holiday - the General has already sanctioned it - so we shall have a royal time Im sure we are still in the line but the Turk is very quiet and keeps his distance - in spite of the weather the men are in wonderful spirits - one cheery soul outside my dug out is singing now 'I tiddle dy Ity take me back to Blighty' - Im sure thems my sentiments too.

Im longing to hear what you think of all our fighting and the capture of Jerusalem - I havent been to the Holy city yet but Ive been to Jaffa Ramleh and Ludd which are ever so interesting - German banks - hotels & buildings predominate everywhere. Im afraid poor Milsom is still very ill - Im sorry for his missus who is in New Zealand - she is such a good sort and was ever so good in India. I do hate this war. I think of little Gretchen[13] every day and wonder how she is getting on - I shall have quite a lot of new nephews & nieces to get to know when I do reach home once more.

No more news just now and its getting too dark to write and there are no candles or oil nowadays - so goodnight dear old girl with my very best love.

from Stan

*****

---

[11] Major DS Watson was Mentioned in Dispatches and won the DSO. He joined the Regiment as Lieutenant on April 1st 1908 and left with the rank of Lt-Col on August 28th 1923 (*BoR* pp.73, 74, 120).

[12] Capt J Duke was with the Regiment when they left for India in October 1914 and was awarded the Order of the Nile 4th Class from Egypt , and the Order of the Crown of Italy [Chevalier] (*BoR* pp.13, 75).

[13] Gretchen (see note 1914/3). Her first child was expected in January and there are several references to this event before Stanley received the news. Christine Hyde was born January 8th 1918.

No. 18/2

28th Jan. 1918
E.E.F.

My dear old Elsie,

I have just returned from a weeks leave in Cairo with Major Urwick and have had a delightful time - I wrote you a long letter from the Turf Club there but I hear the mail boat was sunk. I sent you also some silk handkerchiefs with I'm afraid were in the same boat - if these dont reach you please let me know for they were insured and I can get compensation. They were made by the Egyptian harem ladies and I wanted them to arrive somewhere about your birthday with my best love and good wishes!

We ran up to Alexandria for a couple of days to see Milsom and our other woundeds - we were lucky to arrive just in time to see Milsom on his hospital ship, for he had already embarked and by this time is well on his way home. He looked very well though still in pain and unable to walk but I quite envied him his trip to England and it made me quite home-sick. I am afraid he will never come back to us and as he, Banes and I were always inseparable, it makes me very unhappy. I hope to go to Jerusalem next month for two days and shall climb up that mountain overlooking the city and plant a few of the wonderful spring flowers which are growing up everywhere here round Banes' grave. I was so looking forward to finding some letters from you on my return yesterday but nothing has come and it makes me very fed up - but today a wonderful parcel came from you of baccy soap - a memo book and all sorts of useful things - so many thanks dear girl and a big hug! But I want so much to get your letters and to know what you think of all our fighting and the doings of the dear old Somersets - I wonder if you got my letters describing those terrible times? Cairo was very gay and amusing but I think I enjoyed my two hot baths a day more than anything and as I had slept in my boots and clothes every since I was in Cairo last October you can imagine how delightful it was to get into pyjamas again. There are no signs of food controllers and rations in Cairo and with its perfect climate I can't imagine a more perfect spot to live in in these awful times. Lady Allenby is simply charming and does everything possible to give officers on leave a good time - she gives 'At Homes' and small dances[14] - I actually had a one step and a waltz and it made me feel quite young again. Sheppheards Hotel where we stayed is the acme of luxury and some of the menus we tackled were wonderful - to celebrate the Majors D.S.O. he gave me a dinner which included a large bottle of Irroy 1906 and from the hors d'oeuvre to the savoury I think was the best and most expensive dinner any city in the world could produce at the present time. The feelings and joys of short leave can only be experienced by those who have been 'through it' as we did last November! I saw quite a lot of Karl who is very fit but still a 'B' man on account of his rheumatism.[15] It is horrid to be back in the line - I found the Regiment in

---

[14] 'Allenby obtained with some difficulty permission for Lady Allenby to go to Egypt. She arrived in October 1917 and went to the Villa Heller at Gezira. Her influence in the English community in Egypt was, in its way, as great as Allenby's at the front. She took part in the direction of the Red Cross, working in finding occupation and interests for the convalescents, and for officers and men on leave, and similar activities.' AP Wavell *Allenby* op. cit. p.196.

[15] Karl Jones was appointed Cypher Officer at HQ EEF in 1918, O/c Cyphers EEF 1919.

the same old spot and its raining hard and very cold and cheerless - the Colonel has gone home on leave for a month - I envy him too and hope my turn will come soon - my great fear is that by the time the C.O. is back it will be necessary for us to begin another advance and then of course I shan't be able to get away however I shall hope for the best. I am always thinking of Gretchen these days and wondering how she is getting through what I imagine is a very terrible yet very wonderful time of a girls life - I am hoping to hear all is well soon. I have much arrears of office work to tackle so cannot scribble anymore now - if this reaches you near your birthday please accept a birthday kiss and my most loving wishes - it is too depressing to think it is nearly 4 years ago since I last saw you and the damned old war is more complicated and awful than ever - Ive come to the conclusion it will fizzle out and one day we shall wake up & suddenly find Peace has been declared and we can go home - may it be very soon - Best of love dear girl

from Stan

*****

No.18/3

Feb 4 1918
E.E.F.

[Passed by censor No. 3983]

My dear old Elsie

At last I have all your letters - many thanks dear girl - the last is dated Jan 4th but up to that time apparently none of mine had reached you but I find that all the E E F letters were held up and everybody is frightfully annoyed about it. But I hope you have heard from me long before this and that some of my descriptions of the fighting have reached you. Your letters were a great joy to me - I used to get a lot of letters but all my old friends 'cept you have long ago forgotten me and never write now but I expect it's my own fault for I get little time to write to them.

I told you in my last letters that I had been on leave in Cairo with Major Urwick - it did me a world of good and cheered me up no end but I still get horribly depressed now I'm back with the Regiment for I'm always thinking of the old days when I was surrounded by my pals who are nearly all killed or wounded and so my dearest girl I look forward more than ever to hearing from you and I only hope your busy life will never prevent you writing - I shall always remember how good you have been ever since I embarked on Oct 10 1914 - what ages that seems away! I'm awfully sorry to hear Mrs Brown has been so ill again and can quite imagine how tied you are - You musnt get too thin else there'll be nothing left of you I get fatter and fatter in this mountain air and campaigning always seems to suit me - do you realize we are fighting in hills as high as Snowdon - so we ought to keep fit eh and are now quite accustomed to mountaineering but it's real bad country for ones boots! Next week we go out of the line for two weeks rest and it will be a nice change - a night never passes in quietness - always there are wires coming thro' and things to be done and an Adjutant's life these times is a very restless one. Did I tell you our Colonel is home on leave now and Major Watson who came back from England a little while ago has gone to Cairo for a 6 weeks course so Urwick and I are running the Regiment again. I have told you I think that I hope to get home on leave about April - so do please save up a little of your holidays so that may see you either at Elm Grove or at Hale or anywhere else you like to fix up - I shall send you a cable as soon as ever I know I am really off - it all depends on the Colonel and the operations out here! If there is to be another big advance this Spring Im afraid I shall have to stay and of course I shouldn't like to be away from the dear old Regiment when theres any heavy fighting after going through so much with them - but I hope for the best I think of little Gretchen every day and wonder how she is and I am anxiously awaiting news - it seems a wonderfull thing to me that she should be a mother and I only hope her best dreams may be realized.

With best love to you dear girl and ever so many thanks again for your welcome letters.

*****

No.18/4

13.2.18
E.E.F.

[Passed by Censor 3983]

My dear old Elsie

We are out of the line now and are in tents and dry ground near Ramleh - we have had some vile weather but now we have plenty of shelter and the sun is shining so we are ever so happy and comfortable.

And now we are busy polishing our buttons and cleaning up - it is a job to get rid of weeks & weeks accumulated mud It is so nice to be doing a bit of peace time soldiering all in honour of H.R.H.[16] - our band instruments and bugles which we haven't seen for months have been sent up and it is such a treat to hear music again. It will be a great day for the Regiment I am on the best of terms with the General[17] these days and dined with him last night and had a great time - our band played at dinner and afterwards we danced on the stone floor of the school house in which he lives - its wonderful how childish a few men can be when they get together and the band tunes up No letters have come from you and we hear of at least two mail boats from home being lost at sea - it is very sad Im longing to hear if my letters have ever reached you. I hope Mrs Brown is better now and that you can have more rest and Im anxious to get further news of little Greta too

These are only a few lines to let you know I am well - I am very busy now with all these preparations and will try to send a longer letter in a few days

Best love dear girl

from Stan

*****

---

[16] Arthur, Duke of Connaught, 1850-1942, third son of Queen Victoria.
[17] Brigadier-General Colston, GOC 233rd Brigade.

105

No. 18/5

My dear old Elsie

We are off again tomorrow and are full of bustle today packing up and getting ready - we have had 3 delightful weeks of comparative comfort here and I shall be sorry to leave my tent and olive grove and many other comforts which we dont get when fighting the Turk in those stoney hills yonder. We are a fine Regiment again now and are stronger in officers & men than we have ever been - most of our wounded have rejoined. The Dukes visit is put off for a few weeks and I hope we shan't be altogether disappointed for we have had a very busy time smartening up & cleaning everything since weve been out of the line - H.R.H. is going to present the decorations recently won on this front and I expect he will give me my Military Cross so I shall have to practice pushing my chest out. Ive just had 2 letters from you dear girl - the last dated Jan 29th many thanks they do cheer me up no end - I expect the excitement of battle again will make me forget for a time all those horrible times of last November and December. We dined our General last night and gave him a wonderful dinner - he is a topper and got ever so cheery. Ill enclose the Menu Card and also the song we sang to the tune of "another little drink wouldn't do us any harm" The Padre composed it!
I'll write whenever I can - best love dear girl

from Stan

*****

No.18/6
This OHMS envelope has written on it: "Salved from Submerged Mail" and is addressed to:
  Miss Elsie Hyde
  "Highcroft"
  Minchinhampton
  Glos.
The next two letters have clearly been wet and are difficult to read. They were written in ink, which has run.
The letter starts in pencil but continues in ink after the first half page; the pencil is obscured by the ink seepage, but the rest of the letter is possible to read:

17 March 1918
EEF

My dear old Elsie

... I little thought a few years ago that I should be taking part in such an historic ceremony. The weather yesterday unfortunately was stormy and at the last moment it was decided to adjourn to the large building in Ramleh town known as the Convent It was rather a pity as the whole thing would have looked better in the open air. The Duke drove up in a car with the Commander in Chief[18] and we gave him a "Royal Salute" and then he came over to the Guard of Honour and I

---

[18] General Allenby , see note 1917/29.

was introduced to him and to the Commander in Chief. He then inspected the men and chatted away the whole time asking questions about the Regiment and he stopped and spoke to many of the men - Afterwards he shook hands with me and complimented me on a very fine body of men. And really they did look well & our band of 48 men and buglers were paraded with us and created quite an impression.

The next thing was the presentation of decorations and there were such a great many of General Staff Officers and all the brass of the Army in Palestine - I had to march up to have my Military Cross pinned on and it is such a handsome thing - Im having it engraved and sent home for the Pater to keep for me for Im sure I should lose it out here. We now have a long trek back to the Regiment all through the hills - just before we left we advanced about 6 miles on our front but thanks to our artillery we met with little opposition - I suppose we shall keep on slowly advancing but where our final objective out here is Im sure I dont know. The Colonel is still on home leave but is really due back now - I wish he would come for Im anxious to get my application for home leave sent in. Im longing to see you again dear girl and it cheers me up no end to have something to look forward to. I heard last night that Geoffrey Clarke[19] has won an M.C. - he commanded my old company in the fighting last November and did most wonderfully well. Many thanks dear girl for your letters which come fairly regularly now - I hear there has been another home mail since we left the Regiment and Im hoping there will be something waiting for me Im awfully fit & the wonderful hill air suits me well and I think Im getting more cheerful than I have been lately. Goodbye dear girl.

Best love

from Stan

*****

No. 18/7

Also salvaged, date missing

My dear old Elsie

I had a lovely lot of letters from you this month, thanks ever so much dear - the last is dated Feb.18th. Im back with the old Regiment again at last - I was away 10 days and it seemed ages - I hate to be away really. It was a long march from the Rest Camp 20 miles all through most wonderful hills. We are going to advance gradually still further and my letters in the near future may be irregular again but Ill send a few lines whenever I can. We have received many congratulations over the Guard of Honour stunt and it's nice to feel everyone is pleased. The position we are in now is almost indescribable - I thought nothing in the World could beat Switzerland but this seems grander and more vast - you would love the wild flowers I wish I could send you a bunch - outside my dug out arum lilies, black & white tulips - orchids and 20 other kinds and colours I cant name - its a glorious sight. Im awfully fit and couldnt be other wise in this hill air.

This is only a short letter this time - best love dear girl

from Stan

*****

---

[19] Lt GP Clarke gazetted to Battalion December 4th 1914, won the MC for his part in the action before El Jib (*BoR*, p.74).

No. 18/8

April 7 1918
E.E.F.

My dear old Elsie

Your last letter of Mar 14 came today and I thought I would send you a few lines right away to tell you I am all right.

I hope little Ronald will soon be quite well again and am glad to hear you are getting fat or fatter I should say. I dont know how you do on the restricted rations. The Colonel is back again but we are so much 'in the fighting' now that Im afraid my chances of leave at present are very small but I still hope it will be O.K. We are gradually closing in on Shekhem[20] and the dear old Regiment is doing splendidly and adding fresh laurels almost every day. Fortunately up to now our casualties are not heavy but we are up against Germans[21] now and its very strenuous campaigning in the mountainous country. We hear all sorts of rumours of great doings in France[22] and I only hope & pray our wonderful army can hold out and kill & keep on killing Huns until they are bound to give in! It is really awful this waste of the worlds manhood. We are all excitement today for we have a big thing[23] on in few hours time - it means a lot of work for me but I dont care a bit so long as the old 1/5th do well and Ive no fear of that. The Pater writes very cheerful letters thank goodness and I had a very welcome letter today too from little Gretchen who is bursting with pride over Christine. I do hope my letters are reaching you. I have written quite a lot lately

Well best love dear girl and loving thoughts always

from Stan

*****

---

[20] now Nablus.

[21] Liman von Sanders, German hero of the Turco/German defeat of the Allies at Gallipoli, had become C-in-C of the Turco/German army in Palestine on March 1st 1918.

[22] The Ludendorff offensive in France had begun on March 31st.

[23] Attack to secure the line Berukin-Arara-Rafat.

No.18/9

undated but post marked 30 Apr.18 field Post Office 233
[Censor's stamp as before. Written on piece of squared paper from a field note book]

My dear old Elsie

Just a few lines to let you know I am fit and well still. Im afraid many of my recent letters to you have gone astray for I have written constantly but Im glad the handkerchiefs rolled up for I had quite given up hope of them ever reaching you. I wrote you a long letter at the same time the parcel was sent but that evidently is at the bottom of the sea. I wonder if my letter describing the recent fighting our here has ever reached you I miss old Urwick ever so much and hope he will soon get over his wound and be back with us

The men of the dear old Regiment are really magnificent wonderfully cheerful after all they have gone through lately - I think I told you in my last letter that the General had written us a note congratulating the Regiment on what it had done. My leave Im sorry to say is hung up for the time being - I cant tell you the reason just yet because it would be disclosing operation secrets but I must be patient a little longer and hope on. Im so glad you are fit but you _must_ keep cheerful and I really think the damned old war cant last many more months - the bloodshed in France just now is really awful.

Best love dear old girl

from Stan

*****

No. 18/10

undated, postmarked 24th May 1918, censored

E.E.F.

My dear old Elsie

Ive just heard that a mail boat with 3 weeks mail has been lost at sea and so Im feeling very fed up. Letters are the only things weve got to look forward to and I havent had one from you for ever so long and now I shant hear for simply ages - its sickening. You will be glad to hear we are going out of the line for two weeks rest in a few days and on the 28th I am going down to Cairo for 10 days with Frank Calway - I am looking forward to it. Its about time Im sure that I had another bath and it will be lovely to sleep in a real bed again. I will write you a long letter from Shepheard and hope youll get it this time I can imagine Minchinhampton is looking quite beautiful this time of year and I only wish I could take a look at it - I often dream my leave is sanctioned but there really seems no chance of it just now - if only things could improve in France[24] it would help matters - we get only scanty news of the great struggle in the West - it must all be perfectly awful. I am always busy and Im glad it is so - it helps to keep one cheerful - poor old Urwick came back from hospital with his wound healed and now he has gone down

---

[24] The Allies had lost ground, lives and material to the German advance on the Somme and south of Ypres.

again with fever - I miss him so much   I wonder if my letters describing the Guard of Honour to the Duke of Connaught and also all the ones describing all our fighting last month have or will ever reach you. Best love dear girl - hoping you will keep quite fit through the summer

from Stan

*****

No.18/11

June 3 1918
Jerusalem

My dear old Elsie

I little dreamed I should ever write you from the Holy City but here I am and having one of the most interesting times of my life. In my last letter I told you I was off on May 28th to Cairo for 10 days leave with Frank Calway during the time the Regiment was out of the line resting. Early on that morning I packed off my kit & servant quite early meaning to follow on my horse but a wire came with orders for the Regiment which made it necessary for me to stay and Frank was very sick because he had to go off alone and so was I - I cant tell you what all these orders were about but I shall not be able to get away for more than 2 days for some time to come and have a very busy time ahead. As a sort of consolation prize the Colonel[25] offered to take me to Jerusalem for two days and of course I jumped at the idea & here we are - the Colonel is a charming man to be away with & has a wonderful knowledge of Scripture History - he makes me feel so ashamed

Anyhow we are having a wonderful time - today we have been to Bethlehem and thoroughly viewed all the sights - the Church of the Nativity - the Stable and Manger where Christ was born - the village where the Shepherds lived & the fields where they "watched their flocks by night" - Rachaels tomb - the place where Boaz met Ruth - In the distance we saw the Blue Mountains of Moab where Ruth came from to work in the fields near Bethlehem. This afternoon we have 'done' the Holy City & seen many wonderful things - the Holy Sepulchre - the Mosque of Omar - Pilates House - the Mount of Olives - the Garden of Gethsemane - Calvary & a hundred other things I shall never forget. Tomorrow I am taking the Colonel to El Jib to show him the battle fields of last November & where the old Regiment fought and suffered last November 23d - I am looking forward to it so much - at Bethlehem I bought for you a little chain, of beads made of mother of pearl - it is just a little memento for you & I will post it tomorrow - the Syrians of Bethlehem work in this mother of pearl and it is quite their industry - I have put a couple of charms in the chain - 1 representing the Star of Bethlehem the other the Crusaders Cross - You probably will never wear it but I wanted you to have something straight from the Holy Land I am posting you some photographs too. I will write you again in a day or two with a fuller description of all my doings. I have not had a letter from you for some time again - it is very sad - I hope some of mine are reaching you now - with best love dear girl - I wish you were here to enjoy all this with me

from Stan

*****

---

[25] Lt-Col Cooke-Hurle

No.18/12

8 June 1918
E.E.F.

My dear old Elsie

I wrote you a letter from Jerusalem and I am now back with the Regiment - I have sent you some photos of some of the places I have seen - it has all been very interesting and I should have liked to have stayed longer.

I spent a day taking the colonel over El Jib and the battle fields of last November. It all brought back wonderful memories - I found poor old Banes grave and tidied it up and put a wall of stones around it - it was a very sad day in many ways.

Of course we went to the Mount of Olives and I enclose a twig[26] from one of the Trees - it is supposed to bring good luck. We also walked through the Garden of Gethsemane and on to Mount Zion where we were shown the Tombs of King David and Solomon & also the place of the Last Supper. I really know more about Biblical History than ever I did before altho I fancy I got a prize at School once for an essay on the 'Life of Christ'! The mails are still very disappointing and I havnt had a letter from you for ages again - I hope mine are reaching you better now We go into the line again in a few days time - everyone has enjoyed the rest & change but of course it has been much too short - I wish it would all end - my leave seems further off than ever but I always hope to be allowed to get away some day. The Colonel has been awarded the D.S.O. in the Kings Birthday Honours - we are all very delighted about it - I am longing get another letter from you & hope you are very fit - Best love dear girl

from Stan

*****

No. 18/13

undated, post mark 3 July 19, no address.

My dear old Elsie

My best thanks dear girl for the book you sent me & which came a few days ago - I havent had a chance of starting it yet but it looks very exciting I am looking forward ever so much to the parcel you mention in your last letter - you are simply too good to me I wish I could be in England now - it must be delightful - but my home leave seems impossible just now - and even 10 days in Cairo is out of the question for some time Major Watson has gone to Hospital with fever and poor old Urwick is marked 'Base 2 months' - this makes me Second in command of the Regiment and I shall be an acting Major for a little while but for goodness sake dont address my letters as 'Major' as I shall be down to Captain again before very long. We are in a fairly comfortable part of the line now but of course the heat and the flies are very trying and we are passing through quite the worst time of the year just now I get very cheerful letters from home still except that the Pater has a touch of lumbago! I havent heard from Gretchen for ages & ages but I guess all her time is taken up with little Christine - Excuse this scribble I am very short

---

[26] The twig survives in the envelope with this letter.

111

of candles and the wind keeps blowing this little bit out I get very cheerful letters from Milsom he is still in Hospital & on crutches but his wife has joined him now from New Zealand so he is delightfully happy - she was torpedoed in the Atlantic and lost all her kit and had a good swim[27] - I wish you could meet them We are very bucked with the news from Italy[28] and long for further details of what seems to be a great victory for the Allies. The Colonel keeps very well indeed and we are the greatest pals - he feels the loss of all his original officers - Do you know - of all the officers who went to India with him originally only T. Moore & myself are left at present - out of about 30 It is very sad isnt it

Hope you keep fit and by the time this reaches you you will be thinking of packing up for your holidays - I do hope you get good weather

Its the longest 4 years I've ever known

Best love dear girl

from Stan

*****

No. 18/14

July 18 1918
E.E.F.

[Envelope readdressed to Gwynant, Park Rd., Hale, Cheshire]

My dear old Elsie

After waiting a long time I was delighted a few days ago to get three letters from you - the latest dated 25th June - many thanks dear girl for them - I also received the parcel quite safely it gave me the greatest possible pleasure to open it and the contents are lovely - the pipe is a beauty and I am smoking it hard already. The tins of things are a very welcome addition to our stores. I have been seedy the past ten days and on the verge of going into Hospital - the weather has been terribly hot and my old Mespot fever has turned up again - I have dosed myself with quinine and hope I shall get fit soon but I get a rotten temperature every night and get a sort of shivering ague I want to hold on for in about 2 weeks time we go into rest again for a short period - we have had a long trying time in the line now The Turk has been very active lately - he attacked us very stubbornly a few days ago - the Colonel was away on duty at Jaffa and Major Watson was still in hospital so I was left in command of the Regiment - It was very exciting for a few hours but our fellows did splendidly and the Turks did not succeed in getting further than our wire - considering that he fired more than 1600 heavy shells at us we had very few casualties.[29] Major Watson is back now I am glad to say and is very well again - poor old Urwick is still at Alexandria - he has been away nearly 3 months now

---

[27] The ship in which Mrs Milsom sailed was torpedoed off Ushant on May 19th 1918. She was rescued by the destroyer escorting the convoy. There was no swimming involved because the skilful destroyer captain laid his ship alongside the sinking vessel. But her wedding presents (and golf clubs) were lost. (Information from SFC Milsom, 1996).

[28] The Austrian offensive had failed in June.

[29] One officer and three other ranks were wounded in this bombardment which consisted of '1600' shells (Stanley's letter) or '600' shells (Battalion War Diary).

You will soon be off for your holidays and I do hope you will have good weather and a real enjoyable time

I shall be thinking of you and wishing I was home on leave

Please write and tell me exactly how Gretchen is and little Christine too

With much love

from Stan

*****

No. 18/15

July 25 1918
E.E.F.

My dear old Elsie

Just a few lines to let you know I am better and hope after all to keep out of Hospital - we go out of the line in a few days time and I shall be able to have more rest and a quiet time

I am tired of the summer - since March we have lived under a boiling sun and I think it gradually saps up ones energy and extra strength

A soldier is always grousing - we curse the wet & cold and then we curse the sun I wish it was all over! And I really think these latest events in France[30] may prove to be the turning point dont you? We only get very short telegrams & long for fuller particulars I am looking forward so much to your next letters - I get so fed up when no English mail arrives

I do hope you will get really fine weather for your holidays and I am sure you will have many happy times

With best love dear girl

from Stan

*****

---

[30] The Second Battle of the Marne, July 16th-18th. The Germans exhausted themselves without making any great breakthrough and with British & American help the French recovered some of the ground they had lost.

113

No. 18/16

My dear old Elsie

You will probably think I am lost stolen or strayed but I am safe and sound - very weary and full of fever but still "carrying on"

I have been away from the Regiment for 15 days and out in the blue on some special reconnaissance work for our General and have been unable to post any letters - Yesterday I came back and was delighted to find 3 letters from you - the last July 28 Many thanks dear girl I was thinking of you during your holiday time and now I suppose you are back in old Minch again - all the better I hope for your change - I was so sorry you had been unwell - it was a great pity - the photo of Gretas lovely baby reached me quite safely - she seems a beautiful baby and Im sure you must have enjoyed fussing with her - I expect they are at Elm Grove now and am sorry you couldnt go as the Pater would have so much enjoyed seeing you once again. I have quite made up my mind to give up all idea of leave now - I think the war will be over soon now and the Colonel has asked me to see him through with it now. You see dear girl - I am the only officer who has kept out of Hospital & been with the dear old Regiment through everything and so I have taken on a good deal of responsibility and the Colonel leans on me a goodish bit now - Old Urwick has gone to Ceylon on leave - his missus is still there so we shant see him again for at least 2 months - he has been away ever since last May and I have missed him so much.

I wish I could tell you about the work I have just been doing for the General - it has all been most interesting and I have been in the saddle all day long - often doing 40 miles a day - I have got such a nice mare now - dark brown with 3 white stockings - you will I expect realize that we are to move to another part of the front altogether - I have been making maps and taking photographs and getting all the information I can

Any day I may be off some where else so it has been necessary to find me an assistant adjutant to carry on the usual battalion work - a nice boy from St Helens who says "a"s like you do and always amuses me - we call him "Pills".[31] A year ago we were in the trenches in front of Gaza - do you remember - it seems years & years since those happy days when I could see poor old Banes most days and Milsom too. I wonder and wonder when I shall see you again dear girl - I have every hope of that happy day being within the next six months - It has been a very long 4 years! Someone told me this riddle which is very applicable to me - why is the E.E.F. like a tea strainer? Because so few <u>leaves</u> get through! I must get on with some work now - so cheerio dear girl - with best love

from Stan

*****

---

[31] 'Beecham's Little Liver Pills,' source of the wealth of Sir Thomas Beecham, orchestral conductor, were made in St Helens, Lancashire.

No. 18/17

My dear old Elsie

When I wrote to you last a few days ago I had just returned from a tour of duty of reconnaissance Work - I was only with the Regiment a couple of days when off I went again on another joy ride for special work. I am now in camp on the banks of the River Auja[32] - it is so strange to be in the plains again after about 10 months spent in the Mountains We get a glorious bathe in the river before breakfast each morning and for the rest of the day I am in the saddle riding about over an entirely new country to me - it is all very interesting but these are hard days and I am very tired at the end of the day. I expect to be here 4 days then I have to go on to Jaffa for one day then back to the Regiment.

I hope my special work will soon be over as I dont like to be away from the Battalion so much as I have been lately - This part of Palestine is very much like the old Gaza district of a year ago it seems simply years and years ago when we were in those trenches. I wonder how you are and if you are safely back in Minchinhampton - the mails have been very lazy again - your last letter was the one dated July 28 which is 6 weeks ago - I am feeling better now but there is such a lot of sickness in this country now and a whole lot of our officers and men are in Hospital most people go down with sand fly fever but I think it is probably the Spanish Influenza which seems to be going the round of the World[33]

I will write as often as I can but for a bit my letters will be written under difficulties

Best love dear girl

from Stan

*****

No. 18/18

My dear old Elsie

I am sending you another short letter to let you know I am safe and well

The last time I wrote I was on the Auja - I have since been to Jaffa and am now back with the old Regiment once again

Jaffa was very nice - I got a lovely bathe in the sea and what pleased me even more got some real fresh butter and a fresh egg - the first since last January!

The town & port are very much ruined now but at one time it must have been a very fine place - of course I was taken to see the House of Simon the Tanner![34]

---

[32] The River Auja flows into the Mediterranean just north of Jaffa.

[33] This pandemic is believed to have killed more victims than the total number of casualties in the Great War.

[34] 'And it came to pass that he [Peter] tarried many days in Joppa [Jaffa] with one Simon a Tanner. (Acts 9.43) whose house is by the sea side' (Acts 10.6).

I am so glad to be back with the battalion again and I hope I am fixed for a time - we are very busy with preparations for something I may not write about but you can probably guess by my letters and by my movements the last few weeks - Things are likely to be very strenuous and that is why I am writing a short letter when I can. No more has come from you since one dated July 28th - it is a shame and it makes me feel so cut off from the world and everybody

I do hope you keep well the news from France[35] must thrill old England with joy - of course we are all delighted beyond words and we long for detailed news

Best love dear girl

from Stan

*****

No. 18/19

18/9/18

[no address, envelope enclosed in another with the green cross - & addressed in careful writing and signed Fred Stoodley[36]]

My dear old Elsie

First of all let me tell you dear girl we are on the eve of great events out here and long before you get this letter I hope all the world will have had good news from the Palestine Front. You will probably have gathered from my recent letters that there was "something doing" out here - I have had a very heavy time and a lot of responsible work and I only hope all will go well.

I cannot stay to write more than a few lines tonight - but I must send you my best thanks my dear for the most delightful birthday parcel which reached me quite safely yesterday - just in time for these operations and all so very nice and useful You must choose all the things so very carefully and it is so sweet of you dear My birthday will be spent again this year in the thick of soldiering - next year Im sure I shall be in dear old England

I was so pleased to hear you enjoyed the last part of your holiday so much and that you were quite fit & well

I am much better - I think excitement and hard work can cure most things

Best love dear girl Goodbye - or rather au revoir dear old girl

from Stan

---

[35] August 8th was the German 'Black Day' when the Allies launched their greatest and last offensive.

[36] Fred Stoodley was Assistant Quartermaster of the Battalion. For many years afer the war, Stanley and Elsie received from him an annual parcel containing asparagus and lilies of the valley.

No. 18/20

My dear old Elsie

Just a hurried line to tell you dear old girl I have been through another great battle (and I hope the last) and am safe and well - We have had a glorious victory and as far as one can tell the whole Turkish army has been destroyed or captured.

My last letters Im afraid have been short and uninteresting but I expect you will have gathered from them that we were going to have a stunt on this front.

The past six weeks or so I have been all over the country doing special work - the Regiment moved from the mountains on to the Plains near the sea about Sept 17th and at 4.30 am on the 19th. the great attack began. It was a wonderful show and successful beyond all expectations. The Regiment took part in the first attack - we went over the top above a terrific artillery bombardment and drove the Turks from their strong positions which had been holding us up for months - Once past their defences we got them on the run and captured hundreds of prisoners

After 4 days strenuous work we were brought out to rest and are now in the Tul Keram[37] district and the cavalry are doing the mopping up miles & miles ahead

The whole thing was so sudden and so successful that thank Goodness our casualties were slight and altogether it has been wonderful time

I will write more in a few days. I am longing for another home mail now

Best love dear girl

from Stan

*****

No.18/21

Oct 15 1918
no address

My dear old Elsie

A cablegram came from you today - it has taken a long time partly owing to dreadful delay in the offices during all the fighting and also from the fact that cables are only sent to Alex and then forwarded up the line by post.

I should send you a reply but I cant do so except by posting it with the money to Cairo or Alex

Many thanks dear girl for your good wishes - I am afraid you have been anxious about me and my letters have not reached you

I must say I spent a very funny Birthday this year but I really think this is the last I shall spend in khaki - on Sept 22 this year we were mopping up the old Turks in a most exciting way. Your last letter was dated Aug 23 so Ive no news of you for nearly two months - It is a shame there is so much delay but I know there is a huge mail at Port Said that should reach us in a few days now. All the

---

[37] Tul Keram on the plain of Sharon between Jaffa and Haifa, one-time Turkish Eighth Army HQ.

news is really wonderful and I do think the old Hun has shot his last bolt - the air is full of rumours of Peace - I may spend Xmas in dear old Blighty but that's too good to contemplate and altho Im very optimistic I dont think we can have peace for a few months yet I hope the Powers that be will not make peace until the German Army is quite destroyed and she surrenders unconditionally

We are in a strange position here with no enemy to fight. The few thousand Turks remaining have fled up country so fast that even our cavalry can't find 'em - I wonder what will happen to us - they are almost certain to send some of the Divisions to another front, at present we are working feverishly on the railway. It is still very hot - what a long long summer it has been- I used to love the sun but now I long to feel the rain on my face and a bit of mud under foot - We have had perpetual sun since April. I am better but still very tired and want leave badly - I shall try to get down to Cairo or possibly Luxor when the weather cools a bit - My hands are tied up at present as I got into the Turkish barbed wire in the attack in the semi light and the scars got sceptic [sic] - I have to have hot foments 3 times a day which is such a nuisance I dont mind much so long as I can keep out of Hospital - I had enough of Hospital in Mespot & India I wonder what you people at home think of our little show out here - I am longing for your letters and the home papers which will have the account of the Palestine fighting

I hope I thanked you properly dear for the last parcel you so kindly sent me - my birthday one I mean - it arrived just in time for the attack and all the little things came in ever so useful - even to the Boracic ointment The soup squares were delicious because for two or three days we were very short of rations - Now I think of it dear girl will you please send me a nail brush for Xmas- I hate to ask for things but you always tell me to and I simply cant get a decent nail brush in this country. Do you remember the pair of ebony hair brushes you gave me - I have always had them with my kit and use them every day in the little bit of hair I have left!!

Old Urwick has gone off to Ceylon - he sent me a farewell note - I hope he will come back soon but Im afraid it will be quite two months before we see him - I do miss my old pals - poor old Banes - Milsom" & I used to have such happy times - It is going on for a year ago since that dreadful fighting for Jerusalem & poor Banes was killed Nov 22nd I have long letters from Milsom - he is still on crutches and has a small house at Worthing - he has his wife with him and is supremely happy but very fed up to be inactive and away from the old Regiment - My last letter from home came a long time ago but the Pater seemed well except for his lumbago - I think the Babe is expecting Karl home on leave soon - it is a shame if he gets home before me - he has seen no fighting and has had a cushy job away down at the Base - but thats the way of the Army!

Cheerio & best love dear girl

from Stan

*****

Oct 29 1918
no address

My dear old Elsie

No letters have come from you for simply ages - I am longing to hear from you again and to know what you think of our great victory out here. I cannot understand the delay in the post for your last was dated Sept. 16th six weeks ago. I hope my letters have reached you. I wrote you quite a long one the other day. My poisoned hand is better but still tied up and I am really very fit now - at present I am bitten dreadfully by mosquitoes!

I am away from the Regiment again and temporarily on the Staff of the Division - there has been so much sickness and nearly all the Staff Officers have gone to Hospital so they have borrowed me for a week or two only on the stipulation that I return to the Regiment as soon as possible I should simply hate to have a staff job and it would be a disappointing finish to the war - I never want to be away from the Regiment

My job at present is finding billets and camping sites for the winter for the Division. I am at Haifa where we shall probably spend the winter unless we are suddenly moved to another front - it is very nice here but very malarial[38] at this time of year and the mosquitoes bite like the devil. I am living on top of Mount Carmel in what was a large German Hotel. It has the most delightful outlook I have ever seen. The sea is perfect blue and Acre across the bay looks charming. The feeding at present is very bad but one can put up with that - I have had a real hot bath today the first since last January!!

The Regiment is 30 miles or so south of Haifa but will be coming along as the railway progresses - Our cavalry have got on splendidly havent they! I hear Aleppo has been taken today and I suppose Alexandretta will be next and then we shall have the whole of Palestine. When things settle down I hope to go to Damascus & Beyrout both of which are very interesting I hear - but of course it is very difficult to get about this country. I have been to Nazareth & the Plain of Esdraelon - Caesarea - Kishon River and several other interesting places.

I have heard no recent war news from France but it is all a wonderful advance and I am always wondering how long the Hun will hold out!

We seem to have quite finished our little war out here and unless we go to another part of the World I suppose I shant see another shot fired - the great thing now is to keep out of Hospital almost every one gets ill and I am looked upon rather as a 'wonder' to have kept fit all the summer and without leave too! This will probably reach you about Xmas so I will start wishing you a happy time - I shall be thinking of you all the time - I shant be able to send you a present which grieves me very much but I will get you something when I get to Cairo next. It

---

[38] A bacteriologist explained his wall chart to Gen. Allenby: 'these charts are the seasonal incidence of malignant malaria in the Plain of Sharon and I think that is the reason why Richard Coeur de Lion never got to Jerusalem . . . he came down the coast in September.' AP Wavell *Allenby* op. cit. p.195.

seems so funny to write about Xmas - I was hoping so much the damned old war would be over this year. I hope you keep fit dear old girl - how I wish the post office people would get a move on,

Best love dear girl

from Stan

*****

No. 18/23

Oct 31st
no address.

My dear old Elsie

I have just heard we have made Peace with Turkey and of course I am overjoyed and thought I must write you a few lines - It is a fine thing to get Turkey out of the way - she should never have come in against us and I must say she has fought well - Now - the question is what will happen to us? I have had no orders and am carrying on my job here at Haifa - all my plans are practically completed and I think I should be able to forward my report tomorrow - and then in a few days I hope they will let me go back to the Regiment - I am sorry to be away from them for Peace-night - but it cant be helped.

No English mail yet - I am very fed up - there must be a good many letters about somewhere

The summer still hangs on here - it is as hot as the devil still - I must go down and have a bathe in the sea tomorrow it looks so blue and tempting.

Cheerio dear girl - lets hope Austria & Germany will soon follow Turkeys lead

Best love

from Stan

*****

No. 18/24

dated Nov 4th. 1918
no address

My dear old Elsie

I have had a letter from you at last dear girl dated 24th. Sept - I hope some of mine have reached you too - Isnt the war going gloriously well for us! I am so excited and feel sure it will all be over before we are very much older I am still at Haifa doing my Divisional job but I hear all plans are altered now and I quite think the Division will go down the line instead of up - it would be nice to get down to Alex or some civilised place for the bad weather. We are all wondering so much what will happen - apparently with so many Americans coming over they do not need us in France - I somehow feel my fighting is over and candidly I am mighty pleased. I am sorry Mrs. Brown is ill again but hope all will go well for her - you must be having your hands full and I hope they will allow you a bit more coal now times are brighter for us! I hate being away from the Regiment but the Colonel is very good and keeps me posted up with everything that goes on - it will be a fine thing when the hot weather goes - youve no idea what an enormous amount of

120

sickness there is out here just now! I am so much looking forward to some more letters from you - now the submarines must go from the Mediterranean there should be no delay.

Best love dear girl and I hope your rheumatics are quite better

from Stan

*****

No. 18/25

dated Nov 19 1918
no address

My dear old Elsie

You will I know be pleased to hear I have been awarded the Croix de Guerre - I was so surprised late last night to get the following wire "Capt. Goodland MC 1/5 Bn SLI awarded Croix de Guerre - Permission to wear decoration granted - Commander in Chief sends congratulations also Divisional Commander"

So dear girl Ive got a memento of the Palestine Campaign as well as the Mespot one and as I can also wear the 1915 star Im getting quite a breast full of ribbons - so Im very gratified. When the news arrived most of the officers were in bed but they all turned out (the Colonel included in pyjamas) and we made merry in the Mess until the small hours - it was a great time & everyone was very kind about it. Ive got back from Haifa all right - of course all my plans were futile for instead of going to Haifa for the winter we are going down to Egypt" - probably in the neighbourhood of Cairo - of course when I was sent away no one realized the situation would have changed so quickly Isnt it simply grand how well the old Country has come out of the gigantic struggle and I am such a proud soldier now - I found my old Regiment had got back to the Ramleh neighbourhood- and now we are only waiting until the trains can take us back across the Canal - a matter of two weeks or so, I cant tell how long it will be before I am sailing home but Im afraid it will be some months before the Regiment is demobilized and I have a busy time in front of me. But I am rested now and quite fit and fat again and very cheerful

No letter from you dear girl since I last wrote I am looking forward to your next so much - I hope Mrs. Brown is better and with you once again

Best love dear girl and all good wishes

from Stan

*****

No. 18/26

dated Dec 3 1918
no address

My dear old Elsie

We are on the move again and this time thank goodness we are going the right way - a step nearer home and demobilization. Our destination at present is Kantara which is on the banks of the Suez Canal - very likely we shall move nearer Cairo or Alexandria later on and so to night we are busy packing up and there is great excitement for we entrain at daybreak tomorrow! At last there are signs of winter here - the nights are cold and rain is coming - we shall escape at Kantara all the unpleasant wet & mud of Palestine This beastly Flu is attacking

121

us and unfortunately several of our men have died - isnt it hard luck to peg out now the fighting is over I am looking forward so much to your next letters - Your last was Oct 30th so the post hasnt improved much has it - I do wish it would a fortnight ought to be quite long enough to wait for letters now! The Colonel has gone to Cairo again on leave - he wanted to miss this move and I dont blame him - he says hes going to take things easily now. Demobilizing is going to be a bit busy - my days are full now with grouping and codeing all our men - 900 of 'em I often wonder what I shall do after its all over - if I were 10 years younger I would love to stay in the Army but Im very old now - and feel it too sometimes. Im sure I could never settle down in Taunton again so suppose I shall make a fresh start at something in London or some big centre - I fancy there should be some good openings in the commercial world when the country settles down - if you hear of a good billet going nurse it for me dear girl - will you? I cannot stay to write more now.

Best love dear girl

from Stan

*****

No. 18/27

dated Xmas Day 1918
no address & no envelope

My dear old Elsie

Just a few lines on Xmas Day to let you know I am thinking of you and wishing all the time I was home in dear old England

I have had a curious Xmas - better by far than last year when I was up to my knees in mud & rain and had no dinner because the fire wouldnt burn! This year I have spent most of the day in my office for I am frightfully busy with all the demobilization papers - Already we have sent home 9 officers and about 60 men - these are miners police & students etc. Goodness knows when it will be my turn to go! My thanks dear girl for your most welcome Xmas letters & for the beautiful pipe & nail brush - It is kind of you old thing and I wish I was near a shop of some kind to buy you something. I am sorry to hear of the death of your girl pal - everyone seems to have some sort of trouble to bear. I do hope Mrs. Brown is quite better now and that you are all having a very happy time. We are still at Kantara and I fancy we shall be here until the end for it is quite near Port Said from which port most of the ships are sailing I am afraid I shall not be able to write one [a letter] I seem to get no time to myself these busy days - All day long I am arranging to send officers and men home & dont get much chance of working out my own salvation - I havent a notion as to what I shall do after the war but feel something or other will turn up - the Colonel says I must stay on in the Army but I dont know! If I were 10 years younger I should like nothing better

Best love dear girl & many loving thoughts
from Stan

Please address my letters as Captain - sometimes Im a Major (acting) but more often a Captain!!

*****

No.18/28

Regimental colour post card, on which Stanley has written, 'Greetings for 1919.'

CHAPTER SIX

1919

The Background.

The acute problems generated by the nature and speed of the collapse of the German and Austria -Hungarian Empires had their counterparts in the Middle East where, as the Ottoman Empire disintegrated, the principle of self-determination embodied in President Wilson's famous Fourteen Points was embraced as eagerly as in Central and Eastern Europe.

As the war had gone on British civil and military control of Egypt had become progressively stricter. The Egyptian people had been assured that they would not be called on actively to help the Empire defeat its enemies but the British turned to requisitioning, particularly in 1917 and 1918. For instance: the demand for labour to build roads, railways and water pipelines could be met only by the recruitment of fellahin (peasants) whose reluctance to leave their land and families was overcome, often with brutality, by native local officials at whose back stood civil and military authorities enforcing martial law. The Egyptian Expeditionary Force could not move without camel and donkey transport and the fellahin found that their precious beasts of burden were commandeered, as was their hay crop, compulsorily purchased for the fodder of the cavalry divisions. Compensation was paid and the wages of labourers and cameliers were good but the disruption and hardship endemic in a clumsy system of enforcement built up a mountain of anger and resentment. In the cities the students, clerks and lawyers complained that their chances of promotion in the civil service and the professions were blocked by the employment of Englishmen, many of whom were less well qualified than themselves. Since their arrival in the 1880s the British had proclaimed their ultimate ambition to educate the Egyptians into self-government but by 1918 it seemed that such a development had been indefinitely postponed.

There was relief among all ranks of Egyptians when the Turkish attacks on the Canal were repulsed but as the front line was pushed further into Sinai, Palestine and beyond, the war became both irrelevant to Egypt's political interests and, in the eyes of nationalists, an exercise in European imperialism. The leading exponent of Egyptian aspirations to independence was Saad Zaghlul, who had held office as Minister of Education in Lord Cromer's time but had since fallen out with the British administration. Soon after the armistice of November 1918 Zaghlul placed himself at the head of a self-appointed delegation and asked permission to go to London to present Egypt's case for self-government. Referred to the Foreign Office, Zaghlul's proposal was turned down flat, as was a similar request from Egypt's official representative, the Prime Minister, who had been a good friend of the British throughout the war. Thus were informed Egyptians taught the bitter truth that their country was of no significance in a post-war world whose leaders had many more important matters to consider. It emerged that President Wilson supported the status quo of the Protectorate and without

American sympathy Egypt was friendless. To add insult to injury Egypt found it invidious and hurtful that, by contrast, the Sharif of the Hejaz, now calling himself King, was invited to send his son Faisal to Europe, where he was received by King George V at Buckingham Palace and accepted by Wilson, Lloyd George and other Allied leaders as the Arab spokesman for the independence of Greater Syria.

Discontent in Egypt simmered in the winter of 1918-19 and boiled over when Zaghlul was arrested on March 8th and deported to Malta. There was an explosion of rage and the country lurched into anarchy; 'self-elected bodies, calling themselves Committees of Public Safety usurped the functions of authority in the towns, and Soviets of Sheikhs ruled the villages.'[1] The schoolboys and students of Cairo, numerous andvolatile, took over the streets, hijacked the trams and built barricades. Unlucky Europeans and other foreigners were assaulted; some were murdered, including eight Englishmen killed on the train bringing them back to Cairo from a visit to Luxor. The railway and telegraph systems were extensively damaged and Egyptian civil servants, either willingly or under intimidation, came out on strike.

The British Government could ignore Egypt no longer and took action. General Bulfin, Allenby's deputy, hurried down from Syria, organised mobile columns strong enough to put down armed rebellion, restored order in the countryside, repaired the railways and summarily punished those communities which had resorted to murder, thus adding to the long history of authority reacting with exemplary and arbitrary force to outrages on what native inhabitants see as armies of occupation. Allenby himself, who had been summoned to Paris to take part in discussions on the future disposition of Syria, was precipitately appointed Special High Commissioner in Egypt charged with bringing the attempted revolution to an end, inquiring into the grievances which had prompted it and meeting such as were found to be justifiable. He arrived in Cairo on March 25th; on the 31st he telegraphed London expressing his intention of releasing Zaghlul from internment, and made the public announcement to this effect on April 7th, provoking a great outburst of triumphal joy on the streets of the capital. There were some further outbreaks of lawlessness but the civil servants returned to work and the country was relatively calm by the end of May. His admirers praised the wisdom of Allenby's surprising clemency; his detractors, of whom there were many among old Egyptian 'hands' denounced the folly of giving way to violence and blamed 'that jackass' Allenby for the dangerous and humiliating loss of face suffered by all those associated with the British régime.[2]

Soon after sending Allenby back to the Residency at Cairo the hard-pressed British Government had announced that Lord Milner would lead a Commission to inquire into Egypt's long-term future, but it did not arrive until December 1919. The commissioners had been judiciously selected and were thought to be broadly sympathetic to Egypt but their terms of reference assumed the prolonging of the Protectorate and Egyptian nationalists made sure that Milner and his associates were booed and boycotted. Back at home in March 1920 the Commission began

---

[1] PG Elgood *Egypt and the Army*, Oxford, 1924, p.349.
[2] Carman & McPherson (eds.), *Bimbashi McPherson. A life in Egypt*. BBC Books, 1983, ch 14, passim.

EGYPT, 1919.

the painful process of preparing their report; by August it was ready, with the recommendation that Egypt should be granted its independence subject to the reservation of vital British interests, including the permanence of military bases and control of the Sudan. Unfortunately these recommendations were leaked before they had been put before, much less approved by, the Lloyd George Government, itself a quarrelsome coalition. In Egypt Zaghlul and other nationalist leaders competed in denouncing the concessions the British insisted on. Eighteen more months of turmoil and indecision ensued before Allenby was able on February 28th 1922 to issue a Declaration announcing that 'the British Protectorate over Egypt is terminated and Egypt is declared to be an independent sovereign state.'[3]

Stanley Goodland in 1919.

For Stanley Goodland as for many others after the Armistice of 1918 the future remained uncertain. There was a strong argument for his seeking a regular commission in the service in which, with his good record, he now felt entirely comfortable. The resumption of his interrupted civilian career in the fine art trade suggested a viable alternative, if a suitable opening could be found.

The 1919 letters convey the situation in which a conscientious war-time soldier found himself. He was guided by intense loyalty to his commanding officers, (Lt Col Cooke-Hurle who relinquished command in February, to be succeeded by Lt-Col Urwick) and to the 'dear old Regiment.' As Adjutant he was directly involved in implementing the demobilisation process; the War Diary records the departure of officers and other ranks in twos and threes and larger parties. When the Egyptian troubles began in March the Battalion had been reduced to about 200 men but the laconic entries for March 25th & 26th record the arrival of a total of nine officers and 623 other ranks from the demobilisation camp at Kantara.[4] The task of re-equipping these men, asserting authority over them and moulding them into a coherent unit must have been acutely difficult; no wonder there were 'many anxious times with the management of the mixed crowd we have with us.'

It was with this 'mixed crowd' that the 1/5 Somersets went by rail from the Canal to Cairo and on March 29th set out for Upper Egypt, some by river steamer, others escorting the construction train repairing the permanent way. It was the train party which was fired on from Shobak el Ghaffara, about 70km from Cairo, on March 31st. The terrible punishment visited on the village is described without comment in Stanley's letter 19/10.[5] After a brief concentration of all four companies at El Wasta the Battalion was again split. Two companies stayed at Beni Suef, while Battalion Headquarters and the remaining companies continued South by river steamer. Passing Beni Mazar and El Minya they reached Mallawi on April 10th, where camp was pitched near the railway station which was found to be undamaged. The villages round Mallawi were inspected, some at dawn, by parties of soldiers accompanying a British political officer. A few suspected

---

[3] Elgood, op. cit. p.369.
[4] WO 95/4690.
[5] of April 7th.

extremists were arrested and in one village a store of gunpowder was discovered, but no resistance was offered - perhaps the fate of Shobak el Ghaffara had been widely reported.

On April 21st, Easter Monday, the force at Mallawi travelled North on the restored railway to Beni Mazar and on May 9th the complete Battalion was re-united near Cairo. Later in May Battalion Headquarters and two companies removed to Suez. Demobilization resumed. In June Frank Urwick, Stanley Goodland, four more officers and eleven other ranks went to Cairo to attend a Court of Enquiry into the Battalion's activities in Upper Egypt in March and April. The hearing lasted a month and ended inconclusively when the lawyer for the prosecution failed to appear in court to make the concluding presentation of his clients' case.

Stanley's last months in Egypt were spent mainly at Port Tewfik, opposite Suez. Cricket, football and party-going occupied some of his time but he feared that the continued unrest in Egypt would still detain him. After many false hopes had been raised he and the small remaining cadre of the old Battalion at last found themselves sailing from Alexandria on Christmas Eve, 1919.

The Letters Written in 1919

No. 19/1

postmark 15 Jan 19
no address.

My dear old Elsie

I hope you wont think me unkind for not writing more often but I have no time My days are full of demobilization and already we have sent off 12 officers and nearly 200 men. Major Watson has gone and so until old Urwick comes back I am second-in-command again. The men are mostly miners students and men over 41 years of age. It is rather sad to break up the old Regiment in this way and I should have liked to have marched up through Taunton altogether but it cant be helped. In a few days I think all the men who left for India in 1914 will be sent home - and there are only 240 left out of the 800 who sailed. Of course I ought to go with this party but the Colonel wants me to stay to see the thing out so I shall be here for another 2 or 3 months I suppose. The Colonel himself is being transferred to the Home Establishment so will go home soon as he says he cant stand another hot weather in the East. We are now in camp actually on the banks of the Suez Canal - one cannot help contrasting this with last winter with all the misery and mud and rain. It is really very interesting here and I suppose the most perfect climate in the World for a month or two - we watch the great liners & transports passing by and longingly wish we were aboard. The men are very happy if a little impatient to be off - they are able to bathe and fish in the Canal and often catch some sort of salmon weighing 16lb. We had quite a good Xmas and a particularly Merry New Years Eve. We managed to get enough frozen turkeys to give the men a good feed and they had plum pudding issued with their rations. Beer was rather short but I think they all had a good drink. It is so peaceful now. You cant imagine what a relief it is to have finished with the incessant noise and anxiety of war! I wish you could see my row of ribbons now - they are so pretty. My M.C. comes first and then the 1914-1915 Star and then the Croix de Guerre - I am entitled to the Star for my service in Mespot in 1915 so I have really been very lucky so far as medals go. I hope you had a Merry Xmas and I am looking forward to your letter telling me about it - I hope Mrs. Brown was well enough to enter into things

Im afraid I have never thanked you half enough for the presents you sent me - please forgive me dear and Ill try to make it up to you one day - I am enjoying the pipe so much.

Please thank your mother for so kindly remembering me too - I will try to send her a line one day for I have so much enjoyed the Xmas Punch Frank Calway is coming to see us tomorrow - he is on his way to Luxor on leave and of course wants me to go with him - but I simply cant! Im afraid I shant get leave any more until Im finished with the Army!

I get long letters from the Milsoms they have a little flat in Harewood House in Hanover Square and I am to be Godfather to a young Milsom who arrives in June.[6] He is still lame and they have kicked him out of the Army much to his disgust. I wonder what Harold & Alice will do now. I havent heard from them since the Armistice but I imagine they will try to get home as soon as possible - perhaps I shall see them pass up the Canal one day! I hope you are fit dear girl and escaping this awful flu' - sorry to say several of our men have died of it lately - It is really very sad after living through the fighting. With best love dear girl and all good wishes

from Stan

*****

No. 19/2

(no envelope) Jan 21st. 1919
E.E.F.

My dear old Elsie

Many thanks dear girl for your last long letter of Jan 1st telling me about your Xmas and Im so glad you spent such a happy time and as you say next Xmas will be happier for all of us. Things are quieter here now the rush of getting the special men for demobilization is over and I get a little spare time and a chance of taking some riding lessons. Major Watson has gone and as the Colonel is at Port Said I am left in command of the Regiment for a few days.

We are still on the canal bank and quite near the Remounts - they are a very jolly lot and have got 6 couple of hounds out from England and hunt twice a week. I went out with them yesterday starting at 5 am and we had a grand run after a wolf[7] he gave us a 35 minute gallop across the open and then got away for horses and hounds had all had enough - I[t] was so exciting and I hope to go out once a week in future. There are plenty of foxes about and an occasional gazelle. There is a lot of shipping in the canal these days and its all very interesting and peaceful after the hell of fighting.

I was expecting Frank Calway tonight he is on his way to Luxor - lucky beggar - I wish I could go with him. My own demobilization still seems three or four months off however. Best love dear girl and all good wishes

from Stan

*****

---

[6] Darrell Milsom was born July 3rd 1919. An RAF officer, he died in a flying accident, March 1940.

[7] There are two kinds of fox which would occur in the vicinity of El Qantara: Ruppell's Sand Fox (Vulpes Rupelli) and the red fox, Vulpes Vulpes which is exactly the same animal as is found in Britain. The wolf, Canis Lupus, does occur in the Sinai Peninsula but is uncommon. It is more likely they were pursuing examples of the common jackal, Canis Aureus. From a letter from Daphne M Hills of the Natural History Museum, Mammals Section. October 16th 1995.

No. 19/3

28/1/19
no address.

My dear old Elsie

Heres another short letter to tell you I am fit and well but still no nearer demobilization! We are in the same spot watching the boats go by and there is a lot of shipping now with troops going back to Australia and some from India and Mespot going home. The Indian troops in our Division are going back to India next month so we shall cease to be a Division[8] then but I dont know what will become of us. In the meantime we continually send officers and men away. 52 went today, I daresay I shall turn up at Highcroft sooner than I imagine - I am looking forward to meeting the Browns & your two little charges. If I get back in time for your holidays I shall ask Gretchen to invite me up to Hale - unless you can spend some time at Taunton - I really think I've forgotten how to talk to a girl - the last time I spoke to one was in India going on for 2 years ago! I will enclose 2 snaps taken of the Regiment on the march a little while ago - you will find me riding with the Colonel. We had a topping hunt yesterday morning - first a fox then a wolf which ultimately got away. My old mare carries me well and seems to enjoy it altho I must ride 12st 6!

Urwick is on his way back from Ceylon at last and we expect him daily - I shall be so pleased to see his cheery face again - he has had a long holiday and I think the Colonel will go home very soon now - he wants to avoid any more hot weather out East   Many thanks dear girl for your last letters which only took 14 days to come - rather different to the old times. I shall never be able to thank you enough for writing so regularly and such cheery letters - Yes I remember well the old dances and I hope Im not too old to dance again with you in the good days ahead - but they say you are horribly out of it nowadays if you dont Jazz and foxtrot and Im not athletic enough to do either

with best love dear old girl

from Stan

*****

No. 19/4

4/2/19
E.E F

My dear old Elsie

Yesterday I went over to Port Said to attend a Divisional Conference with the Colonel - we had quite a jolly day and it was nice to see a few shops and a bit of civilization. I sent you off an amber bead necklace for your birthday with my bestest love I hope you will like it dear - I am very fond of amber and I think the colour should suit you but dont wear it until it has been re-strung - I fancy it is hardly long enough for present fashion & so some day I will find some more to lengthen it. The people in the East think amber charms away illness & evil spirits so I hope these beads will bring you the best of luck.

---

[8] 75th Division.

To day we are having an awful wind and sand storm - it is indescribable but better just now - Last night my tent blew down - it was simply ripped right away so I spent a most uncomfortable night - I think I shall be home now soon - With best love and loving birthday wishes

from Stan

*****

No. 19/5

Feb 17 1919
E E F

My dear old Elsie

Many thanks dear old girl for your last letter (Feb.4) - It is so nice to be in close touch with England once again and it will help matters so much if the mails run on as smoothly as this for the rest of the time I am out here. You will probably be home for your holidays when this reaches you and I hope you will have ever such a good time and fine weather. You will Im sure have a busy time this summer when the new arrival[9] come - Alice tells me I am to have a new nephew or niece this month and I hope all goes well with her and Mrs. Milsom writes out to say there is to be a young Milsom in June to whom I am to be Godfather. Something doing all round! Our demobilization goes steadily on - we have sent away over 200 men the last 7 days which has kept me busy in the Office and I have missed the hunting. The Colonel went yesterday -it was a sad day for those of us who have known him from the beginning - a fine soldier and a thorough Englishman it has been a pleasure and a great priviledge to have been associated with him. He wanted to get home badly and to avoid another hot weather out East and of course his New Forest hounds (of which he is MFH) are always calling him.[10] I cant say yet what the future will bring for me - I promised the Colonel before he left to stay to the end to see the old Regiment through. I am very fit and enjoying the Canal bathing. The days are stoking up already our so-called winter is over

With best love dear girl and all good wishes for your holidays

from Stan

*****

No. 19/6

Feb 25 1919
E.E.F.

My dear old Elsie

You are probably busy packing now & getting ready to be off to your holidays

I do hope you will have ever such a good time and nice weather. England seems to have had a severe winter & our fellows who went home recently have written out complaining of the cold. I do hope the sun will shine when I get back. I hope you are better dear girl - this "flu" is a nuisance - lots of men are dying out here with it. There is little news - we are still patiently 'carrying on' - I think I told you the Colonel has gone and I miss him so much. Demobilization is very slow

---

[9] Alison Brown was born on May 27th 1919.

[10] Lt-Col Cooke-Hurle was fatally injured in a New Forest hunting accident in December 1923.

130

just now - I think Headquarters are busy forming the Army of Occupation and havent time for anything else. I hope you spent a happy birthday dear and that the amber beads I sent you turned up. I shall think of you at Hale this next fortnight - please remember me to you mother & sisters & give Christine a kiss from her uncle - with kindest thoughts and best love

from Stan

*****

No. 19/7

Mar 3 1919
E.E.F.

My dear old Elsie

I was so very sorry to hear in your last letter that you were laid up in bed - I do so hope you got better quite quickly and that it has not prevented you going away for your holidays - I am thinking of you at Hale now & hoping the weather is kind - what a dreadful winter you have had.

Thank you dear so much for the 'Bystander' which I havent seen for months & months and which I enjoyed so much. Things are very much 'as you were' and we still patiently sit on the Canal bank - I hear they have been asking questions in Parliament about the Somerset L.I.[11] - so that may hasten our demobilization. Yesterday the New Zealand with Admiral Jellicoe passed through - it was thrilling sight and our men turned out and gave the Navy a good cheer which was loudly returned - the Canal is very busy now - 8 big liners have passed this afternoon - the hunting is over worst luck - but the weather is too hot now for scent - horses & hounds - I shall miss the early morning gallops - the Colonel must be well on his way home now - we miss him so much - but Urwick of course 'carries on' well and I suppose I shall be Major again soon!

With best love dear girl
from Stan

*****

---

[11] These questions concerned the 1/4 (not the 1/5) Somerset Light Infantry in Mesopotamia who had had no home leave since embarking in October 1914 and, as part of the Wessex Division, had been promised by the late Lord Kitchener if they volunteered for service overseas they would be 'brought home before the end of the war' to resume employment 'before the great rush took place.' (Hansard February 19th 1919).

No. 19/8

My dear old Elsie

Very many thanks dear girl for your last letter from Liverpool (Mar 5) and I am so glad your rash has gone and that you are feeling really better. I do hope you have had a nice holiday - at any rate you must have enjoyed being with your people again and it is nice that your are able to send such a good report of Greta and her little family. I hope you will return to Highcroft strong and ready for your strenuous summer We are living in a state of war out here again - isnt it a nuisance! I wonder if the home papers have told you anything about the unrest among the Egyptians - they are ungrateful swine and I hate them all we have made their country rich & prosperous & filled their pockets with money and now they are shouting "Egypt for the Egyptians" & murdering Europeans all over the country. They must be taught a lesson and I wish they would publicly hang the ring leaders It will delay our demobilization and home coming & upset everything

The mounted troops and armoured cars are out and we have been cut off from Cairo & Alexandria for several days owing to the railway and telegraph lines being cut. The Australians & New Zealanders who were due to sail for home in a day or two have been mobilized again and gone off into the country and they are mad about it and have sworn to kill 200 Egyptians for every white casualty! I hope the winter at home is nearly over & Im trying to imagine how beautiful the country will soon look - Youll have to be patient some time longer Im afraid before you see me - If I have to stay out here another year I shall try to get leave during the summer but everything is at present very unsettled and uncertain We are still on the Canal bank and our few remaining men are kept busy patrolling the railway & used as guards and escorts - it is really a very busy time. The Australian Navy passed through yesterday on their way home - it was an interesting sight and we gave them a good cheer.

With best love dear girl & all good wishes

from Stan

*****

No. 19/9

My dear old Elsie

Just a few hurried lines to tell you I am off on yet another campaign I think I told you in a letter a few days ago that there was very serious trouble in Egypt We were hurriedly trained to Cairo and are now off in a few hours right down into Southern Egypt to fight the Bedouins. The rail is destroyed so we are going down some hundred of miles by steamer on the old Nile It has been a wonderful time of preparation and Ive had no rest - Im cursing too because I thought the fighting was all over for me for all time

We had demobilized practically all our men - just 200 left - and suddenly all demobilization was stopped and the thousands of men in the Demob camp were drafted into any Unit consequently we are made up to 800 strong with all sorts and look a very funny crowd - weve got Scotties - Connaught Rangers - Yeomanry - Rifle Brigade It isnt like our old men and its a hell of job to get proper organisation & discipline I pity any Egyptian or Arab we come up against - I dont think there will be many prisoners taken!! for our tempers are none too good

Hurriedly we had to change from winter kit to summer helmets and cotton uniforms and I am reduced to 30lb of kit again

However dear girl I must keep smiling It is difficult to get definite orders - I understand we are going off into the blue and may be out for quite 2 months I dont know if I shall be able to write and what makes me feel perfectly miserable is that none of your letters will reach me for ages - I shall always be thinking of you & longing for the time when I shall see you again

With best love

from Stan

*****

No.19/10

April 7th. 1919
no address

My dear old Elsie

So much has happened in the last week or so that I cant remember when I wrote you last - I think however I sent a few lines before leaving Cairo at any rate I meant to but everything was so hurried

I am very fit and we are having a really wonderful trip - I believe rich tourists pay hundreds of pounds for this in peace time

At present we are about half way between Cairo and Assouan and up to now we have only had one little battle - this was on Mar 31st. we had gone inland a little way to guard a construction train which was repairing the railway and were suddenly fire[d] on from a village about 3 hundred yards away - We of course immediately formed up and went to the attack and quickly cleared the village and after rescuing the women and children set the place on fire. We only had 8 men wounded and we left 57 Arabs dead and must have wounded a good many too The village was rich with geese - fowls - vegetables & sheep and of course we looted the whole lot and lived like princes for a few days   Since then we have gone steadily down [up] river on steamers and have met with little trouble - there are a few towns however near us now where there has been a good deal of unrest & where they have murdered white men and women

We shall surround these towns and try to find the leaders and shoot them - the damage done to the railway is enormous   Nearly every station has been looted & burnt and the rails torn up for miles.

It is so pretty as we go along but of course its getting hotter every day The cultivation near the river is wonderful - already the crops are golden

133

We are such a mixed Regiment now - I wish we had our own old crowd - we only had 200 or so of our own men left - so we have had 600 men from the demobilization camps pushed at us - they are all Regular soldiers & weve got Manchesters - Connaught Rangers - H.L.I. - Seaforths - Royal Irish etc. - They are very wild especially the Irishmen and of course are frightfully fed up because their demobilization has been stopped

I am looking forward so much to your letters but goodness knows how or when a mail will come - except through aeroplane we seem altogether cut off from the world

Goodbye dear girl I hope you feel ever so fit after your holiday

With best love

from Stan

*****

No. 19/11

April 16 1919
no address

My dear old Elsie

I wonder if my last letters have reached you - it is doubtful and of course no letters from you have come - it is simply sickening to be cut off from the world again like this. I am at a place called Mallawi now it is close to a place called Deirut where a lot of officers were murdered on March 16th. on their return from a holiday at Luxor

I wish you could see this place and that we were having a jolly river trip in ordinary peace time - it is so different now and one goes about in terror of having ones throat cut by a fierce Arab. Old Urwick and I have got such comfortable quarters now - we are living in a large bungalow belonging to an Irrigation Official - there is a beautiful garden with all sorts of lovely trees and palms - the roses are a sight - hundreds of them in full bloom - but of course they dont smell like the English ones - I suppose the sun saps all their smell away - geraniums stocks and all sorts of flowers I cant name are looking just like a show garden - I expect we shant stay here long - a soldier never does when he happens to be comfortable - at least that is my experience

We have had little trouble since I last wrote you but the unrest is still far from satisfactory - we have had to raid several villages in the district and arrest suspects. It has meant a good deal of night work and tiring days

It is six o'clock and the sun is going down into the desert - the pink lights over the sand mountains are wonderful - I fancy I have read descriptions of this in novels - one sees camels and palm trees on all sides - I wish I could sketch. I am very well but have many anxious times with the management of the mixed crowd we have with us There is no news of the length of time we shall be down here - I hope we shall get back to better civilization and a little cooler climate before long

Are the English papers saying anything about our doings - perhaps as usual everything is very hush-hush

Goodbye dear girl with best love

from Stan

*****

No. 19/12

28th. April 1919
no address

My dear old Elsie

I hear there may be a chance of getting some letters away tomorrow so I am sending you a few lines to let you know I am fit and well. Since I last wrote we have moved a few miles nearer Cairo to a place called Beni Mazar - it is in the Minia district where there has been a good deal of trouble. We were all quite sorry to leave Mallawi and our very nice bungalow and altho we are living in a house here it is not half so comfortable and there is a particularly vicious kind of mosquito which is a cursed nuisance.

Old Urwick was left at Minia to conduct the trials of prisoners and will probably be away some time - so I am in command of the troops here - I have got under me - as well as my own men - a squadron of Australian Light Horse - a section of Machine Guns and a section of Sappers & Miners It is quite a nice little command and the people better look out if they give any trouble for everyone is feeling very bloodthirsty. I do wish this rotten unrest here would end so that we could go back to Alex or Ismailia for the summer & get more comfortable and away from the awful heat of Upper Egypt - however one has to be patient. I wish too that they would send some thousands of Army of Occupation men out from home so that our men could be demobilized - it is a shame! I wonder where you are now - perhaps still away in Surrey Anyhow I hope you are very well and I am longing to get your letters - there must be at least 4 for me somewhere Best love dear girl

from Stan

*****

No. 19/13

May 6th. 1919
Upper Egypt

My dear old Elsie

I am thankful to say our job here is nearly over - In a few days, possibly the 8th we are going back to Cairo and getting rid of all these troublesome demobilizable men and getting made up with our proper Army of Occupation men. We shall then be able to start training and organising our New Battalion. I am looking forward ever so much to finding 4 or 5 letters waiting from you - it has been horrible to be cut off from everybody for so long. I wonder where you are now - you must be back in Highcroft again - I hope you and all the Brown family are very fit The Gippies in these parts are quite cowed and peaceful now but I fancy it is only skin

135

deep and at any moment a very serious outbreak may occur - the position is critical and I really dont know what the outcome will be. The World seems very loathe to settle down doesnt it? Im very fit and some days quite enjoy my varied experiences but Im very fed up too sometimes and want to get home badly

Cheerio dear girl Ill write you a decent letter from the comfy Turf Club Cairo before long I hope

Best love

from Stan

*****

No. 19/14

May 21 1919
Suez

My dear old Elsie

My dreams of a comfortable time in Cairo with lunches at the Turf Club and dinner at Shepheards were quickly dashed to the ground for here we are at Suez the last place God ever made I should think!

But we are seeing more of the world and I should think few Battalions in the War have done more travelling than we   I was only able to go into Cairo once to do some hurried shopping and to see Karl - I had tea with him and spent about an hour   He was very well but of course frightfully love sick and home sick. We were kept on tender hooks all the time expecting a hurried move so we could not do much or wander very far   We arrived here 2 days ago and now I hope we shall get a bit of peace   It is really too hot to do much and we will just have to exist until about next November   There is a good deal of trouble and unrest here - all the docks people are on strike and the Student class very riotous. Did I thank you dear for all your letters and the book you so kindly sent me - I have loved those naval yarns and I shall read them again - the childrens party on board the Battleship is a charming yarn I think

I am wondering so much if Alice and Harold will soon be passing through - I do hope they will send me word and I shall try to go along to Port Said with them. I hope you are fit dear girl and that you are having summer weather at last - I do wish I could get home but it seems almost impossible at present - I should love to be home for Whitsun - I try to keep my pecker up

Best love dear girl

from Stan

*****

136

No. 19/15

My dear old Elsie

I am so delighted to get your letters and Tatlers regularly now - it makes such a difference to ones existence in this God forsaken country!

Very many thanks dear girl. Its Whit Monday - they are having great doings at home and at the old School[12] - I should love to be there - Since I last wrote I have been up at Kantara - 250 men came out from home for us and I was ordered to go and fetch them and sort them out. Tomorrow old Urwick and I have to go to Cairo to give evidence in a Court of Enquiry. The natives of Upper Egypt have made accusations against the British Troops who went down in March and we have to refute them - they accuse us of violence - rape - theft and all sorts of things and I see they have been asking questions in Parliament[13] - It makes me wish we had killed more of the swine. The[y] produce witnesses who are paid to lie and I believe women are going to appear at the Court who will swear they were raped. It is disgusting and makes me so angry. Our men wouldnt dream of touching the women and children. I will try to write you again from Cairo

My Colonel called to see the old Pater a little while ago - The Territorial Force Assoc. is trying to get the cadre of the 1/5th. home so I may be sailing before long. They are also persuading me to stay on as adjutant of the new Battalion at home! Best love dear girl

from Stan

*****

No. 19/16

June 19 1919
Turf Club Cairo

My dear old Elsie

I think I told you I was going to Cairo to give evidence in a Court of Enquiry so here I am enjoying a thoroughly luxurious time with old Urwick.

The enquiry is likely to last another week - there are about 60 of these damned Egyptians all swearing the most abominable lies. It is really ludicrous to see the awful looking women - black as coal and ugly as sin - who come up and swear they were raped by British Tommies - It is all a put up job by the Nationalist party out here. However it gives Urwick and I a very pleasant holiday.

We are down at the Court in the morning - afternoons we go to the Sporting Club and watch the Cricket & polo. I wish I had brought my flannels up as I

---

[12] 'The School Commemoration in 1919 was, not unnaturally, a solemn affair. Dr. Whittaker [Headmaster since 1899] preached most eloquently at the special service when the roll of the dead was called [He] was visibly moved as he evoked the homes left desolate...' John Brown *Independent Witness*, Taunton 1997, p.246.
[13] Hansard records a long debate on May 15th 1919 concerning behaviour of British troops and expressing confidence that they would not have practised violence, rape, theft, etc.

should have been able to play games - the last time I played for the Regiment versus Suez I made 102 not out - so I've still got a good eye I'm glad to say. Your letters come very quickly and regularly now & the Tatlers too many thanks, dear girl.

And do you know - I really think I shall be home soon - We have just been told that the Cadres of all 1st. Line pre-war Territorial Units like ourselves are to go home as soon as possible in order to reconstruct the new Territorial Army. This means I shall go with the Cadre and all the records - papers and property - If they want me to stay on as Adjutant for a year or so at home I think I shall do so and in the meantime look out for something to definitely settle down in. I am wondering if the old Boche is going to sign.[14]

No news of Harold & Alice passing through yet - I may be home first after all - Cheerio and best love dear girl

from Stan

*****

No. 19/17

June 21st. 1919
Majestic Hotel Alexandria

My dear old Elsie

I seem to be always on the move now. Soon after I posted my last letter to you I was ordered to go to Alexandria to see Army Headquarters about some details connected with the Regiment - principally about demobilization & reinforcements etc. I have had my interview this morning and am going to the Races this afternoon and back to Cairo by the night train. I was thinking of you this morning when walking along these wonderful shops and I was tempted to buy you a wonderful dressing gown in pink and embroidered by the ladies of the Harem here - also a string of Lapis Lazuli beads[15] which are very hard to get now-a-days - Please accept these with my fondest love and as a little thank offering for all youve done for me and especially for what youve been to me thro all these horribly [sic] years of war. I thought the beads would look best strung between your amber ones they will make the necklace a better length. But you must do as you like with them - only they are much more valuable than the amber beads. G.H.Q. told me today they thought that I should be on my way home with the jolly old cadre soon. The Court of Inquiry in Cairo is going as well as possible for us - the native witnesses are getting tied into splendid knots - the old women are most amusing - they come and swear they were raped by the Tommies and go into minute details! I should have to blush if it wasnt all so horribly false - I hope I shall back a winner this afternoon but I never get much luck and these damned Egyptian jockeys wont ride "straight" and honest

Best love dear girl from Stan

---

[14] The Treaty of Versailles was signed on June 28th 1919 between the Allies and Associated Powers (which included the USA) and Germany.

[15] The pink dressing gown and Lapis Lazuli beads are still in the family, 1998.

No. 19/18

July 4 1919
Turf Club, Cairo

[Stamped: 'Passed by Base Censor E.E.F.']

My dear old Elsie

I am still in Cairo but hope to return to the Regiment two days hence. It is very nice here and so luxurious but frightfully expensive!

I was under cross examination from a Gippy barrister for two days - it was very fatiguing and I felt more like hitting him than answering his damn silly questions!

The Court has already found out that natives have been bribed and threatened with death if they dont appear to give false evidence - the Nationalist Party here are really the scum of the Earth!! My dear Ive had my photo taken as you wished [see frontispiece] - it was dreadful ordeal - I will send it along when ready - I hope the parcel from Alex has rolled up.

Glad you enjoyed the summer weather - I remember how burnt you used to get with a white mark on you cheek where your bonnet strings used to come. It is good news too that Mrs. Brown and the new baby are getting on well - I'm sure you must be having a very busy time.

No more news yet of the Cadre going home but I will send you a cable when I know something definite.

I get many cheery letters from the old Pater still - his last was full of the Whitsun gatherings at the School.

Karl is in hospital again - I have been to see him two or three times - I wish they would invalid him home for he will never be fit in this country.[16]

Many thanks dear girl for your last letters and Tatlers - Eve's letters are better than ever and I love her descriptions of the ladies summer fashions!!

Best love from Stan

*****

No. 19/19

July 19 1919
Port Tewfik

My dear old Elsie

Im afraid I have missed writing to you the last two weeks but since I have been back from Cairo I have been seedy with what we call Nile boils and have felt so depressed that Ive written no letters. I cant describe quite what Nile boils are like - they are sort of sceptic [sic] sores - nasty hard things the size of a pigeons egg. I thought I should have to spoil my record and go into Hospital but the medical orderly here has made hot fomentations almost hourly for me and I am now practically fit again. I suppose my blood is a bit wrong but after 5 years in the East that is not to be wondered at. I have been back with the Regiment about 10 days

---

[16] Karl returned home in November 1919.

now and was very glad to return. The Court of Inquiry was really a "wash out" in the end - the last 2 days were given over to the Barristers on either side to make their summing up speeches. Our man gave his address quite well and the day following the Native Barrister was billed to give his address - the Court assembled in due course but the Native Barrister failed to appear & so the Court simply closed - the native wrote to say he had a more pressing engagement. It only shows how futile the whole thing was. I believe the Military Authorities are now going to take action for perjury against some of the native witnesses. What worries me and annoys me so is that this possibly will mean that Ive got to stay in this rotten country until these new proceedings are over - however I try to keep cheerful in spite of Nile Boils. The night before I left Cairo they had a great victory dinner and dance at Shepheards. Urwick and I went of course and it was really a very wonderful show. I'll enclose the dinner menu if I can find it. The dancing was extraordinary and quite frightened me. We didnt dance at all - in fact Im sure I could not possibly do these funny new Jazz steps - the attitudes of the dancers were so intricate and looked more like a perpetual cuddle than anything else - as the old lady in Punch said "I hope they really love one another". The Peace celebrations here on July 14th/15th were quite a success and the men had a good time The French people who are very influential here gave a sort of carnival but I wasnt well enough to go. Todays mail brought 2 letters from you June 28th. and July 7th. also a lovely Tatler - Many thanks dear girl Ive been reading the Tatler this afternoon & have enjoyed it - I think Eve and Silent Friends better than ever. The mail also brought news of the birth of my god son - the Milsoms baby - everything going well thank goodness - but strange to say the kiddie was born on July 3rd. which is the same day the one that died in India was born! News from home continues good - I fancy Greta is there now - Marco West[17] has been staying at Elm Grove. Taunton seems to be waking up and is quite gay with tennis and dances. Muriel Wrenn was married on July 10th. - quite a big affair I believe[18] - I must turn in now into my little camp bed. It is very very hot here now, quite the worst time of the year

Cheerio dear girl - with best love

from Stan

*****

No. 19/20

Aug 8th. 1919
Port Tewfik

My dear old Elsie

Another week of Army of Occupation and waiting for "Der Tag". I have no more news of my home coming except a long letter from the Colonel today telling me all about the new Regulations for the Territorial Force and saying that I am

---

[17] Female friend of 'the Babe'.

[18] Muriel Wrenn, the eldest daughter of Alderman W A Wrenn, had performed in the pre-war Taunton Operatic Society. She was married to Mr Arthur Walker of Liverpool at St Mary's Church, Taunton.

bound to be home very soon now. Unfortunately men & officers seem so scarce that we have little hope of any more men being sent out here from home and altho the country appears to be quiet there is in reality a great deal of discontent and rifles are being smuggled into Egypt in large quantities so that any day fresh trouble may break out. I wonder what you are doing now - it is Saturday evening and it has been a broiling day - now it has developed into a sand storm and I am in my tent getting what shelter I can but in a short time everything including my little camp bed will be covered an inch thick with desert sand - It's a cursed country this - And yet it can be lovely some times Last night for instance Mrs. Norman the wife of the British Consul here gave a wonderful picnic up the Canal on her launch

I can[t] describe the beauty of a full night moon on the water here & it was so delightful we did not get back until 2.30 am. We went about 30 miles & landed & played twos & threes and other childrens games after supper There were about 10 ladies & 12 men in the party - we had a gramophone and sang all the way home One record took my fancy so much - it was song by Violet Lorraine in the "Bing Girls" - I think called "So he followed me". I hope my photo will reach you and that you will like it - Old Urwick thought it very good - you will have to make it do until you see me in the flesh & blood a little later on

Goodbye dear old girl with best love

from Stan

*****

No. 19/21

Aug 21st.1919
Port Tewfik

My dear old Elsie

I was so glad to hear the parcel has reached you at last as I was so afraid it had been stolen - I am very pleased too that you liked the things so much. So glad you are going away to Newport in September but I fancy it wont be much of a holiday for you with all your babies to look after.

Since I last wrote I have been up to Cairo to play in a cricket match for my Divisional team of which I am Captain - had a very good time - I took Karl out to dinner at Sheppherds - he is so pale and thin but is actually going home next week so Babe will be happy at last.

I quite expect to have definite news of my home coming very soon now so you must be patient a bit longer dear girl - I am wondering so much what you will think of me in my photo

Great excitement here a few days ago - the boiler of an Italian warship,[19] which was a anchored in the Canal 500 yds from our Mess, burst and she sunk in 10 minutes - more than 100 poor devils were blown to bits - It was all very distressing

---

[19] Lloyds Agent at Port Said telegraphed on Thursday that the Suez Canal has been blocked since the afternoon of the previous day through the Italian Warship *Basilicata* (a small cruiser of 2560 tons) having sunk near Port Tewfik after an explosion. *The Times*, August 16th 1919.

Glad to say I am quite fit again now and enjoying bathing and games but its damned hot and I long to feel a drop of good English rain on my face.

Cheerio dear girl, Best love

from Stan

*****

No. 19/22

Aug 28th. 1919
Port Tewfik

My dear old Elsie

Many thanks dear girl for your last letter (Aug 12) and the Tatler I am still patiently waiting for news of my home-going - I hope the Territorial Appointments at home have been made by this time and if I have got the Adjutancy I shall surely get a cable soon ordering me home. I have got my English uniforms al[l] brushed and ready and am longing for the day to come I went to Kantara last Saturday to play cricket and saw Karl again - he was at the Demob Camp and by this time I expect he is well on his way home Wont the Babe be excited I will enclose a snap shot of our officers football team - it was taken 4 evenings ago when we played a match against the Sergeants and won by 6 - 0. It is very very hot but we play games every evening for it is the only way to keep fit in this country & then we have a gorgeous shower bath fitted up which refreshes us for dinner - We are really a very cheery lot of officers and get a good deal of fun one way and another

My boils are well now thank goodness with the exception of one on my neck - this doesnt worry me - its when they come on the place one sits down with that they are so uncomfortable I believe Frank Calway has gone home this week - he will probably be getting married very soon - they have been engaged about seven years - awful long time isnt it!

I hope you are well dear girl & not having too many fights with the other P.C.Governesses[20]

Best love

from Stan

*****

---

[20] P.C. stands for Princess Christian. (Elsie was a P.C. trained children's nurse). Family legend includes no record of fights with other governesses.

No. 19/23

My dear old Elsie

Very many thanks dear girl for your last letter Sept 3rd. received yesterday &
for the birthday present and good wishes. I shall find the little leather case so
useful and am actually using it to keep my Piastre notes in.

It is very sweet of you to send me such a nice present for I feel I dont deserve
it in the least. We are having a very special dinner at Mess on the 22nd. and I
expect it will be a very gay night. I did not write to you last week for Ive been
daily expecting news of our home-going - this has come at last for we have had a
warning order saying the Regiment is to be relieved by a Regular Battalion and
reduced to a cadre by the end of this month. This is of course grand news and with
any luck I should be home by the middle of October - We have no orders yet as to
the composition of the Cadre but I shall either go home with it or quite
independently with Urwick I have been busy today looking out my warm clothes
for I expect to feel very chilly in England this winter. I am thinking of you now
at Parrog[21] and hoping you are having fine weather and a real good time

I will keep you posted up with my movements[22] and will send you a cable as
soon as I know a definite date of sailing

Again many thanks dear girl for your birthday wishes & the present

With best love

from Stan

*****

No. 19/24

My dear old Elsie

Five years ago yesterday I sailed from Southampton! Isnt it dreadful to think
of. When I last wrote I think I told you there was definite news of our relief. The
days go quickly by and nothing has happened - Today we are told the relieving
Regt. arrives on the 14th. When they come we shall have to deal with all our
non-demobilizable men - about 300. They are going to the Hampshires at
Khartoum and will go by sea from here to Port Sudan. All this will take time and
I am so fed up that I wonder now if I shall be home for Xmas! Also the Gippies
threaten another rising when the Milner Commission arrives. But I still hope for
the best and for the day when I can send you a cable. Many thanks dear girl for
your last letter (Sept 18) written at Newport. I do hope you had a real good time
and it must have been nice for you to have Leila[22] with you. What a long motor

---

[21] Newport Bay, Dyfed.
[22] Leila Hyde (1896-1982) youngest sister of Elsie.

journey you had! We have been watching with interest the progress of the Railway Strike[23] & wonder what the end will be - the public seem to be playing up well. The Major & I have hired a dinkie little boat & I have been doing a lot of sailing & deep sea fishing - it is great fun. One day last week we caught 148 fish! Thank goodness the weather is cooling at last & these lovely Eastern moonlight nights are simply fascinating

Best love dear girl

from Stan

*****

No. 19/25

Nov. 4 1919
Port Tewfik

My dear old Elsie

Many thanks dear girl for your last letters - up to Oct 21st. - I have not written much for everyday I hope definite sailing orders will come - I think there is no doubt now that we shall sail from Port Said either the 19th. or 26th. Nov. but I will of course send you a cable - as far as I can see Harold & I will arrive home practically the same day which will be very nice and you can imagine how happy the old Pater will be.

The new Regiment has taken over all our quarters and we are now reduced to 4 officers and 46 men - this party I hope will march up through old Taunton as the Cadre of the Regiment - What a day that will be? Cant you get down for it - and what about Xmas dear girl - can you spend it at Elm Grove? I have written to Gretchen to say she simply must get down for it. There have been some very serious riots in Alexandria & minor ones everywhere - we live in very exciting times for the feeling against the British is very very bitter - I only hope we shall be clear away before Milner arrives - I have been mixed up in enough trouble & strife to last me my lifetime Our heavy baggage is going home all the way by sea & everything is packed up & ready - we shall go via Marseilles - so should reach home about 10 days after leaving Port Said. You will be pleased to hear G.H.Q. have decided at last to make me an Acting Major from last Feb 27th, & old Urwick an Acting Lieut. Colonel so that is very nice and will give me quite a nest egg of back pay

Harold reaches here about Nov. 17th. & I am wondering so much if I shall see him - possibly they may put us in his ship!

Best love dear girl

from Stan

*****

---

[23] Railway strike September 26th to October 5th 1919.

144

No. 19/26

Nov 29. 1919
Port Tewfik

My dear old Elsie

We are still in the same old spot - wondering & wondering when our orders will come. The country is so unsettled & feeling is so bitter against us at present that G.H.Q. are very nervous about depleting the E.E.F. of troops. Still I am going to Cairo on Monday to see G.H.Q. and hope to get some definite news then - they have promised to get us home before Xmas so they will soon have to get a move on. The brightest news I can send you is that I am now a Major and dated back to Feb 27th. - which is of course very nice - Urwick is a Colonel from the same date and we are very delighted. We are giving a little dance tonight as a sort of celebration of our promotion and a farewell. I wish you could just slip over for it. I have learnt the Jazz roll for the occasion - about 70 guests will be there and all the Sisters are coming - they are not allowed to dance in public really - but this is a private affair and we have called it an "At Home". I was delighted to see Harold Alice & the baby as they passed through - the Baby[24] is a beauty - Alice wasnt very well & was in bed so we had a cheery time in the cabin. I thought Harold looked very war-worn - much more so than I. I dont know what to say about my plans when I get home - if I get the appointment of Adjutant of the new Regiment I shall have to get busy almost at once but when Xmas is over I mean to put in a week or so with Greta at Hale. If I dont get the appointment I shall take a longer holiday & then go to London to see what business openings there are about. Many thanks dear girl for letters & Tatlers. I hear that Marseilles is closed down & that we shall probably go home all the way by sea.

Best love

from Stan

*****

No.19/27

Dec 6 1919
Port Tewfik

My dear old Elsie

Just a few more lines to let you know that the people at G.H.Q. have promised to send us to Port Said on Dec 8th. That will be a step in the right direction but I'm now told there isn't a boat going home until Dec 17th. and in that case we shall spend our Xmas at sea & arrive home about New Years Eve. It's simply sickening but G.H.Q. are very nervous about things out here and are not at all keen on sending us away at all. Cairo was very nice & full of people - I was only there a day and a half and had a great rush round settling up Regimental business & buying some clothes for myself.

But it isn't at all safe - there is shooting going on in the streets & very bitter feeling against us - it is a God-forsaken country. Best love dear girl

from Stan

---

[24] John Goodland, born in Burma February 28th 1919, died November 18th 1978.

No. 19/28

My dear old Elsie

Just a few lines to let you know we have got a move on at last and arrived here yesterday - thank goodness we are now a step nearer home

We do not know yet when we embark but there is a boat leaving Alexandria on the 17th. and we hope to get on her - this means Im afraid that we shall spend Xmas at sea which is of course a bitter disappointment to us all but Im sure weve pulled every available string in this country to get away earlier

I think we go home all the way by sea so we shall probably reach England somewhere about New Years Eve - I shall most likely spend Xmas in the neighbourhood of Gibraltar - tossing about and feeling anything but festive! We had a wonderful send off from Suez yesterday and I shall never forget it - all the Station turned out to see us off - We were inspected by the "Base Commandant" and Bands came down and played and people put out flags in our honour - we were very friendly with the R.A.F. at Suez and they sent a formation of planes to escort our train as far as Ismailia - I think old Urwick & I were snap shotted 100 times - and we really felt quite like Royalty.

Im sure no one had a more hearty 'send off' - all through the war wherever we have been weve made friends and there are some at Suez who I hope to meet again at home some day

I came across Jack Harcombe today - he is an old Taunton School pal who I daresay you have met - he is on his way to East Africa & came on shore on the chance of seeing me and I came across him in the main street by great good luck

I shall be thinking of you at Xmas time dear girl and wishing you the very best - and it will not be many days now before we meet again

Best love dear girl

from Stan

*****

No. 19/29

[Regimental Christmas Card]

A Merry Christmas
and
A Happy New Year

from Stan

No. 19/30
Cable dated Port Said 22nd. 4 pm handed in 11.40 am received at
Minchinhampton
11.56 am 26 Dec 19.
addressed:
To Hyde Highcroft M'hampton

"Sailing Alexandria on Teutonic"[25] 24th

Goodland

*****

No. 19/31
Telegram handed in Plymouth 4.15pm received Minchinhampton 5.15pm
6 Jan 20.

To Hyde Highcroft M'hampton

"Arrived safe and well best love Stan"

END OF LETTERS

---

[25] *SS Teutonic*, 4611 reg. tonnage, managed by White Star Line for the Shipping Controller. Built 1889 in Belfast.

HOMECOMING

Writing on November 4th (letter 19/25) Stanley had suggested to Elsie that she try to be in Taunton for the homecoming of the cadre of the 1/5 Somersets.[1] It is not known when they were re-united but Stanley's return to Taunton was a low-key occasion. He was one of the party of ten, of all ranks, which reached Taunton Station at about 10.30 pm on January 6th; the remainder of the cadre had gone straight from Plymouth to a demobilisation centre.

There was no marching through Taunton but next day there was a civic reception and luncheon for which the three officers, two warrant officers and five private soldiers paraded, with the support of the Depôt band. The Mayor presided and the guests included many officers who had come home earlier, including EF Cooke-Hurle, now a full Colonel. He was among those who made speeches, followed by Frank Urwick, Stanley Goodland and the wag of the party, Private WS Hayes. Stanley reflected 'that hitherto I thought the proudest moment of my life was when I marched off in 1914 in the uniform of the Somerset Light Infantry. I feel that that moment has been eclipsed now that I have marched back to my native town as one of the representatives of that fine old Regiment'. The idea for what became *The Book of Remembrance* was already in his mind: 'I hope some day someone will set down in writing and in detail the full record of the Regiment in the Great War. I think it would be a good thing for the people of Somerset . . .'[2]

---

[1] See also letter 16/14.

[2] *Somerset County Gazette*, January 10th 1920.

AFTERWORD

Stanley and Elsie were married at the Unitarian Chapel, Hale Barns, on September 18th 1920. They made their first home in Golders Green; later, they moved to Merton Park and then to Wimbledon - each of these last two houses standing within a mile of the family home of Harry and Babs Milsom.

It is probable that before the wedding Stanley had found employment in the West End showroom of Malletts of Bath, distinguished dealers in fine art. He remained with Malletts for the rest of his working life as a partner and, when it became a limited company, a director and eventually managing director. Early in 1930 he undertook a pioneering visit to the United States. His base was New York City but he also went to Philadelphia, Pittsburgh and Boston. He had with him some old silver and a portfolio of photographs of furniture. Despite the Depression which followed the recent Wall Street crash he did successful business with dealers and private collectors, greatly strengthening Malletts' connection with the American market. William Randolph Hearst became a good customer and, at home, that avid collector of antiques, HM Queen Mary, valued Stanley's judgment, awarding him a personal warrant which Malletts displayed until his retirement.

Stanley's loyalty to the 'dear old Regiment' was lifelong. He kept in touch with his old comrades and, until Frank Urwick's death in 1936 there was a special reunion of Messrs Urwick, Milsom, Goodland and their wives every November. Stanley also attended the annual commemoration service for the Buffs, held in August in Canterbury Cathedral. He was equally devoted to Taunton School and its Old Boys Association. For many years he played for the Old Boys in their annual Whitsun cricket match against the School XI. He supported the rugby football club of the London Old Tauntonians, helping them to buy a playing field at Ruislip, Middlesex, where a new pavilion was built.

From 1939 to 1945 Stanley worked in Civil Defence, becoming Chief Air Raid Warden for the City of Westminster. Though the most valuable of Malletts' stock was stored underground in Bath he kept open the showroom at 40 New Bond Street and lived there in a gloomy flat on an upper floor. Elsie remained in Wimbledon, working at the first aid post established at the headquarters of the Lawn Tennis Association. Each came unscathed through the Blitz and V1 and V2 bombardments. At the outbreak of war, their children were evacuated to Bath to stay with a member of the Mallett family.

Stanley retired in 1952 and he and Elsie bought a West Somerset cottage in the area to which he had been sent as a recruiting officer in 1914. They both lived long lives. When they married in 1920 Stanley was on the eve of his 37th birthday and Elsie was 31. Yet they were able to celebrate their golden wedding day in 1970. They each died aged 90, Stanley in 1974 and Elsie in 1979. They are lovingly remembered by their two children and their spouses, and by seven grandchildren.

APPENDIX

The El Jib Affair

The Book of Remembrance of the 1/5 Somerset Light Infantry provides a factual account of five and a half years service. The Battalion's War Diary, written by Frank Calway from May to October 1917 and thereafter by Stanley Goodland, records events in the obligatory laconic and dispassionate style. This Diary is in the Public Record Office, file WO 95/4690 which contains the papers of the 233rd Infantry Brigade. For example, Brigade Orders survive, in all their close detail, for the night raid of October 6th 1917 as does a copy of Lt-Col Cooke-Hurle's report on that 'stunt' written immediately after its successful conclusion.

As well as Stanley Goodland's letters to Elsie, and the letter he wrote to 'the Pater' which was printed in the *Somerset County Gazette* on January 26th 1918, two more documents add colourful detail to the story of the 1/5 Battalion's campaign in Palestine. Harry Milsom wrote, *'My Experiences During the Operations in Palestine, October 18th to November 30th 1917.'* This exists in a number of typescript copies and was begun soon after the events described and completed during his convalescence in England as he recovered from the severe wound sustained in the attack on El Jib. A junior officer's tale, it is uninhibited in its revelation of the excitements, confusions and miseries of war. When on leave in Ceylon Frank Urwick wrote and printed 'for private circulation' a 24-page pamphlet entitled, *'Some Fighting in Palestine' by A Major (Acting Lt-Col) DSO of the Light Infantry.'* This senior officer's record is more restrained but no less vivid than Harry Milsom's. A few days before the start of his final illness Stanley Goodland, then almost blind, asked that Frank Urwick's booklet be read to him. Some of the comments he then made, 56 years on, were duly noted and are reproduced here.

Milsom's and Urwick's accounts are too lengthy to be quoted in full but there now follows part of their description of the most glorious and tragic episode in the Battalion's wartime history - the attempt to capture El Jib.

The 1/5 Battalion had already distinguished itself in the sharp action of El Mesmiyeh on November 13th. As Lt-Col Cooke-Hurle had been admitted to hospital in Cairo before the Third Battle of Gaza, Major FD Urwick was in command and 'the Regiment behaved splendidly ... and were much complimented.'[1] For his brilliant leadership that day Frank Urwick was awarded the DSO.

The Battalion again distinguished itself at dusk on November 20th when in rain and mist it took a leading part in rushing the Turkish position at Kuryet el Enab. Another battalion involved was the 2/3 Gurkha Rifles, of the 232nd Brigade. 'To General Bulfin [Commander, XXI Corps] ... the first news of the success came when, above the rattle of musketry and the boom of the Turkish artillery, there were heard the shrill cheers of the Gurkhas and the deep-throated roar of the

---

[1] War Diary 1/5 Somersets. November 13th 1917 WO 95/4690.

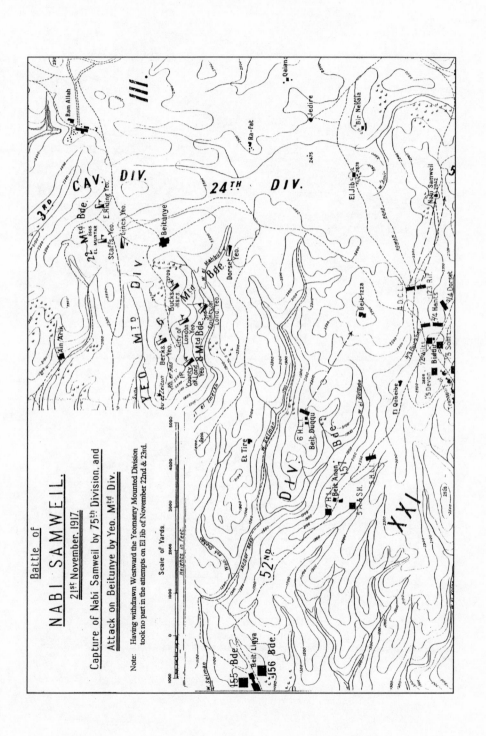

Battle of
NABI SAMWEIL.
21st November, 1917.

Capture of Nabi Samweil by 75th Division, and
Attack on Beitunye by Yeo. Mtd. Div.

Note: Having withdrawn Westward the Yeomanry Mounted Division
took no part in the attempts on El Jib of November 22nd & 23rd.

Scale of Yards

0   1000   2000   3000   4000   5000

Heights in Feet.

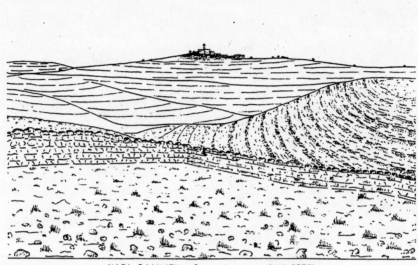

NABI SAMWEIL: from the west (hill 2878).

EL JIB: from the south-west.

Map compiled by Historical Section (Military Branch).
3000/30.

Sketches from Falls; *Military Operations*, op.cit.

British troops, followed by regimental bugle calls.'[2]   On November 21st the Somersets marched to Biddu by way of the old Roman road, 'though this was merely a track over the mountains which necessitated moving in single file ... where the track reached its highest point [we] got a splendid view of Jerusalem, about seven or eight miles away' (Urwick). 'We ought to have been much impressed at this glad sight; it certainly was magnificent but I fear the majority of us were very callous and irreverent.   The truth is that we were all dead tired, foot-sore and feeling "fed up and far from home" ' (Milsom).   That bitterly cold, wet night (and the Battalion was still in its desert kit) the Battalion bivouacked just South of Biddu. 'For a long time we got no sleep, as one or the other's teeth would begin to chatter and the vibrations would keep the other awake' (Urwick).

The Attack on El Jib: Day One, November 22nd 1917

'This Useless Adventure'

For the day's operations the 1/5 Somersets were put under the command of Lt-Col A Armstrong, officer commanding the 1/4 Wiltshire Regiment. In Lt-Col Cooke-Hurle's continued absence Major Urwick still led the Somersets so it was inevitable that Brigadier Colston should give the senior officer charge of the force whose objective was the capture of El Jib and Bir Nebala. In his old age Stanley Goodland characterised Lt-Col Armstrong as "a madman who never cared two hoots about his men" but Urwick's account, though critical of his leadership, stresses Armstrong's gallantry 'which was beyond all praise . . . It was a marvel that he was not hit that day, as he walked about in the firing line regardless of the attention of enemy snipers, and was always one of those men who do not know what fear is.'[3]

Lt-Col Armstrong's plan was to attack El Jib and Bir Nebala from the North-West - that this was wholly reasonable, the next day's events were to show. To achieve this he took his force North from their bivouac area at Biddu, himself leading the advance guard of two Companies of the Somersets. The main body consisted of the Somersets' two remaining Companies and Headquarters Company and, following them, Armstrong's own 1/4 Wilts Battalion. The country North of Biddu and West and North of Beit Izza was soon found to be exceptionally rocky and steep, while much of it was under observation from enemy gunners and riflemen. 'On the way we flushed a fine fox with a large bushy brush: a few forgot the business in hand and tried to bayonet 'the varmint' but the fox was the easy winner and got clear away' (Milsom). As time passed the Companies scrambling up and down precipitous slopes became scattered and jumbled; control was difficult.

---

[2] Falls, *Military Operations II*, p.194. W T Massey, *How Jerusalem was Won* Constable 1919, pp.139-40.

[3] Lt-Col Armstrong was mortally wounded when reconnoitring ahead of his battalion, September 19th 1918. Falls *Military Operations II*, p.479.

Instead of placing himself in a position from which he could direct the entire force under his command Lt-Col Armstrong personally led the advance guard. The Somersets' officers began to realise that he was persisting in keeping to a northerly line of advance long after he should have turned eastward. 'We were attacking the wrong objective altogether, a fact which our Intelligence Officer [2/Lt Bradford] confided in me' (Milsom). '(I) at last caught up with Lt-Col 'X'.[4] I pointed out to him that to reach El Jib we were moving about 80 degrees out on compass bearing. We . . . had a good view to the North. Lt-Col 'X' pointed to a village a shade East of North and said. "That is the only village I can see; it must be El Jib and I mean to attack it." The village he pointed out was Beitunye, about five miles away, and I told him so, but he would not believe me. We then continued to move northwards.'[5] (Urwick).

Now Lt-Col Armstrong ordered the two remaining Somerset Companies to join the advance guard. 'I have never in war been in such a funny position as I was that day. Lt-Col 'X' after commanding two of my Companies all the morning had now taken the remaining two, with the intention of leading my Battalion himself in the attack, instead of issuing orders to me and acting as if he was the Commander of the entire force. Not being in the best of humours, or knowing quite where my duty lay and feeling that lives were being uselessly thrown away, I kept my headquarters and Lewis guns . . . I was much depressed during the afternoon by the number of our casualties in this useless adventure.' (Urwick).

On the hill top from which Lt-Col Armstrong planned to lead the next stage of his operation Milsom reports: 'Orders and counter-orders flew about. But at last and much to my relief I located Captains Major and Banes Walker; in order to reach them I had to cross a bullet-swept piece of ground and half way over I tripped and fell headlong. My efforts to scramble into safety caused considerable amusement to Banes Walker but not to me, as the beggars were pumping lead at me. But Banes was the same in action as he was in mess, seeing humour in everything and most delightfully casual. A few minutes later he himself was shot dead, though I never knew it until the evening.' (Milsom) '[Banes Walker] was one of my best friends, and had proved himself a good and fearless soldier and was also an excellent horseman, and a sportsman in every way.'[6] (Urwick)

Further progress being impossible the 1/5 Somersets stood fast until dusk allowed them to retreat to Beit Izza, carrying their casualties with them. 'It was a sad and melancholy business, this retirement, and very, very slow owing to the difficulty of carrying the dead and wounded down the steep rocky ground. I was very thankful to find our CO and Adjutant quite safe. I told them all that happened and my own private opinion of it too, for the strain of the day had told on me, and we had lost too many good NCOs and men.[7] Besides I was much upset by poor Banes Walker's death. Of course it is a soldier's duty to obey orders and above all not to criticize; but I am convinced if our own CO had been allowed to control

---

[4] Urwick tactfully does not name Armstrong, nor his battalion.

[5] From the map, this village could have been no more than 3000 yards distant. The village in sight may have been Ram Allah, but was certainly not El Jib.

[6] Gerald Banes Walker was 28. See note 17/40.

[7] The *BoR* lists two sergeants, three corporals and two lance-corporals among the dead.

152

our part in the show the attack would not have been such a ghastly failure, neither would so many valuable lives have been recklessly thrown away. Needless to say I got told off very properly for having given way to overwrought feelings.' (Milsom)

So ended the first day's campaign for the capture of El Jib, with the Somersets bivouacking about 500 yards south of Beit Izza. Their War Diary records the casualties: one officer killed, nine ORs killed, three officers wounded, 23 ORs wounded, two ORs missing. The 1/4 Wilts had been deployed to protect the advance guard's right flank in the afternoon and covered its retreat; their War Diary lists two ORs killed and 19 wounded.[8]

The Attack on El Jib: Day Two, November 23rd 1917

'The Valley of Death'

Before the weary officers of the 1/5 Somersets settled down to sleep late on the 22nd, they had learnt that in the morning they would be required to make a direct attack on El Jib. Early on the 23rd Major Urwick accompanied Brigadier Colston to a small hill 'from which we could get a good view. El Jib is a natural stronghold ... and looking at it from the West, as we did, it stood out about 2000 yards away, a high-terraced rocky hill, with the village standing on the left shoulder. On the right were the lofty slopes of Nabi Samweil, and on the left was high ground and ridges leading forward from Beit Izza. The approach to El Jib was through a valley 600 to 700 yards wide ... Altogether it looked a very strong position to take without artillery support, and with a Battalion which had been so reduced it could only go into action with about 400 bayonets' (Urwick).

The Nabi Samweil ridge on the South side of the valley was dominated by the mosque built over the alleged site of the tomb of the prophet Samuel. The mosque had been captured late on November 21st and on the 22nd had been subjected to furious Turkish and German counter-attacks and artillery bombardments during which 'the shrine of the Prophet, which was supported by four ancient and massive silver lanterns was smashed to pieces by a direct hit.'[9] The British clung on at the mosque but the Turks still occupied the northern slopes of the ridge, there being no artillery to dislodge them.

'Immediately our extended lines emerged from the end of the valley the enemy left off shelling Nabi Samweil and opened a very heavy fire of HE and shrapnel on us. The men advanced in perfect formation as if on parade. Soon the leading waves . . . came under intense machine-gun and rifle fire and suffered heavy casualties. The enemy machine-guns were situated on the northern slopes of Nabi Samweil, in El Jib itself and also on the slopes and ridges to the left . . . The Battalion was therefore subjected to the most severe enfilade fire but went pressing on, without a check, right up to the terraces of the rocky hill. Seeing the

---

[8] PRO WO 95/4688.
[9] Falls *Military Operations*, II, p.203.

three leading Companies, despite losses, pushing on so bravely and knowing how few we were in number . . . I sent in the reserve Company and also the fighting part of my HQ with Captain M[ajor] my second-in-command' (Urwick).

'Directly the artillery barrage was passed the bullets began to fly around and the air was full of them. Every other man seemed to be falling, it was terrible the lines just melted away. One bullet went through the pugri[10] of my helmet. It didn't worry me as I was far too concerned about the progress of the attack, but I felt I should 'stop one' soon. The next instant my right foot went out of action, there was no pain simply a numbing shock. As luck would have it there was a low heap of stones a few yards in front, and to this I vigorously hopped. The blood was spurting in a thick stream from my ankle, but a man named Pennell (one of my Lewis gunners, the only one left in the Company by this time) hastily slashed the boot off and bandaged the ankle with my field dressing; also to stop the bleeding he improvised a tourniquet round my leg . . . I popped my head over the stones and a hail of bullets pattered round so I hastily popped it down again . . . There was only a handful of my Company near and they were mostly wounded. Dusk was our only hope and for that we waited, praying that in the meantime no bullet or shell would come to finish us off. It was the longest day I have ever known; the loss of blood made me weak and feverish and I was much upset by this second catastrophe' (Milsom)

'It was found that when the attacking waves reached the rock' (on which El Jib stands) 'that the terraces were so high and steep that it was almost impossible to climb them, but the men went forward with wonderful bravery and small parties actually succeeded in reaching the village, where they were wiped out' (Urwick). In the *Book of Remembrance's* most emotional passage Stanley Goodland and Harry Milsom wrote, 'It is to be recorded in these annals with real pride that three Lewis gun sections succeeded, with great difficulty and bravery, in scaling these terraces. They were all either killed or taken prisoners and their guns lost, but their deed remains an heroic example for all time.'[11]

'The enemy's fire of every description continued throughout the day . . . Every officer who went forward with the Companies was either killed or wounded. Captain G.[oodland] asked me to allow him to go forward and see what he could do, but I knew the position was quite hopeless, and that he would only be throwing his life away, so I refused . . . Of personal experiences of that day, early in the advance a bullet struck the satchel of my box respirator which had luckily slipped round to the front, passed through it and the middle of the tin containing charcoal, then through my thick riding breeches and struck me in the lower part of the stomach. It had been fired at a considerable range and these obstacles broke its force and turned it sideways so that although making a bruise it did not break the skin.'[12] (Urwick)

---

[10] Hindi for turban, but referring here to a cloth wound round a helmet to increase the wearer's protection from the sun.

[11] *BoR* p.54.

[12] Stanley Goodland later recalled that Frank Urwick, inspecting the damage "took down his breeches in the middle of the battle". In its obituary of Urwick the *Light Bob Gazette*, vol.XXXIX, no 4, Ocotober 1936 remarked that 'it was said of him that under the hottest fire he was more cheerful than usual.'

'How the day dragged on. I thought the sun would never go down. But at last it grew dusk and as I was unable even to hobble along they got a stretcher and carried me back . . . All the wounded could not be got in for the Turks came down and bombed them . . . Poor young [2/Lt WA] Hannaford's body was never recovered. [2/Lt G] Clarke and [2/Lt] Foster were both wounded, and as I was being carried back I heard someone say, "Here is Capt Major, stone dead". So poor old Major had gone, too! It appeared he was wounded early in the day and killed outright by a shell whilst crawling to cover. Again I was greatly relieved to find Major Urwick and Capt Goodland both safe and sound and they were equally pleased to find me still alive.' (Milsom)

'At nightfall the Battalion was ordered to withdraw to the same bivouac area it had left in the morning . . . Our wounded were collected . . . We managed to bring back Captain M.[ajor]'s body and buried him that night, close to our bivouac. Our Padre read the burial service, with myself, the Adjutant, Captain C.[alway] and one or two men standing by. After all we had gone through that day, this simple ceremony I shall always remember as one of the most impressive in which I have ever taken part. Captain M.[ajor] was a fine Christian gentleman, and very brave soldier[13]. My last recollection that night was of poor M.[ilsom] who was badly wounded in the foot, and I, who had settled down by the side of his stretcher both enjoying a cigarette from a fifty-tin which Captain C.[alway] had very kindly given us - a very valuable present, as we were all out of smokes of any kind by this time' . (Urwick)

'Our Medical Officer - a splendid fellow - bandaged me up and at the same time confided in me that he did not think I should see much more of this war; however, I did not worry overmuch at this bit of news, as I was feeling particularly tired of war just then.' (Milsom).

In the Battalion War Diary for November 23rd, which Stanley Goodland must have written that night, the casualty list shows: two officers and eight ORs killed, three officers and 132 ORs wounded and 32 ORs missing, most of whom were later numbered with the dead. Urwick notes that in January 1918 the 74th Division, which occupied El Jib weeks after the fall of Jerusalem, returned 27 identity discs to the Battalion. 'I believe they also buried two men they could not identify.' The Roll of Honour in the *Book of Remembrance* carries the definitive list of those who died on November 23rd: three sergeants, and 39 private soldiers, as well as the two officers already named.

---

[13] Arthur Oswald Major was aged 42, and from Bridgwater. His obituary in the *Somerset County Gazette* of December 1st 1917 says that 'he had been prominent in many useful spheres in the town'. He was actively identified with political and church matters.' He had represented Somerset at both hockey and association football.

After The Battle: November 24th, 25th & 26th, 1917

'A Well-earned Rest'

NOVEMBER 24th: 'As I was being carried away on a camel to the nearest Clearing Station the brutes shelled our convoy: it put the wind up me horribly as one felt so helpless stuck up on top of a camel, and such a target, too! But no-one was hit, luckily.' (Milsom)

'Early next morning an unlucky shell wounded nine more men. I saw the Brigadier and finding we were allowed a well-earned rest, I asked if I could move the Battalion further down the valley where the steep sides would protect us from shell fire, which request he granted . . . That night as G.[oodland] and I settled down . . . we said, "Thank goodness we shall get a night's rest to-night"; but so uncertain is the life of a soldier we had not been asleep long when we received orders to be ready as quickly as possible to march back to [Kuryet el] Enab'. (Urwick). After a night march blundering across open country the Battalion hit the Roman road which 'since we came along it on the 21st had been made into something that deserved the name of road and was now passable for artillery . . . We arrived at [Kuryet el] Enab 0030 and bivouacked under the hill which we had taken on the 20th'. (Urwick)

NOVEMBER 25th: 'Remained in bivouac at [Kuryet el] Enab. Some of our wounded passed down that day in motor ambulances and I shouted to M.[ilsom] as he went by' (Urwick) 'The last I saw of my poor old Battalion there was but a handful of them, Companies commanded by sergeants and corporals! Still the CO and Adjutant carried on - and kept smiling too - a perfectly wonderful couple.' (Milsom)

NOVEMBER 26th: 'The [233rd] Brigade marched to Junction Station . . . The men's boots were very bad, owing to the rough, stony hill work. In one or two cases the soles had completely gone and the men had tied sandbags to their feet. But the 215 men who were left were all hard nuts, and glad to be alive, and they sang cheerily throughout the march.'

'So ended the part played by my Division in trying to cut the North communications of Jerusalem.' (Urwick).

BIBLIOGRAPHY

Unpublished Sources

Goodland, Edward Stanley, *Letters to his fiancée Elsie Hyde, September 1914 to December 1919.*
Milsom, Harry Lincoln, *My Experiences During the Operations in Palestine, October 18th to November 30th, 1917.*
Urwick, Frank D, *An Account of Some Fighting in Palestine in 1917.*

Newspapers etc.

The Light Bob Gazette, Taunton (the Journal of the Somerset Light Infantry)
The Tatler
The Times
Somerset County Gazette, Taunton
West Somerset Free Press, Williton

Public Record Office, Kew

WO 95/5121, 2nd Bn Dorset Regiment, *War Diary*
WO 95/5175, 1/5 Bn East Kent Regiment (the Buffs), *War Diary*
WO 95/5175, 37th Dogras, *War Diary*
WO 95/4690, 1/5 Bn Somerset Light Infantry, *War Diary*
WO 95/4690, 233rd Infantry Brigade, orders & reports
WO 95/4688, 1/4 Bn Wiltshire Regiment, *War Diary*

Official Publications

Falls, Captain Cyril, *Military Operations Egypt and Palestine from June 1917 to the End of the War,* (in 2 parts, with a box of maps), HMSO, 1930
Moberly, Brigadier FJ, *The Campaign in Mesopotamia, 1914-1918* (in 4 volumes). HMSO, 1923-27
Pirie-Gordon, Lt-Col HA *(ed) Brief Record of the Advance of the Egyptian Expeditionary Force from July 1917 to October 1918.* HMSO, 2nd edition, 1919.
Hansard: House of Commons Debates, 1919.

Regimental Histories

Goodland, ES & Milsom, HL, *The Book of Remembrance of the 5th Battalion (Prince Albert's) Somerset Light Infantry,* Chiswick Press, 1930
Atkinson, CT, in *The History of the Dorsetshire Regiment, 1914-1919.* Henry Ling Ltd, Dorchester 1932.
Moody, Colonel RSH, *Historical Records of the Buffs, East Kent Regiment 1914-1919.* Medici Society, 1922
Wyrall, Everard, *The History of the Somerset Light Infantry (Prince Albert's) 1914-1919* Methuen, 1927

Other Works Consulted

Barker, AJ, *The Neglected War: Mesopotamia, 1914-1918.* Faber, 1967.

Braddon, Russell, *The Siege.* Mayflower Books, 1969.

Brown, John, *Independent Witness. 150 Years of Taunton School* Taunton School, 1997.

Brown, Malcolm, *The Imperial War Museum Book of the First World War* Sidgwick & Johnson, 1993.

Candler, Edmund, ('Eye-Witness') *The Long Road to Baghdad.* Cassell, 2 vols., 1919.

Carman, Barry & John McPherson *(eds.), Bimbashi McPherson. A Life in Egypt.* BBC, 1983.

Elgood, Lt-Col PG, *Egypt and the Army.* Oxford University Press, 1924.

Falls, Cyril, *Armageddon, 1918.* Weidenfeld & Nicolson, 1964.

Halpern, Paul G, *A Naval History of World War I.* UCL Press, 1994.

Hopkirk, Peter, *On Secret Service East of Constantinople.* John Murray, 1994.

Massey, WT, *How Jerusalem Was Won.* Constable, 1919.

Massey, WT, *Allenby's Final Triumph.* Constable, 1920.

Reynardson, Captain H Birch, *Mesopotamia, 1914-1915. Extracts from a Regimental Officer's Diary.* Melrose, 1919.

Swayne, Martin *In Mesopotamia.* Hodder & Stoughton, 2nd edn, 1917.

Wavell, AP (Lord Wavell), *The Palestine Campaign.* Constable, 1928.

Wavell, AP (Lord Wavell), *Allenby. A Study in Greatness.* Harrap, 1940.

Wavell, AP (Lord Wavell), *Allenby in Egypt.* Harrap, 1943.

INDEX

161